Finding the Magic

A HISTORY BOOK, HOW-TO BOOK, PHILOSOPHY BOOK AND MOST OF ALL, A LOVE STORY

By
Dan Sumerel

Finding the Magic

ISBN: 1-890306-23-1

Library of Congress Catalog Card Number: 00-132654

Second Printing

Jacket front cover photo by Roni Bell.
Jacket back cover photo by Susan Sexton.

Warwick House Publishers
720 Court Street
Lynchburg, Virginia 24504

Thank You...

In life we often do not realize it when we have a profound impact on the life of another. The experiences that brought me to the point of writing this book were often influenced by people that had just such a profound impact on my life. I need to thank those people so they know their input was important and appreciated. My deepest thanks to each of you.

My ex-wife Lisa. Even though our relationship didn't work out, I will be forever in your debt for introducing me to the world of horses and thereby changing my life forever.

John DiPietra, Bobbi Richine and Linda Fisher. You offered help and encouragement to a beginner, without which I would not have begun. You were important to me then and still are today.

My friend Dawn. You showed me how much better I could be and helped me get there in more ways than you will ever know.

Ray Hunt and Buck Branaman. Two master horsemen who opened my eyes to a better way of dealing with horses. They taught me that the word *cowboy* does not need to be a verb meaning a rough way of handling a horse. And that sometimes I could learn a lot from people that don't say a lot if only I tried hard enough.

Gunther Gable-Williams. A man I had admired from a distance for so long. In the brief time I spent with him he confirmed many things that I had figured out, but didn't have the confidence to truly believe in on my own. A true character of the highest level.

A special thank you to the Janiak family, Linda, Kelly, and Michelle, of Hunter's Creek Farm in Lynchburg, Virginia, for their help and participation in the photographs.

And to the many people who have encouraged and supported me as I changed and learned. For their trust with their horses, and the education that provided.

Dedication

This book is dedicated to a handful of horses that changed my life. It would be unrealistically romantic to embellish the actions of those animals with human traits – something people often do. But in fact they had such a profound effect on me by simply being the horses they were. And it was by simply just being a horse they opened my eyes to their world as well as gave me insights into my own. I am a very different person than I was before I met the horses. For that gift, I will be eternally grateful.

For...

Raj, Shazi, Cisgo, Kasty
and especially, my friend Sunny.

Sunny in Colorado. Sunkist Sir Beau. Photo by Roni Bell.

Table of Contents

Introduction

Right now I would like to plant an idea in your head; the idea that there may be a more effective, faster and even safer way to influence the behavior of a horse than what you have been used to. For the past six years I have had the privilege of traveling across the U.S. and Australia, working with virtually all breeds of horses and almost every discipline – from racetracks to horse shows to western events of every conceivable type. That opportunity has provided me an observer's perspective on the horse/human relationship and the problems so often present. It never ceases to amaze me how much of the horse/human interaction I see involves a struggle. You have no doubt experienced that struggle first hand from time to time yourself; often subtle, although occasionally even a violent struggle. A struggle that is based on a lack of understanding and communication between two very different creatures that actually can work very well together. Not unlike many marriages. Sadly, that struggle is accepted by many people as *normal*, and tolerated because of a lack of understanding. And just to set the record straight, I do not mean that as a criticism of what some of you or any of your trainers may have done with a horse in the past. I have made many mistakes with many horses due to my *lack of knowledge at that time*.

Most of us do what we think to be best. This book will not ridicule or criticize anyone except those using cruelty as a supposed training method. I would not question the wisdom of those who built the 1951 Chevy in 1951, even though today we build vehicles that are so much more capable in every dimension. I would, however, criticize anyone who insisted on *STILL* building '51 Chevys, knowing we can do so much better.

As we learn, we have a responsibility to use that knowledge. The ideas and philosophy contained in this book are the end product of the efforts of many people whose lives date back hundreds of years before me. It has been my good fortune to be in the right place at the right time, to learn from some incredible people, and then apply my own interpretation to what I learned and adapt it further.

It was also my good fortune to come into the horse world as an adult rather than growing up around horses, like many of you. Although I would consider growing up around horses to be about as good a childhood as any kid could have, I am referring to my attitudes as an adult, and how they affected my perspective, as I entered a whole new world I knew absolutely nothing about. Unlike a child giving credibility to information as being valid *simply because it came from an adult,* I was willing to question what other adults told me about horses often just because it didn't "feel" right to me. Throughout my life I have learned to follow my gut instincts despite outside influences. If something doesn't feel right, then we should pay attention to that feeling and question it – a position children aren't as quick to take when directed by elders. Children grow up being taught about horses by adults displaying the *normal* way things are done. Often, what we accept as *normal* is so inherently wrong for the horse. This book will ask you to examine much of what you may have considered *normal* with horses in the past. In those situations where I challenge the *normal*, I will attempt to explain the reasoning behind my position as well as offer alternatives to replace the *normal*. To simply criticize something without offering a better alternative is a bit shallow.

Unfortunately I see too many adults who blindly accept something said or done by a "supposed" expert in the horse world. No more than I would expect you to blindly follow everything I put forth in this book, just because "I wrote a book," I would expect you to question anything you see or hear if it doesn't "feel" right. If more of us would pay attention to our intuition (especially when dealing with animals), and question those things that make us uncomfortable, much of the struggle

I referred to would soon disappear.

A wise man once told me, "If prayer is your attempt to talk to God, then your intuition is God attempting to talk to you." Are you willing to listen? Regardless of your personal, religious, or philosophical beliefs (and this book will not attempt to present any religious positions) I feel I would be incomplete if I were to only present "how to" techniques without also presenting an understanding of the dynamics involved as the source of those techniques.

This is not just a book about horses, but about the horse/human relationship. And, remember, it takes two to have a relationship. So we must be as attentive to ourselves as we are to the horse if we are to create the best possible relationship. My experiences with the many horses and people that provided me the information for this book gave cause for me to constantly question myself; often teaching me as much about myself as I learned about the horses. For all the horses I have been able to help with the application of what I have learned, I truly believe that the changes that have occurred within me as the result of my work with them has left me the greater benefactor of those involvements.

It never ceases to amaze me that much of the knowledge and understanding of the horse, which has been around so long, is not being applied more universally than it is. This is far from the first book devoted to this area of study. Why are people, often with twenty-thirty years of experience in horses, so far off base when it comes to understanding the very animals they make their living with? I feel there are several reasons.

First, there are always large numbers of people who are content to "just get by" with whatever is the quickest fix possible. They don't eagerly seek new and improved ways of doing things. They have a bunch of horses to get through their "training factory," and they just want to get the horse to do what they need done. And fortunately (or unfortunately for the horses) horses are compliant enough to let that happen far too often. They often endure so much unnecessary abuse, just because they adapt so well. The same adaptability that helped them survive for millions of years could now be said to be working against them. If they had been less adaptable, perhaps we would have left them alone. No other creature has been so successfully assimilated into working for us. (Yes, I know dogs are closer friends, but they didn't help us work and build in the way the horse did.) You don't see people riding around on elks or giraffes either.

Second is what I call *human arrogance*: we are the top of the food chain, so the horses simply MUST do our bidding. I am not totally against that attitude, as I see too many situations where people have little or no control over their horse, and that puts them and their horse at risk. I do firmly believe you *must* control your horse. But I do differ with the approach most often used by people of that attitude to gain a response from the horse. It frequently involves the *unnecessary* use of force and inflicting pain on the horse, most often applied by the excessive use of equipment. Many humans can even be quite cruel (both mentally and physically), showing little or no consideration for the horse. That is a position I cannot understand, nor will I accept. And remember, it can be just as cruel to the horse when the cruelty is based on ignorance, and perhaps not intended to be cruel. "I didn't mean to be cruel" or "I didn't know" is of little consolation to the horse suffering the abuse.

Third, and perhaps the most common reason many horse people are still struggling with their horses, is because they have never been in a situation where they could learn to really understand what makes their horse tick. How he works and what motivates him.

For us to learn, we need to have the information presented in a fashion WE can understand, and hence implement ourselves. We cannot learn what we don't understand. And we cannot use what we don't learn. Since the horse is made up of an infinite array of subtleties, many of the marvelous aspects of horse behavior and social structure go totally unnoticed by a less informed observer. We must first understand the horse and the world he came from in the wild. We must understand what millions of years of evolution created, for that is what we have to work with. The four thousand or so years we have been handling horses has not dramatically changed his nature. Let us not be so arrogant as to assume we even *could* undo what it took fifty million years to create. Once we understand the horse and his true nature, we may even ask ourselves, *why would we want to change him?* By first understanding the horse, we can then develop techniques or tools to best influence his behavior. Most people try to affect horse behavior by applying human logic – doing what makes sense to us. But what makes sense to him will not make sense to us. A very popular book entitled *Men are from Mars, Women are from Venus* does a great job of teaching men and women how to stop expecting the opposite sex to respond to things the way they do, because we're so different in our very nature. It won't happen. Men think and feel differently from women. Which causes them to react very differently in most situations. We have argued about this for centuries, but it is a reality of life. If we acknowledge that we are different and then interact with each other by taking those differences into account and allowing our understanding of those differences to guide our actions, we become more effective in our inter-gender relationships. If we can stop making our spouse *wrong* for being *different,* we might be able to get along better. The same is true with our horses. They are not like us, nor we like them. To proceed with our horse while only considering what is logical to us and never trying to understand their point of view is not only less effective, but unfair. It is my belief that we must understand their perspective and adjust our behavior accordingly. That approach is better for them and better for us. It is to that end that I offer this book.

CHAPTER 1

In the Beginning

Historically speaking, horses have been on our beautiful planet about fifty million years. Since there are a number of very well researched scientific books on the evolutionary history of the horse, I won't go into great detail about the scientific knowledge relating to the horse's evolution. For anyone who would like to broaden their perspective on horses in general, I'd strongly recommend Stephen Budiansky's *The Nature of Horses* and Frank Dobie's *The Mustangs*. But what I do want to discuss are several aspects of the horse's nature, both physical and behavioral, that came out of that evolutionary process and directly affect us today. I believe that one way for us to become more effective with our horses is to begin by studying what happened during that fifty million years to create the horse as we know it today. Not what we'd like him to be; not what the movies portray him to be; but the reality of the horse. And all too often when I see someone having a problem with a horse, it is due in great part to the *human's perception of the horse* being too far off base from the *reality of the horse*. Perhaps by understanding what happened to make the horse into what he has become, we can better understand this incredible creature we love so much. And in my humble opinion, the reality of what the horse really is is far greater than the image of the simple, big puppy dog so often portrayed by Hollywood.

Much of the information I have read regarding the evolution of the horse has been both enlightening and thought provoking, though often leaving more questions than answers. One of the most thought provoking aspects I have read is the great debate regarding the actual effect evolution had on the development of the horse, if any. In other words, many people believe that evolution is a refining process that *evolves* a better creature. Little by little, traits of no value disappear and new traits offering improvements show up and endure.

Most people today believe the species that have survived are superior to those that did not. There's actually a lot more to it than that. And the facts seem to bear out that evolution deals more with immediate survival than any long-term plan for improvement. Any change to any creature that was not of immediate benefit – in other words, didn't help the creature survive in the short term, was not likely to be around long term. The creature had to survive *TODAY* if his traits were to be passed on to future generations. True, improvements may have evolved and frequently did, but it does not prove that what exists today is superior to what is extinct. One example is the effect of dramatic climactic changes, sometimes sudden, and how that could wipe out a certain species. Many of the horses' ancestors existed for millions of years, only to die off suddenly for that very reason. At several times in history, there were many forms of the horse on the planet. Large ones and small ones at the same time, both evolving successfully. Single-toed (hoofed) and multi-toed branching off in their directions. There is still much debate on why some vanished while others survived. But any creature that survived for three to four million years, only to vanish during a climactic crisis, should not be considered a failure of evolution. More realistically, it was the result of being in the wrong place at the wrong time.

And by the way, when you do take a look at the evolution of this beautiful planet of ours, it would be relevant to notice that for millions of years, long before humans did anything mechanical or electrical or atomic, there have been incredible climatic changes, including the Ice Age, etc. This planet has repeatedly cooled and changed in quantities we would consider nothing short of catclysmic today, based on our limited time of observation. These climactic changes frequently caused the disruption of life, as it existed then, to change and even cease at various levels.

One example is the dinosaurs. If the "bigger is better" theory held water, where are all the dinosaurs? This beautiful planet that we consider our home is a very dynamic, active planet. And just because it changes over time spans that we can only comprehend, but not experience, we should be a bit more humble in our attempt to quantify our ability to influence the overall scheme of things during our brief time here.

Human arrogance is very self-perpetuating – and very limiting to our thinking. For us to think any change in our planet must be because we caused it is the height of arrogance. As bad perhaps as someone thinking they can simply change their horse into something he isn't, after he took millions of years to become what he is. I am not saying that we humans do not have the *power* to change this planet; obviously a nuclear war would do just that – in a most negative way. But there are far too many of us trying to protect everything on the planet from *us*. Including horses. There are those who would tell us that we are abusing the horse when we ride or use them at all. And I will be the first to admit that many humans do abuse their horses. I wrote this book to help change some of that by educating others the way I have been educated. But I will not subscribe to the view that doing anything with a horse that he would not do in the wild is abuse. I have seen too many horses that really enjoy their human activities (not activities natural for the horse). The sparkle in their eye and their passion in performing are not indications of a creature sustaining abuse. Horses are naturally curious and playful creatures and they like to do things. When they perceive it as fun, they will do it with passion.

My interest in the evolution of the horse was primarily related to how it had affected his natural behaviors. Yet you must keep in mind that in order to study the behavior of the horse, one should not omit the study of the physical nature of the horse as well. By physical nature of the horse, I am not just talking about the way he looks or his ability to go fast, I am talking more about the way his physical make-up affects his life and behavior, not to mention his physical limitations. My work with BioScan and dealing with the numerous physical problems horses endure (mostly man-made) has given me a perspective

3

on the physical nature of the horse that often conflicts with the norm. [See Chapter 9, The Physical Horse.] Obviously the environment the horse has survived in was instrumental in his evolution, and many of his physical changes were necessitated by, or results of, that environment.

For example, some people believe the horse to be a creature that has evolved into the large, incredible running machine we have today because of his need to survive by fleeing from his predators. The speed part may be true, but the size part is not necessarily so. Size alone does not predict speed. The cheetah can outrun a horse and is quite a bit smaller. Even the fox and the greyhound are only slightly slower, yet dramatically smaller. In fact, there were times during the evolutionary history of the horse where several species of our horses' predecessors were getting larger while several others were getting *smaller*. Think how that would have affected *our history*, had the larger Equus become extinct and only the smaller versions survived. What would Napoleon and Attila the Hun, not to mention John Wayne, have ridden? Also, consider the fact that speed alone does not guarantee survival. If that were true, all the little animals would have died off. A deer can out maneuver a horse and that maneuverability is often more important than sheer speed.

> ITEM- I have, on several occasions while on horseback, tried to catch deer in open country. It didn't work. The speed of my horses Sunny or Kasty was not the problem. It was the sudden turns. Large animals, like horses, especially with humans on top, can only turn so fast. Frequently the horse can execute the turn closer to that of the deer's capability, but the human usually becomes a projectile, and even though the absence of the human does a lot to free up the mobility of the horse, the deer still wins. Once in the woods, the agility of the deer IS the deciding factor. And how in the devil do they go through the woods so fast with all those horns on

4

their heads not getting tangled up in the trees? If I could only get my dressage saddle on the back of a large buck....

Overall, the evolution of the horse is quite a success story, I think. Starting as a little dog-sized animal, they took fifty million of years to evolve into the magnificent creatures we focus on today. Even the full-size horse we know today as Equus, has been around about five to eight million years or so depending on who you ask. The mere fact that they *did* survive for so long, when so many other species did not, is a credit to their adaptability and a lot of very good luck. Since the extent of luck in their survival is a debate without end, let us focus our discussions on their adaptability. I feel the adaptability of the horse is truly *THE* key to his survival. In fact, there are many experts who believe the current horse as we know it would not have survived the last ten thousand years were it not for his adaptability that enabled him to be *domesticated by man.*

The horse has several things going for him when it comes to being adaptable; mobility, diet, and social structure. We'll talk about each separately even though they are all related and overlapping.

Mobility of the horse is what got us interested in him in the first place. I'm sure of that. His beauty may have been an attraction, but in the primitive world where survival was more urgent than having a pet, it was his ability to cover ground that was of premium interest. From the horse's point of view, it was his mobility that also saved his life in more ways than one. Obviously, the ability to run from predators is what most people think of first. Yet, being mobile enough to find food and water was usually a far more important asset. Horses in the wild are known to travel fifteen to twenty miles a day and more, just grazing and being a horse. That's six hundred miles a month. In North America, certain wild herds were known to travel from Colorado to New Mexico and over to Oklahoma, then back to Colorado each year. Had they been less mobile, they could easily have starved when the food ran short during a drought or severe winter. We will get into how the mobility of the horse is related to his mental condition and behavior in the chapter on control. But for the moment, just remember this: he is bigger, stronger, faster, and hence more mobile than you or I. Which means he can *PHYSICALLY* out-perform us in every way. That is fact, based entirely on his mobility as compared with our mobility.

Diet is an area that I am sure saved the horse from extinction as much as his mobility. The first little horses were what's called "browsers," animals that eat rather rich vegetation such as leaves of trees, which have higher levels of nutrition than grasses. During periods when vegetation became more sparse, our early horses began to adapt their diet, eating what they could find, namely grasses. This required more physical changes such as stronger jaws to handle increased chewing, and tougher teeth for eating grass with more dirt in it, as well as intestinal changes allowing the digestion of those grasses. Did you ever stop to look at what a horse actually eats and how much energy (mobility) can be derived from so little intake? I'm not talking about the junk most people feed their horses, much of which is based more on human perception than horse reality. But what did a wild horse eat, and survive quite nicely on for all those years? We humans have some strange ideas about eating, and subsequently on feeding our horses. I base that not on any scientific study, but on simple observation of the incredible number of excessively overweight and out of shape people I see. *AND*, by the things I see people feeding their horses. I have seen many situations where unmanageable and out-of-control or neurotic horses had their personality completely changed for the better, simply by a change (usually reduction) in diet. Not unlike seeing a five-year-old child screaming and running around like a demon, while mom gives him another candy bar as he chugs down his caffeine and sugar-loaded soft drink. The point is that *diet* and *mobility* have a certain interdependency which many people overlook. If your horse is being fed lots of grain and alfalfa hay, he *NEEDS* to have access to more exercise in order to work off the energy that his intake produced. Not getting the opportunity to work off his excess energy will likely produce an accentuated stress level in the horse, usually resulting in some forms of unwanted behavior. If you are using your horse for endurance racing (my favorite horse sport) and he is being asked to go a hundred miles a day over rough terrain, you need to be sure his intake is sufficient to provide for the needs of his added mobility.

The *social structure* that a horse lives within is a marvel of efficiency. It not only works and has helped him survive, but it provides us an incredible system of interaction that when *we* understand it and embrace it, can open the horse's world to us like few other creatures on earth. The horse is a prey animal that lives in herds. Prey animals are herbivores (plant eaters) that are usually eaten by predators who are carnivores (meat eaters). As a prey animal, the horse's job each day is to survive and not become lunch to any predator, while the predators try to catch him for lunch. To that end (survival) horses use their social structure in the herd to avoid capture. The horse's first line of defense is the collective awareness of the herd to *ALWAYS* be on guard against attack. Seeing the predator before he gets too close allows the herd to stay safe. As a horse, dropping your guard for even a moment can mean death. By nature, they always expect the worst.

The second line of defense is the mobility; the ability to run away. If you stay *very* alert, the running away is less necessary and much less urgent.

The final line of defense is to fight. The herd may group together with their heads in, which means any approaching predator is facing a lot of angry, fast-kicking hooves – a rather formidable defense. The predator will seldom attack a group of horses in this defensive posture. A single horse will try to fight if cornered, but is usually not as successful. A horse knows that by the time everything has gone wrong and he is fighting alone, at close range he is in imminent danger and probably about to die.

7

To facilitate some form of order to this herd or group living system there *must* be leadership. And horses know that inherently. If you ever put two or more horses together that do not know each other, they will immediately begin to posture and test each other to establish who should be in charge of this herd. Character always wins out. Often it is not the largest or even the strongest horse (although those traits are a part of the selection process) which takes control. It is often not a stallion as many people believe, but rather a mare that ends up on the top of the pecking order. I have often seen herds in the pasture where it's a little 14.2 mare that runs the show, and has the bigger 16 hand horses running for cover. And that pecking order goes all the way down through the herd so each horse knows his place and who is above him and who is below him. Why? What if the herd were split up and some horses were surprised by a group of predators? Who would lead which group? What if the herd leader were killed? Who would step in and take charge and make the immediate decisions needed to survive? In any group, there will always be a leader and a chain of command, not unlike any military group. It is efficient and necessary for survival.

Humans often misconstrue this struggle for hierarchies as dangerous behavior for their horses and attempt to solve it by separating or even isolating the animals. This is a serious mistake based on ignorance. In a natural (wild) environment horses seldom have any real physical contact that causes harm to other horses. Over ninety-five percent of horse arguments end with *no physical contact*. When people have an argument with their horse, over ninety percent of the time the result *IS physical contact* from the person to the horse. Who is really more effective? The horse's basic approach of posturing and displaying aggressiveness in order to establish their position in the herd is designed to *AVOID* the need for the bloody conflicts. Such battles would deplete the herd of many of the very best animals and diminish the chance of survival for the species. When wild horses *grow up together,* they learn the social skills that allow them to become effective members of the herd and enhance their chance for survival. Think about this: in any herd of wild horses, how many *geldings* are in the herd? How did they ever survive without humans there to separate them and protect them from themselves? More about this in a later chapter.

There are three basic situations that will create an environment where actual injuries are likely to occur: during struggles relating to breeding rights, territorial battles during a scarcity of food, or being crowded together with a lack of sufficient space/room to move. The third is usually a problem in domestic horse environments and seldom appears in the wild. Too many horses in too little area. Somebody gets kicked or bit. Add to that too much unnecessary rich food, creating excessive energy, with insufficient room to work it off, and you have a typical domestic horse problem. Add to that, horses that have been separated too much and not allowed to learn the social skills provided in a more natural environment, and you have a crisis waiting to happen. An avoidable man- made crisis at that. I know many of you will argue that you can't have your expensive colts and fillies running around together, the potential risk is too great. But let's be clear on the problem: it's not horses, it's money. I can show you many excellent horse ranches/farms (I say it that way because it seems that people say horses live on ranches out west and on farms in the east. I don't know if the horses know the difference, but I sure can't tell it. I always thought ranches had cattle, and farms had corn and potatoes. But then where exactly does that leave the horses? I don't know. I grew up in the city.) that keep *ALL* their colts together in one giant pasture, and *ALL* their fillies together in another. And they have nice, rather well adjusted horses with excellent social skills. Throughout this book I will continue to relate most of what I present about horses to the conditions and situations that allowed them to survive for the fifty or so million years they have graced this planet. And they did so *without human help or control*. Remember that fact the next time you start to impose a human value on your horse. If you tried to survive in the natural lifestyle of the wild horse, eating grasses while wandering across the wide-open spaces, staying ever alert for predators and enduring all four seasons without shelter, you couldn't – anymore than they could – be truly happy in some of the human designed, unnatural environments we force them into. But they do try. We must not take advantage of their inherent willingness to adapt, by letting ourselves overlook what is truly natural and in most cases better for them. True, we have changed dramatically the environment they now live in, and adjustments must be made for that. But above all, as it was so well said by the famous TV star MR. ED, "A horse is a horse, of course." As silly as that line from the song seemed, it is very profound. The horse is not a dog, nor a child, nor anything else *BUT* a horse. And that is, in reality, more than we could have ever wished for in our wildest dreams. Today, most horse problems are created by us. Unfortunately, the horse is dependent upon us to solve those same problems. Let us try to better understand him and then use that understanding to adjust our behavior and be fairer to him. The rewards to this kind of approach are incredible for us both.

CHAPTER 2

How'd This All Start?

There is a lot of speculation on exactly when man first got involved with horses. And there is a lot of speculation as to whether people first used horses for food, to pull a wagon, or to ride. I am sure, knowing there are many parts of the world where horsemeat is still considered a desirable dish, that the idea of eating a wild horse when it was all that stood between man and his family starving or not, was an idea with great potential. I am not making any judgments on or attempting any social comment here on what you choose to eat. The living conditions of human beings varies greatly around this world of ours so it may be unfair to make overt judgments regarding what we would or would not do, under conditions we have never had the misfortune to experience. I have never been on the verge of starvation, and I hope I never am. But it is the nature of our planet that some creatures eat plant life for food, which allows them to grow up and potentially become food themselves for other creatures that eat meat for food. Such is the *reality* of the Prey-Predator relationship within our environment. I did not design it that way, nor can I change it. Having said that, it is my position that due to my involvement with horses and respect for their remarkable nature, I cannot consider them something for food. I must also place the dog in that same "not for food" category.

We should also be realistic in understanding how much of the domestication of the horse and other animals was our fault. And how much of it was not. It has been shown in dogs, for instance, that originally the wild dogs/wolves probably sought us out as much as we them. They benefited from our scraps, our fire and much more. There were factors present in certain other species that have their roots in the very origin of those species that affected the *possibility* of domestication. In other words, of the nearly four thousand species of mammals that have been around for the past ten thousand years or so, why have so few been successfully domesticated? We have tried. But just because we try to domesticate does not mean we get our way. Many factors have to be in place for domestication to occur, including physical traits, mental traits and the needs of us humans. Some animals were domesticated for food, such as chickens. Some were domesticated for labor, such as oxen and horses. Cows and sheep can also provide numerous additional benefits to humans in the form of food and clothing, etc. Dogs are more complex in that they have and still are used for food in some cultures, but initially they provided warning to danger, and eventually companionship at a very high level. As human needs have changed, the proliferation of certain animals has also shifted dramatically, yet of all the animals during the existence of this planet, only a few have successfully connected with man in domestication.

ITEM- At this time there are over seven million horses in the United States, more than at any time in history. The only time there were nearly this many horses in the U.S. was at the end of WWI when horses had still been used for the war effort. At the end of WWI, after many horses had served so well, millions were simply slaughtered since there was no way to care for so many horses in the peace time environment. Some were sold to countries that used them for food. It is a sad commentary on us humans, at how we can be so callous with living creatures as to simply use them and then throw them away. The wars themselves serve as comments on our barbaric nature towards our own kind, so we should not be surprised at our cruelty towards animals. It goes without saying that the horse played a major role in the building of this country, as well as most of the rest of the world. Even as late as the beginning of the last century, we depended on the horse for so much of our transportation it was incredible. With the development of the car/truck/tractor we became far less dependent on horses for work. There began to take place a shift in our *need* for horses to we *wanted* horses. It should also be noted that today there is less *NEED* for horses than at any point in our history. Sports, pets and business – we *WANT* horses today, we don't need them as we did before.

I am also sure, from all I have read, that the earliest signs of people riding horses predates the wheel by several hundred years. And I guess you could have used a horse to pull a non-wheeled (sled) vehicle. Since a sled is much harder to pull on dry ground, the idea for needing something large to help with transport may have originated before the wheel itself did. But it is my humble opinion that we *rode* horses before we *drove* horses. I could be wrong, and many very learned people still argue the idea. In fact the whole concept of capturing a wild horse when no one *really* knew what, if anything, could be done with it after capture, seems incredible to me. Did you ever really think about the very first situation that started this whole "ride your horse" thing? A few thousand years ago, someone got tired of walking and decided to try to get on the back of a horse. That's without doubt an oversimplification, but the basic idea is probably the way it went. Somebody, somewhere, had the magic idea to attempt to catch, get on and then ride a horse. No barns, no saddles, no how-to books or videos. Just an idea to ride this big, fast, not-even-wanting-to-be-touched animal called a horse. Whoever he was (I openly say he, because even though today there are far more women into horses than men, the first riders were probably not a she because women back then were still stuck in the kitchen and unliberated.) I have to admire him. He was either very brave, very desperate or very stupid. Perhaps a bit of them all. (He also didn't have a computer to keep him inside all day.) You see, even though a wild horse and the horses we ride today are incredibly similar, the most significant change that has taken place as the result of domestication is the acceptance of humans. Most horses now days accept people. In the wild they do not. They fear any creature they do not know, and do all they can to keep great distances between them and what they fear. Think about it. Most people don't like getting on a horse that's not well trained. A well-trained, easy to ride horse brings a much higher sale price than an unbroken equivalent. What was it like for the first guy who had to figure a way to catch the thing and then try to get on it? His desire must have been incredible. (Or maybe he was just really bored since he didn't have a computer.)

And, as if the task by itself was not awesome enough, can you imagine the harassment he must have endured from his friends' comments when he told them what he planned to do? "You know those big fast animals we see running around off in the distance? The ones we can never get near? I'm going to catch one and ride it." One thing I'm sure is true, there were pessimists back then too. Just as it is today, there have always been those that seldom *do*, but are expert at killing the dreams of those that want to try. I imagine they tried to tell our first "horseman-to-be" that he would be killed attempting such a crazy stunt. I'm sure they used that age old line of "it's never been done before." (Always remember that almost everything we do and have today fell under that heading at one time.) Or, that he could never control such a fast, powerful animal even if he did get on. Fortunately for us, he had the courage to ignore them and pursue his dream even though the reality is that many people were no doubt injured and killed trying to tame the wild horse. The learning curve that followed for the human trying to make the horse a useful tool for man was long and difficult. The struggle that ensued between man and horse was not pretty. Man is a predator and a very aggressive predator at that, with an undaunting will. Many horses did not survive their encounter with this new two-legged predator. I say new because remember, the horse has been around for fifty million years, and man for much, much less. So we were the newcomer on the block compared to the horse. He had survived and was now facing a new threat unlike anything prior. The goal of the horse in the face of this new threat was to simply survive. The goal of the human was to conquer and control. For all our superior intelligence, we were totally egocentric in our approach to most situations and our quickness to resort to force to get our way was still the norm.

As with any new endeavor, there evolved many differing approaches to the horse taming process, but most involved the man forcing the horse to submit. Unfortunately, this is still the primary approach used today. Our intelligence and our dexterity (the opposing digit theory) allowed us to think of and then create "things" to help us in our environment. We made ropes and fences and all sorts of things to help us get control of the horse. The endless list of stuff we make to go on the horse continues today. If you don't believe me, simply go in any tack store. Horses don't "build" much. They simply exist with what's available. They also don't attempt to change the way things are. We, on the other hand, as the "supreme being" on this planet, used our superior intelligence to overcome the horses' superior strength and speed, changing the way things were and forcing the horse into our society. Hence the struggle, and the pain that ensued. We had not yet learned how to best use the intelligence we had been given. Many of us still have not. We were and in some ways still are, very much like the animals we claim superiority over and wish to control; we rely on force to get our way – the strong take what they want and survive. We have too often been content to resort to force to obtain control.

But somewhere, sometime, there was some guy that wanted a better way. His compassion was stronger than his ego. He had the ability to respect and empathize with a living creature very unlike himself. Very admirable traits. Yet, if I think of myself possibly being in his position, I must honestly admit to perhaps being affected by several other very human traits of less noble origin. I say this because when you read the following chapter on my beginning in horses there are several similarities between him and me. Not that I could ever claim to have near the character or courage of these first pioneers in the horse world, but that we were in fact both subject to the same human frailties. Being pragmatic, (and I believe the severity of living conditions in times past would have forced a high degree of pragmatism) our brave, first horseman-to-be would have been at least somewhat directed by not wanting to be hurt. And somehow the risks of starting a physical struggle with a creature so much larger and much faster than he, would have seemed, well, illogical. Perhaps even a degree of fear entered here. Boldness and stupidity often cross paths with disastrous results in the horse world. And was there no degree of laziness back then? I think there was. Speaking strictly from my own perspective, if I can do something in two days by being smarter, then why spend a week struggling unnecessarily?

I like to think the first horseman-to-be was a little guy. Lacking size and strength, he had to rely more on his brain. I'm 5'8" so I relate well to this concept. You see, being small can be an advantage in the way it affects one's perspective on life. If you're a big strong guy, you have often been able to use your size and strength to get you through life's troubles. Although a big guy can be as gentle and compassionate as anyone, it is all too common for people with great physical strength to resort to the use of that strength as a *normal* problem-solving tool. That is one reason why so many women are good with horses. When a person of great strength is handling a horse, his size and strength are much less a factor. A 295 pound pro football player is one powerful guy. Yet compared to a small horse, only 900 pounds, the football player is a toy. Look at the numbers, 295 to 900. And many horses can reach the 1500-1900 pound bracket. To put it another way, a 100-pound woman is about the same 1/3 proportion to our 295-pound football player as the football player is to the 900-pound horse. Most women grew up in our society knowing they cannot rely on their physical strength to solve their problems, so they are more readily adaptable to seeking other means to their ends. They are often quicker to use their brains over their brawn. Also, many women, who have at some time in their lives experienced first hand what being forced to do something is like, tend to empathize with the horse on another level as well.

So if we assume our first horseman-to-be was a small guy, it would make sense. He had to find another way, other than relying on just force, to capture and control the horse, and if he was to be able to ride. And his approach to his problem of how to control the big fast horse would have been to first study his "subject." His more aggressive contemporaries would probably have referred to the horse as "adversary" since they thought in terms of winning a conflict and dominating the animal. But as you will often see in this book, the very words that you choose to describe someone or something sets the tone for the initial phases of that relationship. Choose your words carefully and become more effective. By studying the horse, our little horseman-to-be began to learn about the nature of the horse. How the horse lived, what motivated him and most important, the *horse's* language and social structure. All creatures are products of their society, and they will react to others based on what they are programmed to do by their social environment and their instincts. Horses are far more instinctive than man, so their social structure is much less flexible than man's. Man is the only creature that can develop a philosophy and hence change his way of being. A horse can only be a horse, and can never be anything else. Their very survival depends on their place in their very structured social group, their herd. As our horseman-to-be began to understand this aspect of the horse, he began to unlock the mystery of how to control this incredible animal by using the horse's own social programming.

As time went on, a new approach in dealing with horses began to develop, based on interacting with the horse as if the man were another horse. By learning the horse's language and social etiquette, the idea evolved that perhaps we could win over the horse to want to be with us. By earning his respect, using his social value system, we could end much of the struggle between man and horse, and change the very nature of the relationship. This was not an overnight discovery, but more realistically a long, drawn out process developed over centuries by many, many people. Sometimes I wish I could have been there to see the face of the first man to actually apply this more benevolent approach successfully to a horse, and get the horse to join him willingly.

Even though I wasn't there then, I do get to experience the same feeling over and over each time a new student in one of my workshops gets a horse to connect with her and willingly join her for the first time. The glowing smile of the student, sometimes even accompanied by a tear as well, is always one of the most touching aspects of my work.

That very first time when a horse joined with a man, willingly, because the man had changed his approach, had to be one of those "oh so important" moments in history, the significance of which was probably lost at the time. That moment proved that the horse and human could have a better relationship, where the horse could have a life involved with man, but more devoid of the fear and struggle that was so common before. All great achievements have that incredible moment, where the theory ceases to be a theory and becomes a reality. Much the same as when man dreamed of flying, and the "theory" that man could fly was a challenge; it had never been done before. If they had subscribed to the idea that the past equals the future, they would have never flown. But the past does *not* equal the future unless we allow it to. On the day Orville and Wilbur actually flew, at that moment, that glorious moment, the theory of flight became a reality forever. And changed our world. During the moment that the first man joined with the horse in language and manor, to the great joy and acceptance of the horse, the world of the horse was also changed forever. The *theory* of a horse/human relationship based on understanding, communication and trust, instead of forceful dominance, had been transformed into a reality. From that moment on, there have been people who were able to have a *different* relationship with horses than that known to most people. Far better than *normal*. Unfortunately, most people are satisfied to marvel in wonder at what those "gifted few" are able to accomplish with horses, and attribute their results to some inherent natural gift or talent. The reality is that it's less a gift and far more a level of knowledge that permits such a relationship to occur. Sadly, this benevolent, yet most effective, approach to interacting with horses has not become the norm. Even today when we fly in space and technology rules our lives, the simple understanding and communication of the horse is unknown to most horse people.

Most people have never been exposed to this level of knowledge. Some have seen it but have not had an instructor effective enough to help them understand what they were seeing. Some people simply didn't spend enough time with it to become successful using it. If you are in any of those categories, you are about to leave that behind right now. Your past need not equal your future. But understand one thing before we go on. This way of interacting with horses is so soft and subtle to human observation (as well as foreign to human logic) that it often goes unnoticed and overlooked. It appears to be magic. That is where the image of the Horse Whisperers came from. The ordinary horse people were so blind to the subtleties of what the true horsemen did, that the success of those Whisperers with the horses was attributed to "magic" or "whispering in the horse's ear." Such is not the case. The magic is not magic at all. It is simply a way of interacting with a horse that is based on the horse's world and how he sees that world. It can be learned by anyone who wishes to learn it, and applied on any horse, by anyone that has learned it. It is easy to do, but as with most things that are easy to do, it is also easy *NOT* to do. And as we tend to be creatures of habit, we are often not eager to embrace ways that are "different" from our own patterns of behavior. We are comfortable with the *normal.* For many of us that resist change, the use of this different approach will take effort on our part to achieve. In many cases, continuing efforts. Learning is a process, and the person you can become once you complete the process may surprise you no end. If I am any example, I will tell you that what I have learned from the horses has both touched me and changed my life in so many ways I cannot begin to list. It has allowed me to touch the lives of so many others, both horses and people, and to help them not just solve problems, but also become more of a team; removing the struggle from their relationship and letting them be at peace with each other. And that gives me great pleasure.

CHAPTER 3

Dan, This is Horse.
Horse, This is Dan.

It was the fall of my 40th year on earth and I was married and living in Lakewood, Colorado. A great place to live and, as is usual in life, some things were going very well and some things were not. If you have not yet been forty, just wait, you'll soon appreciate what I mean. I had enjoyed a reasonably exciting life, some success, but for the most part, I had been known for doing things I liked to do rather than doing a "job" to make a living. In fact, my life had revolved around cars, motorcycles, and mechanical things like that since I was just into elementary school. Even as a young boy, all I did was build model cars and airplanes. And motorcycles. My bicycle was always *really* a motorcycle to me. I can remember whenever the older guys would go by on a motorcycle I would lose all focus on anything else and even give out one of those '*OHHHHH*' type of sighs that girls did for Elvis. I loved engines and going fast. I still do. There seemed to be a special attraction to engines and their sounds and power; for me that was almost overwhelming. As I got older and actually began to really *have* cars and motorcycles, I did seem to have a bit of a knack with them. I was racing before I ever finished high school, just at the local level, but with a good degree of success. This was in the 60s when the Corvettes, GTOs, Mustangs and all the rest ruled the automotive scene. If you had a Corvette or a GTO the girls loved you. And the motorcycles. There were the established favorites, Harley, Triumph, BSA, Norton, etc., all being challenged by the new Japanese invasion: Honda, Yamaha, Kawasaki and more. It was truly an incredible time to be a teenager, and it cultivated my love of engines, speed and power that would shape my future forever. As exciting a time as it was, there was almost *NOTHING* in my life during that time that related to horses. Except, ironically, I used the word 'horse' almost constantly in my youth, in unending discussions about horsepower. But there was definitely nothing else from my growing up that could be related to a horse environment. Had you told me at any time in my life, even up until past my 40th birthday, that I would become totally consumed in the horse world, I would have laughed in your face.

Obviously, unlike many of you, I did not grow up around horses. I had not had a life-long love affair with the horse, nor had I spent enormous amounts of time dreaming of riding horses. In fact, other than two brief stints at summer camp (ages 9-10) I had almost no involvement with horses at all. I thought they were pretty, and that was about it. Yet here I was, forty years old and going out to buy a horse. But not for me; for my wife Lisa. (The women always seem to be trying to get us men to widen our horizons.) Lisa had talked about growing up with horses and how she missed them so much. She had ridden throughout her childhood and participated in shows and all sorts of horse events, but had been forced to sell the horse when she went off to college. To be totally frank, I must admit that the relationship was not going very well and I hoped that buying the horse might provide a new hobby that could bring us together. (In hindsight it now seems so silly to have even considered bringing something from *outside* the relationship into the relationship, in hopes of correcting problems that were obviously coming from *within* the relationship. So often we look outside when the solution we are seeking is inside all along.) The idea of buying a horse was not taken lightly and I was very concerned at first, when the lightning bolt of an idea hit me. I *knew* I didn't know anything about horses, and that turned out to be a double-edged sword of dynamic proportions. It would at first almost get me killed, then later open my life up to a career of incredible opportunity. Since the wife had grown up with horses and had years of experience with them, I assumed she knew all about them and I was not afraid of the big step into horse ownership. Would you not also make the assumption that anyone with years of experience in the horse world *does* know about horses? Oh Contrare. Today I am continually amazed at the number of people with vast experience in the horse world, even championships and ribbons in droves, that have a very weak basic understanding of the horse. The assumption that experience equates to knowledge was the first of many mistakes I would make in my adventure into the world of horses.

ITEM - Don't Believe It: I have since learned that when someone says, "Yea, I been around horses all my life. I've had lots of horses...", I do *NOT* assume they know *anything at all* about horses. They may know nothing, or they may know a great deal about all the wrong things that you don't want to learn anyway. It never ceases to amaze me how much bad, incorrect information about horses is passed down from generation to generation as if it were the gospel. So think about this; just because something has been done a certain way for fifty years, does that make it desirable and even more important, correct? NO. We humans are creatures of habit and we resist change with a passion. Even when what you are doing appears to get a result, if there is a better way, (and I like to define "better" as safer, faster, or perhaps just easier on the horse) should we not be willing to consider those ideas? We too often do things because "that's the way they're done." A pretty weak approach. In defense of Lisa, most of what she had been taught was both well meant and quite normal, even today. She loved the horses dearly and would never intentionally do anything to hurt one. But if what she and I knew about horses could fill a thimble, what we didn't know could have filled the Grand Canyon.

So imagine a typical, semi-intelligent grown man that knows *NOTHING* about horses going out to buy one to surprise his wife on her birthday. Stop laughing. I can remember driving out to a ranch to look at a horse for sale and not even knowing what to ask. I tried to be cool and say all the right things. "He really is pretty." "What does it weigh?" "What does it eat?" "Does it bite?" "Why is it so dirty?" "Are his ears OK? They seem to be going in so many different directions so much." And, of course, don't forget the all important question for any true horse enthusiast to ask about a prospective animal, 'How fast is it?" (My years of racing cars made that seem relevant.) Can you imagine what those people must have thought? I was quick to inform them that I was really buying the horse for my wife and she grew up around horses. I would modestly tell them that I was kind of new into horses. As if they needed to be told.

ITEM- I also now look back in amazement that I was lucky enough to buy a really great horse and not get burned by some non-reputable horse trader. There are a few out there you know. I could have been the ultimate sucker and the potential problems I didn't know I was facing could have caused a life-changing disaster. I could have ended up with any sort of walking catastrophe as my surprise birthday present for Lisa; "Surprise Honey, here's your birthday present, Attila the Horse!" Or perhaps, "What do you mean? At least the other three legs work pretty well!" Or even, "Thirty-one isn't old. I just turned forty." Think about that one.

Now don't think I didn't do some research before jumping into this great endeavor, though. I did. I went to a tack store (which was a 'bit' overwhelming [no pun intended] in and of itself to a non-horse person) to do a little knowledge gathering. And boy was I amazed at all the stuff in there. So many things that I had no idea what they were used for or even what they were called. One whole wall was covered with just bits. And bottles of all kinds of things that I didn't understand even *after* I read the labels. I couldn't help overhearing several conversations and my ignorance of the terminology made me feel even more out of place. I knew they were speaking English, because I could get a word here and there, but I had no idea what people were talking about most of the time. Comments about a disease called 'leg aids" got me very nervous and wondering how to avoid catching that one. Needing to cut a "bridal path" seemed to be like having a wedding in a bit more remote environment than I would have chosen. Then I felt better when I realized one couple must have been discussing what a good lunch they had at some Italian place. Yet I still admit I never figured out what kind of pasta their "cavalletti" was. And then the ugly idea of segregation showed up. Right here in Colorado. I suddenly realized the whole store was *VERY* segregated; all the English stuff was on one side and all the Western stuff was on the other. I don't know what might have happened had any of that stuff ever touched, but it would have probably been dangerous. Some of the differences were rather obvious. I had already figured out that most cowboys probably don't hang out with guys that wear red coats and tight pants. Lisa liked the western stuff but I didn't relate to being a cowboy at all. I kinda' liked the red coats, but then I like anything that's red.

Anyway, I had come to the tack store to learn about horses and decide what kind of horse to buy. A man has to explore his options and there are a lot of options in horses. I'd look in a book to see what kind of horse I really liked best and then decide. You don't want to make snap decisions on important (read: expensive) purchases. You need to do your research. You need to know the important information so you can make the right choice. And after several minutes of careful deliberation, I decided I thought the Arabs were the prettiest horses in the book, so that's what I should buy. Also, having vast experience watching horses on TV, and remembering how much I liked SIL-VER, (the Lone Ranger's horse) I decided that gray was the best color. I couldn't imagine why so many people were buying brown horses. And there were so many colors of *brown*. Chestnut, I could understand. But a "bay" was a body of water – blue or green, not brown. I've yet to see a blue or green horse.

And then there were the undecided horses: paints and appaloosas. They couldn't decide what color to be. But then I remembered that Tonto rode a paint, so they must be OK. Enough information. Some people take forever to make a decision, and I hate that. At some point you have to get off your butt and take action. I now knew what I needed to know. So I set out to buy a gray Arabian. What more could a man need to know?

I did hire a veterinarian to check out my favorite prospect, and he turned out to be very fit. The horse I chose was an eighteen year old gelding that had been a very successful show horse for a young girl, winning hundreds of ribbons on him as she grew up. (As I found out older horses are often much cheaper than young ones, I began to see the advantage to maturity.) In hindsight, my reasoning may have been flawed [am I good with understatements or what?] but the fact is that the best horse for *ANY BEGINNER* is an older, mature horse. Buying a green horse for your young child to grow up with is nuts.) As had been the story with my wife, the horse's owner had gone away to college and the family was downsizing to a smaller home so the horses had to go. I could sense the reluctance in the parents to parting with their old friend, so I repeatedly assured them of my sincerity in giving him the best care possible. The father was a large burly man, yet he showed incredible tenderness in dealing with this pretty gray horse. The daughter was not there at all and I think that was probably just as well. It almost seemed at times like I was applying for a job rather than buying a horse. They wanted to see where he would be living and so much more. I wish more people were that concerned about what happens to a horse they sell. Somehow I was able to convince them that I had the resources, if not the wisdom, to care for their friend, and the deal was done. I arranged to have the owner deliver the horse to a facility near our house where we would board him. Since I had no horse trailer that was really the only option open. As you may have guessed, I also had no concept of all the *COSTS* I would begin to incur as a horse owner. The

26

cost of buying the horse is *nothing*. I would soon find out, cost wise, it was the tip of the iceberg.

The wife was very skeptical when I wanted to blindfold her, put her in a truck, and drive her out to see her birthday present, but she did go along with it. I told her she wouldn't get it unless she complied. Neither of us had anticipated that some people, when blindfolded and subjected to movement, such as riding in a car, tend to get motion sickness. I'm not sure if it was the excitement of the event or the movement while blind-folded, or perhaps a bit of both, that was to blame, but I noticed the wife's face looking quite pale under the bright red blind-fold. When she put her head down between her knees, I under-stood the gravity of the situation. Those sorts of stains do not help the resale value of most trucks. After a couple of brief stops to stabilize my passenger's condition, she managed to survive the trip with no regurgiatory outbursts. There were sev-eral friends and my mother-in-law, quietly waiting for us with camera in hand, at the horse's new home for the proud unveil-ing. I helped my somewhat pale wife from the truck and then led her across a small pasture to the round pen holding the horse. She was still trying to guess what she was getting for her birth-day; she could tell she was walking on grass, not pavement, so she guessed I had bought a piece of land. (*Had* I bought land, think how that would have affected my life.) Then she guessed I was taking her down to a lake, so I must have bought her a boat. (Wouldn't that be just like a man to get a wife what *HE* wanted most in the world? 'Here Honey, I bought you a bass boat for your birthday. I just know you're gonna' learn to love fishing as much as I do.' About as romantic to a woman as new bowling shoes for Valentines Day.) As we neared the round pen one of the horses nickered, and I knew it was time. Off came the blindfold, and after a bit of blinking and squinting, I pointed to our new family member and introduced her to Raj, the Arabian. She blurted out in surprise, "You bought me a horse?" (She always did have an amazing grasp of the obvi-ous.) I had pulled it off; she had had no clue about the horse.

Her mom was clicking pictures, she started to cry, and everyone there was all excited and happy. Even today, years later, I still get a good, tingly feeling, recalling that day and the look in her eyes when she saw that horse for the first time. I even think Raj enjoyed it.

From that day on, several times a week, she would go out to the pasture and groom the horse (which I found out meant a lot of brushing his coat and picking at his feet. I didn't seem to think it at all surprising that his feet were caked in, well, you know, since he walked in it all day.), ride, and do all the other horse stuff that horse people do. And when she came home, she would be all happy and cheerful. I'm sure many husbands of horse-owner wives know what I'm talking about. (Too bad more husbands don't find out more about how enjoyable horses are, first hand. It could help some relationships.) I still had little understanding of what the big attraction of the horse was all about. I was still looking at the horse as a big "dog you can ride." An incorrect attitude carried by far too many people to this day. Occasionally I would take a friend out to show-off our horse. I would say all those horse things that horse people say, like "there's the fetlock," and "watch his smooth transition from trot to canter" and the all important, "watch where you step." I really didn't understand any of it (except for the part about watching where you step) but it always impressed our non-horse friends. Impressing someone that knows nothing about horses, doesn't take much knowledge. That was fortunate because I didn't have much knowledge to spread around at that time.

Over the next few months, Lisa rode often, and even I was allowed to mount the wonderful horse on two occasions. A couple of laps around the round pen usually at a walk, was my limit, and to be frank, I had *NO* control during those outings. But I *WAS* riding the horse. Then there came the time that Lisa had to be out of town on business and she informed me that I would have to ride Raj in her absence. "He *NEEDS* to be ridden," she said with great sincerity. I gave a great deal of thought to her statement. *WHY* does Raj *NEED* to be ridden? Does *HE* know he *NEEDS* to be ridden? If he does *NEED* to be ridden, what about all those wild horses that lived for over FIFTY *MILLION YEARS* before people ever rode them? Did they *NEED* to be ridden too and did they feel left out at having *NOT* been ridden? I found myself asking all kinds of interesting questions (at least they were interesting to me) but having few answers. All that aside, you know how wives are, if she says ride the horse, I'll ride the horse.

My first visit to Raj without guidance was an afternoon I wish had been caught on film. Or maybe I don't. Anyway, I arrived at his abode, and he had already been placed in his round pen by one of the staff. I carried the saddle and saddle pad out to him and noticed how heavy they were. It was a western saddle (Lisa's choice, not mine) and I couldn't help thinking that I wouldn't want to run around with that big thing on *MY* back. But he is much bigger than I, and since everybody does it, *it must be OK*. I also had the bridle and bit. (I was learning more new words than I ever dreamed would be necessary. Knowing that to really learn new words you had to *use* them, I tried to talk about horse stuff to all my friends as much as possible. A habit that I soon found out was exercised by all good horse people.) When I lifted the saddle to put it on Raj's back, he decided to move sideways just as I attempted to lower it in place. I caught it before it hit the ground, but it was awkward. I tried again, and once again, he moved sideways. Maybe I should tie him up, so he can't move around so freely. (Aha, control the horse, what a concept?) Then I thought, "Maybe he's trying to tell me something." Naw, he's just a horse. Putting the saddle on had looked so easy when I saw Lisa do it, but to be honest I had not been studying all the details of this obviously complex procedure. I did remember that the horn-thing went towards his head. Once I had succeeded in getting the saddle on the horse, I had to fasten this belt-thing that goes under the bottom of the horse to keep the saddle in place. Lisa had told me how to attach it a couple of times but I didn't remember the over-and-under part too well. Maybe I'll just kind of tie a knot in it.

Finally I had the saddle on the horse. Success is sweet. Now for the bridle. I knew the bit went in Raj's mouth, but again I had not been paying very close attention to Lisa's demonstrations, and it was looking more complicated than I remembered it. I believe this part goes on the top and the reins go on the bottom, so I think I've got it. I lift it all up to put it in Raj's mouth and Raj simply raises his head. I try reaching higher, and Raj raises his head more. He wins. Short people hate it when tall people hold things up too high for them to reach. I try to pull his head down and we start all over again. Instant replay. Then another. I don't really remember how long it all took, but it wasn't very quick and it certainly wasn't pretty. I did get the distinct impression Raj was having a good time. But, finally I had the saddle and bridle on Raj in what seemed to be their normal positions, so it was time to get on. As visions of Roy Rogers running up and jumping on from behind flashed though my head, I carefully put one foot in the stirrup. Much to my amazement, Raj left. I had never had to face this problem in all my years of racing motorcycles. The bike was quite content to stand still until I was happily on and ready to go. It had no agenda of its own. Raj seems to have developed his own agenda. As I clung to the saddle horn and some mane, and anything else I could grab, we were on our way around the round pen. By the end of the first lap, the saddle was beginning to rotate around Raj's rotund physique and I was recalling the many times I had jumped out of perfectly good airplanes just for the fun of it. Somehow I didn't think this particular jump was going to be fun. When I hit the ground I just rolled a little, then got right back up. Dirty, but only my pride was bruised. Raj was standing nearby, saddle cocked off to the side, and I know this may sound strange, but I had the distinct feeling he was laughing at me. He always did have a great sense of humor.

I went over to him and untied the knot in the leather thing that holds the saddle on, which by the way was now less conveniently located on his back. I repositioned the saddle and decided on a tighter knot just to be safe. Fortunately for me, someone of more horse experience than I (which at this point in my life could have been almost anybody including Daffy Duck) had seen my adventure and came to my aid explaining the over and under part about fastening the girth/cinch thing, which I had not remembered before. (More new words to learn and try to use, but I was not sure how to bring the girth/cinch thing into the conversation at my next dinner with friends.) She even offered to hold Raj still until I got on. Great idea. I had even thought of tying Raj up to keep him still, before her intervention. But I quickly realized that once I did get on, I probably wouldn't be able to untie him. And that would kind of negate the entire effort, namely to ride the horse with a greater degree of movement than a standstill. I somehow didn't envision Lisa's idea of riding Raj to mean me sitting on Raj tied to a post. By the time I actually got on, it was almost time to go home. I think I rode a couple of laps in each direction, carefully repeating the key phrases learned by all beginner horse people, "Easy boy, easy, whoa, easy boy, easy." (A few years later I was sitting on a horse in the dark at 5 a.m., waiting to begin a one hundred mile, one day endurance race. The sound of someone trying to calm a very fit endurance horse that was *REALLY* ready to go, by saying, "Easy boy, easy, whoa, easy boy, easy," sent my mind back to Raj and that first solo ride in the round pen.) After our "ride" I carefully removed the saddle and bridle and put Raj back in his paddock. He immediately trotted over to his roommates to discuss his afternoon outing with me. Wish I knew what they said. No I don't.

We had only had Raj a few months before I had another great idea (these things come in spurts as even the most brilliant minds only have so many brilliant ideas to bring up); if we each had our own horse, we could do more together and ride together, which after all was what this horse deal was supposed to accomplish in the first place. I must confess it was a bit boring watching Lisa ride, although she seemed to be far more entertained by the activities generated by my presence on Raj. By now I had spent some time with Raj, our new family member and he had shown great patience with me. Even though he didn't seem to take me very serious, he did appear to be having great fun with me. In almost no time at all, I became very attached to Raj. His older, patient demeanor gave me a chance to survive my mistakes, yet still enjoy the horse. Lisa had actually expressed interest in wanting a younger, more spirited horse. That is when it was decided that we should get a second horse. We actually bought a much younger (read, more excitable horse) from the same people we got Raj from. Wife Lisa happily took the new younger horse and Raj became all mine. At the ripe young age of forty, I now really had my very own first horse.

Once we had two horses, we became more focused on finding something to *DO* with our new four-legged friends. We attended shows, and jumping events, and watched dressage, and barrel racing, etc., etc. Humans have found so many ways to compete against each other on horseback, that it never ceases to amaze me. And the versatility of the horses is the most impressive aspect of it all. Again I was a bit overwhelmed with all of this, but the one thing we really could do together was to go trail riding. In all the years I was involved with motorcycles, the one thing I loved the most was trail riding in the woods. I figured it would be just as much fun to trail ride on a horse. It was. Living in Colorado with the incredible scenery, and riding, either motorcycles or horses in the Rocky Mountains was one of the greatest pleasures I have ever experienced. I have since ridden in many beautiful parts of the world, but the mountains of Colorado still rank as my favorite, and are as good as it gets. Frankly, most of our rides were short, five to eight miles. Most of the people and horses we were around were not fit enough to do more. Lord knows we weren't either. I developed blisters on so many places on my body that I had not even been familiar with previous to riding horses. People at work could always tell when I did a trail ride the day before; even though the signs were frequently different. I would always be happy but I was usually moving a little slower and more cautiously. I never knew one could have so many different ways to walk with a limp. It was also my first exposure to the idea of sitting as an endurance test. Over the next several months several things became painfully apparent; I really loved being around Raj. I knew almost nothing about horses. And I really couldn't ride worth a darn.

ITEM- There Does Not Have To Be A Purpose For You To Have A Horse. As with so many people I have met in the horse world, we began to think about what we wanted to *DO* with our horses. We kept getting asked what do we *DO* with our horses, and we had no acceptable, meaningful answer. "Er, ah, we just *HAVE* them." So often people need to justify their horse by having a purpose for it; showing, racing, jumping, dressage, etc., etc. If you meet a horse person, the first question they will ask is "What kind of horse do you have?" Immediately followed by "What do you do with him?" In other words, what is his purpose? And the response is usually something like, "I show Arabs" or "I have thoroughbred hunter/jumpers," "I barrel race," and so on. Each response opens up endless conversation about past events or competition, and the reliving of special times – except for those that have no specific task for their horse. The most common are those who respond by shyly saying, "I just pleasure ride." *JUST? JUST PLEASURE?* Where did the 'just' come from? I thought people have horses because it is *supposed* to be a pleasure. (Not to mention I think it should be a *pleasure for the horse* as well. More on that later.) Since when does *not* having a big task for your horse to accomplish require an apology? In hindsight I sincerely believe the main purpose in owning a horse (and hence enduring the

33

costs and logistical difficulties of that ownership) is in experiencing the immense, indescribable *pleasure* that being around a horse provides a person. In other words, having a horse is supposed to be *FUN*. And needs no other justification. Although many different people can define fun many different ways, showing or competing with horses can be a very complicated/involved/expensive activity. Too often I see too many people spending too much time, too much effort, and too much money trying all too hard to *ACCOMPLISH* something with their horses in some structured horse activity. And they seem to have lost track of the *fun* aspect of it. Schedules get tight, costs escalate, pressures rise, tempers flare, etc., etc. What could be more fun than climbing on a good horse to go for a ride in the country? Going as fast or as slow as you and your horse desire. No apology necessary. Even today, when most of my waking hours revolve around horses, in both business and pleasure, I am committed to having fun with it. If it ever stops being fun, it will be time for me to do something else.

One day we were at a horse show still trying to find something we wanted to *DO* with our horses, and a man was riding a horse around the arena while the announcer was saying something about Endurance Racing. He said they *raced one hundred* miles in one day. In the woods. Over all kinds of terrain. Rain or shine. And the horse lived. He had won eight of the nine hundred milers he had done that year and became the national one hundred mile champion. The man was John DiPietra. Endurance racing sounded awesome and I simply had to go look at this incredible horse. Back at the stalls, I saw the horse and met the man that rode him. Turns out that John used to race boats, and since I had grown up in Miami, I had a lot of experience with boats, etc. We had some common interests besides horses and he invited us out to ride with him. He and his wife

Bobbi only lived about an hour away from Lisa and me, so we arranged to go for a ride at their place south of Denver. We hit it off together and soon John and Bobbi became friends with Lisa and me. They proceeded to open up the world of endurance racing to us, sharing their knowledge and experience with true beginners. Initially we just did some trail riding together, as they conditioned their horses for upcoming races. As time went on, my interest in endurance riding was sparked. John and Bobbi turned out to be great mentors and good friends. They helped me with so many things about horses, I could never list them all. I will forever be in their debt.

About the same time we met John and Bobbi, we met another endurance rider who lived east of Denver, Linda Fisher. Linda's place was much nearer where we lived and she let us come out and ride whenever we wanted. She was a real go-fast type rider and I thought that was wonderful. Her idea of a trail ride was a big step above what we were used to, but it showed us what a horse can really do. It quickly changed my perspective of what "could be done" versus what we had been doing on a horse. Although we didn't spend a great deal of time riding there, those early rides with Linda helped me prepare for the crisis I would soon face on another horse, Sunny. Linda is a good friend and her input was a great help to me in the very beginning.

The more we rode the more I wanted to try endurance racing. But one of the first problems (of many) that John had pointed out to me was that Raj was too old to start a career as an endurance horse. He was now nineteen and it was not fair to ask him to try something so strenuous at his age. He was a great trail horse and had trotted and cantered all over the Colorado mountains, but not for any long distances or sustained intervals. I would need another horse for endurance riding. A younger horse that could be conditioned to become an endurance racer. My memories of just buying first Raj and then shortly thereafter, Kanaff, Lisa's new horse, were not helping me look forward to another purchase. Looking at horses to purchase and having to deal with the people trying to *sell* those horses had been as bad as buying a used car. But this time I had expert help in my quest to buy another horse. My new mentors agreed to help me find just the right endurance prospect. We looked at horse after horse and finally we found a six-year-old gelding that was well trained and had good conformation. In short order, I now had two horses. In less than two years I had gone from being a total novice to being a total novice owning two horses and in training to become an endurance racer. I was excited, but I was also facing a very serious problem. I couldn't ride two horses (actually I could barely ride one) so I would have to sell Raj. This had to be one of the most difficult times in my short but intense horse experience; selling my first horse. I could not just sell him, I had to find the proverbial "good home." I had become so attached to Raj, he was as much my friend as he was a horse. Even now when I think back to some of the things we went through together, it is clear how incredibly lucky I was to have been around that wonderful horse. Had I gotten a different horse that was less suitable for my novice abilities, my life of today with horses might never have happened. I realized how little I knew about horses at the time, yet my ignorance never kept me from being close to Raj. He was a pet, a friend and a teacher. I don't think you ever forget your first horse. I know I won't.

Fortunately, an adult friend of Bobbi's was looking for an older, gentle horse for her and her husband to ride and keep forever. Bobbi knew they were great people, but I will tell you that I still felt terrible in parting with my friend Raj. I saw him many times after the sale and he was always fit and happy, so I know it was OK. He had a safe, loving home to live out his many older years. I'm hoping all of you can remember your first horse with the same love and thanks that I feel for Raj. He changed my life. Thanks for everything, Raj.

My new horse was Shazi. Actually he came with the name Petey. (pete-ee) I didn't really care for that too much so I looked in a book of Arabian words and found the word "Shaz" which loosely translated to "strong wind" or something like that. Anyway, it sounded better to me than Petey. With a new young horse in hand, I was given some specific advice from John that I really didn't like too much. He said if I wanted to become a top endurance rider I would need to ride a lot and ride alone. The "a lot" part was OK, because I was really starting to enjoy riding more and more, especially after getting a new dressage saddle that helped me ride better. I had been riding in a cheap western saddle. The problem was not the "western" part, but rather the "cheap" part. The saddle had fit Raj, but not me. Nor was the position it put me in very good at all. The new saddle was a big improvement, although I lost the ever-popular horn-thing to hang on to. Dozens of riding lessons didn't hurt either. Also the "alone" had new meaning as Lisa and I were splitting up and our relationship was history. We had actually moved our horses to John and Bobbi's ranch, since it bordered the national forest and offered hundreds of miles of trails. Lisa would keep her horse and I would keep mine. I saw Lisa occasionally. Then John and Bobbi split up also and John went on his way with Bobbi getting the ranch. Things had been changing very, very fast, and I was now a divorced horse owner.

But the part of John's advice that had bothered me the most was still the part about riding alone. I know, many of you are thinking how we always tell people, especially kids to always ride with a partner for safety sake. Ride with a friend to be safe. That's not it. Some of you are thinking it was fear; novice rider alone in the woods, but that wasn't it either. I had spent enormous amounts of time on dirt bikes alone in the woods, literally *flying* along at break-neck speeds, so I had no fear of that aspect. What was bothering me the most was boredom. You see I had spent all my trail riding time riding with Lisa and our friends. We would ride in groups and it was a very social outing. I enjoyed that a great deal. But I did not yet truly understand the nature of riding a horse in the wild. I expected to be bored riding all those miles alone, because I considered that *I would be alone*, and that was *my mistake*. I thought I wouldn't

37

have anyone to talk to. I am almost embarrassed to talk about this, but I do so that some of you might learn from the error of my attitude.

My first serious training ride alone on Shazi was about ten miles of beautiful mountain trails. The weather was cool, the fall mountain air was crisp and clean, and the leaves had all fallen from the trees so the sun shone through more than normal. If you have never ridden in the Rocky Mountains I doubt I can accurately convey with my simple words the incredible beauty. In the fall the leaves change into multitudes of color, then fall, and the whole process is gorgeous. In the winter the green pine trees combine with the white snow to create a different but equally awesome beauty. The evening moon reflecting off the glistening snow can make the night seem as bright as day. In the spring the snow melts and the leaves come back with rich foliage hard to imagine. Then summer. The days go on till nine at night and the hot days make the cool evenings a great time to ride. But this ride was in the fall. It was what I call a "postcard day" since it was so pretty you would expect to see it pictured on a postcard somewhere. I was grumpy before and during the entire ride because I had no one to chat with. I was all by myself. I barely noticed the surroundings or even the horse.

The second ride started out as bad as the first, only because my attitude was so pathetic, but it ended up being one of those days that will always be remembered for the way it changed me forever. It was only a few days after the first ride, but the weather had cooled quite a bit. Endurance riders ride in all kinds of weather, as well as day or night. I *had t*o ride to be ready for my *purpose*, which was to become an endurance rider. Shazi and I started as always, walking first to warm up, then we trotted a ways and depending on the terrain, we would alternate trotting and cantering, even walking in the rougher stuff. After about thirty-five minutes or so we had settled into a nice rolling canter and it began to snow lightly. I was getting angry. I remember saying to myself, "Damn weather. How the hell am

I suppose to have fun riding when it insists on snowing all over us?" I was dressed very well, warm and dry, so it was not that I was uncomfortable. I have never had much enthusiasm for being cold or wet and especially both, so I had made sure I had adequate clothing for my outdoor jaunts. Why was I so unhappy? Because of my attitude. I knew I was going to be miserable so I was going *to be miserable*. The weather was as good an excuse as any for being unhappy to someone that was quite ready to be unhappy. If it had not been the weather's fault it would have been some other excuse. As Dan, the grump, and Shazi rode on, the snow began to come down heavier and heavier. The green began to turn white and suddenly something happened to me. It was as if something hit me in the face and woke me up. Like a hard cold look in the mirror. Shazi was getting covered with snow but he was just happily cantering along. He was OK. He lived in a twelve-acre pasture and was used to being outside, so to him this was just another day to be happy and alive. He wasn't going to let the snow be a reason to be unhappy. This was his environment as natural as could be. As I looked around me at the incredible splendor of the Rocky Mountains, the fresh, pure white of the falling snow, it looked more like a picture post card or a calendar photograph of a place that most people dream of going... someday. And I was in the middle of all this beauty, atop a wonderful Arabian horse, being miserable and taking it all for granted. We were making fresh tracks across virgin snow and experiencing what many people on this planet will never get to enjoy. Talk about needing an attitude check. Still to this day I am not sure why it suddenly hit me as it did, but I am so thankful it happened. I leaned down and rubbed Shazi on his neck and said, "Maybe I need to take a lesson on attitude from you my friend. You seem to be enjoying this and you're the one carrying me." Then, at that moment, I also realized that I was really not alone on these rides. I had never really been alone. I was with my horse. The only reason I felt alone is because I was too wrapped up in myself to notice the incredible beauty all around me. In much of my life I had been taught and had even been teaching others about the importance of being aware of your attitudes, understanding them and how they influence, even control your life. Now I suddenly realized I had fallen into the same trap I had coached so many people out of in my work as a motivational speaker. I was letting my silly attitude about riding alone being so bad, which had come from some emotionally based who-knows-where, control my thinking and interfere with me being happy and effective. Even today as I teach workshops to all kinds of horse lovers, it still amazes me how much time I must spend getting people to recognize that *THEIR ATTITUDES* are getting in the way of their success with their horses. And those silly attitudes, based in myth or hear-say or emotion, are treated as fact by people who should really know better.

As Shazi and I continued our ride together that day in the snow, I smiled a lot and for the first time, I really paid attention to my horse. And I understood what John had meant when he said ride alone…he didn't mean I was alone, he meant I needed to ride without the distractions of *other people*. And when you take away the distractions of other people you find it easier to look inside yourself, where the true solutions to most problems really lie. If I were to become a serious endurance rider I needed to learn more about my horse and myself than I knew at that time. I had to learn how to develop a union with a different species. Shazi and I had to ride together to build up our trust of each other. When you are twenty-thirty miles from anywhere you are depending on your horse and he is depending on you. You must become a team because your survival may depend on it. You must develop your confidence and your skills, and that can only come with miles and miles of riding. You must learn to depend on yourself and your horse in a way the pioneers must have understood, but a way that seems to have been lost with many people today who take their horse hobby much more for granted. Remember this, regardless of what you do on horseback, be it endurance, dressage, barrel racing or trail ride for fun, at some point it all boils down to a person on a horse. There may be fifty thousand people watching and cheering, but the results are always determined by the teamwork or lack of teamwork you have developed between you and your horse. It's true, you depend on your trainer or coach, and numerous other people that contribute to your success. But in the final analogy it all boils down to you and your horse. And the responsibility for that team is yours. You make the choices for the path you *and your horse* take. In the years that followed that beautiful snowy ride, I have had many incredible experiences on horseback in some of the most isolated areas of this country. From Death Valley, to Texas, the Dakotas, Utah and on and on. Those wonderful experiences would not have been possible without the lesson I learned that day in the Colorado snow on Shazi.

Throughout the fall and winter I spent many days and nights riding hundreds of miles with Shazi. We got to the point where we would cover fifteen-twenty miles every time we went out. We started doing a lot of walking but eventually would trot and canter on and on. I wore a heart monitor watch that would display Shazi's heart rate constantly. It was an invaluable tool for conditioning a horse by letting me know exactly how well he was doing and how much he was being stressed. You have to push to get stronger, but pushing a bit too much can cause injuries. As I will talk about in the chapter 'Physical' it is far smarter to go a bit slower, avoiding an injury, than pushing too much and having to wait for that injury to heal. Especially since I was still very new in horses, the heart monitor was an awesome tool in helping me evaluate Shazi's condition throughout each conditioning ride as well as during each race. In the beginning I almost got one for me too. To suddenly be riding three-five times a week, for a novice like me was a real change to my anatomy. We rode in all kinds of weather, and except for the physical pain I was working though, I loved every minute of every ride. Shazi and I were becoming a team and I was becoming a better rider, although not very schooled in the sense of classical riding, but I was learning to move with the horse and not get in his way. I was also getting a lot more fit myself. Initially I had a tough time doing long rides. I got sore so much at first I doubted I would ever be able to do fifty or a hundred miles. You can do all forms of exercise, but few things can get you in shape for riding lots of miles like riding lots of miles. I had been working out since I was in my late twenties, and had at one time managed several health clubs. In fact that's where I had met Lisa. Yet riding had made me feel almost "out of shape" as I was using muscles I was not used to using. Even all the time I had spent racing dirt bikes seemed to have only slightly prepared me for this new adventure. All the motorcycle riding had left me with little fear of speed, which was a notable advantage over more timid riders. It had also taught me another important lesson that I began to apply to riding horses. A smart motorcycle rider soon learns he cannot *make* a motorcycle do anything. He must develop the skill to influence it precisely, and to actually *let* it do what it can. Trying to force a motorcycle to do something against the laws of physics is usually the precursor to disaster. Much the same is true of riding a horse only you must add to the equation not just the laws of physics, but the will of the horse. You really can't *make* much happen. But if you can influence the horse and stay out of his way to let him do what he does best, then you can feel the magic that happens when a horse and a human become a real team.

In my quest to become more fit for riding, I continued to work out with moderate weights, not wanting to add any bulk (weight) at all. Many of the best endurance riders are one-hundred-pound women, and there are very few two-hundred-pounders that have much success, other than to finish in the top ten (often a major accomplishment) and do the rides for the fun of it. I also continued a serious stretching program that I had been on for years. Flexibility is frequently more important than brute strength in many athletic activities. You need strength too, but bulk without flexibility can be a real problem. I had also become a vegetarian, mainly since John and Bobbi were, and they were quite happy to ride a hundred miles with few ill effects, so

I gave it a try. (I was a vegetarian for almost five years, but no longer follow that program.) All in all, I was serious about my riding and becoming an endurance rider. After months of conditioning Shazi, (who was already in pretty good shape when I got him) and myself, we began our first few endurance rides. It was amazing to me how many other areas of my life were beginning to be influenced by the horses. Other interests were falling by the wayside and my priorities were shifting towards the horse activities. Little did I know.

Shazi and I did a couple of twenty five milers just to learn the rules and procedures, as well as gather experience. They really weren't too bad since we had been riding almost that far on most of our training rides. Sometimes even further. But it was hard to not get too caught up in the racing part of it. Often horses would get pulled (taken out of the event) by the vets at the mandatory vet checks due to the horse being too tired or coming up lame. This was usually the result of not enough conditioning before the racing started, or just the simple fact that the rider rode the horse too fast too soon. After the first few twenty-five-milers we went into the fifty-milers. And that was a bit different. These people were serious riders and most of them were good. Their horses were strong and fit also. And they knew the strategy part of endurance riding when it became racing. It is important to point out that at any endurance ride there are two distinctly different groups of people; those that come to race to win and those that come to finish. Their slogan, "To finish is to win." The second group goes to have a good time, enjoy the scenery and the other people with their horses. In other words a big organized trail ride. I did the first few races in the second group. By the fifth race of the year, Shazi was really going well. Due more to his condition and my mentor's guidance than any brilliance on my part, I was riding an incredible horse. We had been doing our homework, so to speak, and it was paying off. He was fit, I was fit, and we both were loving what we were doing. You may wonder how I could be so sure he loved it. Well, it was actually quite easy to tell.

When I went to get him, he'd come running over to me. When I'd saddle him up he never pulled away or resisted at all. When I got on he was always eager to go. I never had to make him go, I usually had to hold him back. Everyone that saw him and rode with us, including John, said he was a true endurance horse. He loved the adventure of just going somewhere and it showed.

We had done our first few fifties at a pretty reasonable pace, and Shazi had fared extremely well. We actually won the Best Condition Award at our second race. Many endurance riders would rather win Best Condition than first place. At most endurance rides the top ten finishers are evaluated by the vets after the race to see which horse looks the best for wear and tear. In other words the most fit. There is a very well thought-out formula that assigns points for each aspect of the accomplishment. The first place rider gets extra points because she went faster and won. But the seventh place may be a 190-pounder and the winner only weighed 102, so the seventh place horse did a lot more work carrying a heavier load and there are points awarded to accommodate that difference. All in all a good system used to select the horse in the best overall condition *after the race*.

Our fifth race was in Fort Collins, Colorado, about an hour north of Denver. The ground was *very flat* and it was a pretty boring ride, but good for practice. Shazi and I had started out moderately, but had no trouble getting in and out of the vet checks quickly, so soon we were up front with the leaders. A good "vet check" can make up a lot of time for you during a race. Endurance rides are divided into various legs of the race, separated by vet checks where the horses have to show themselves to be fit to continue or they can be pulled from the race by the vet. When you enter the vet check area, you are given a "time in" but your important time is the time at which your horse's heart rate comes down to a predetermined resting level, usually sixty-four beats per minute. If your horse is fine, his heart rate will drop quickly. If he is stressed, it will stay up. You usually have thirty minutes in the vet check, but that time does not start until your horse has passed the P&R (pulse and respiration) part of the check-in. Errors here can cost you a lot of time that is almost impossible to make up on the trail. For example, if I gallop into the vet check, passing you walking your horse in, I could get there first. But if I had stressed my horse in doing that gallop, he might take ten minutes to get his heart rate down to the sixty-four level. You may walk in one-two minutes after I did, but your horse could be at sixty-four right then. My "out time" would be seven to eight minutes *after* yours and that seven to eight minute lead would be really expensive in terms of energy costs, and hard to make up by going faster on the trail – one aspect of the strategies involved in endurance riding.

The lead group consisted of about six veteran riders and Shazi and me. As the ride went on, this group had begun to pull

Shazi and Dan jumping a creek during their second endurance ride. Colorado.

away from the rest, even though the pace was not very fast, but the heat was taking a lot out of some of the horses. Shazi was not even fazed. His heart rate was down and he was full of energy. As we neared the thirty seven mile point, Shazi had barely broken a sweat. A veteran endurance rider was along-side Shazi and me, and had been with us since the last vet check. After watching Shazi for quite a while, she yelled over to me, "Boy he looks great today. I don't think any of us can stay with you. Today looks like it could be your first win." I grinned back happily. This could be our day.

From the very first time I visited Bobbi's ranch I had ad-mired a gray Arab stallion that was boarded there. He was not a popular horse because his owner tended to just gallop around, sort of out of control. The two frightened the more timid riders, and the veteran riders just saw this behavior as obnoxious, but whenever I saw this stallion in his paddock, he just looked so… special. At some point the owner moved away and the stallion went up for sale. At first there was a little interest from pro-spective buyers, but even that dissolved quickly, although at the time I didn't know why. He was a light gray with an almost black mane and tail. His knees and hocks were also very dark and his big eyes were captivating. He did have two problems though; he was only 14 3 hand (many people are mistakenly hung up on the need for *BIG* horses) and he had an attitude. A bad attitude. A few people had actually come to the ranch with an interest in buying him, but the results were usually the same. They either never got near him (his choice), as he often chased them away, or if they did manage to get on (and I think it only happened twice in eleven months) they got dumped very quickly, (again, his choice). He began to develop a reputation. And you know how hard reputations can be to dispel. Every-body loved to talk about how "bad" Sunny was. He was this and he was that, and none of it was good. The last few months he got so out of control he had not been shod or even handled at all. Still, watching him run around and strut his stuff was a sight to behold. He could snort and rear with the best of them.

And any horse that dared go near his paddock had to deal with him. He was, as the saying goes, "open for business."

I don't remember exactly when the idea first appeared, but at some point I decided it would be good for me to have a second horse. Follow this: I decided that if I had two horses I could do more races, as you really don't want to do more than one-two hundred milers a month, since it could be too much for the horse and wear him down. So...as some people do, if you have more than one horse you can do more races. Or if one horse develops a problem, you can still keep racing. Great plan, huh? All this from a guy that had not yet even *done* a hundred miler. I had been used to two horses, up until Raj was sold, so I figured I could deal with two again. As logical a justification as all that sounded, there was actually a more profound reason I wanted Sunny. The *REAL* reason I wanted Sunny was because he was *so pretty*. (If you're laughing now, it is most likely because you've been there and done that...right?)

Yet I will admit to having some concern about Sunny's behavior problems. I didn't think he was really a rogue and all that, like everyone said. But still, he'd been for sale for a long time and no one had been able to do anything with him. And it did seem to be getting worse. I still responded to the name "Novice" when someone called, so I didn't have any illusions of knowing what to do with a problem horse. I needed a test. I needed to see if I could handle him. Not actually *ride* him, just handle him. If I could handle him, then I figured, one day I could ride him. You've heard the expression, "Ignorance is bliss." In horses, that is not only not true, it is dangerous.

The next time I went to the ranch I approached Sunny's paddock and with great care, climbed through the fence rails and entered his paddock. He was on the far side of the paddock, about seventy-five feet away. He was snorting and pawing the ground, and all around not looking too happy. We stared at each other for a moment or so, then I said, 'Stop it and come over here.' And I said it like I meant it. I hoped he knew I meant it. To my amazement, he put his head down and walked over to me. As he approached, I glanced around to see if I would be better off diving between the first and second rail or go over the top of the fence to escape his impending attack, if he were to charge. I was entering unchartered territory for me with this activity. I could see the headlines, "Novice horseman killed by angry stallion. Film at eleven." Yet, to my surprise he walked over to me and stood quite nicely. I touched his neck and then began to rub him all over. I quickly felt any fear I had disappear totally. He seemed almost glad to have someone to be with and I immediately began to wonder where his reputation had come from. He was behaving like any normal horse and the whole event went very well. So well in fact I decided to take him for a walk. I got his halter, which he kindly let me put on him, and then took him for a walk all around the ranch. He did occasionally snort at another horse or two, but a quick verbal reprimand ended his aggressive behavior. Children, I strongly recommend that you *NOT* try this at home. Especially with someone else's problem stallion. Fortunately for me, and Sunny, all went well. I put Sunny away, all excited about my new prospect, and proceeded up to the house to tell Bobbi I was going to buy Sunny.

She didn't stop laughing for several minutes. That is, until I told her I had taken him for a walk around the ranch. "You did what!" started a long drawn out lecture and a lot of "don't you ever's." As soon as I could get a word in edgewise, I went right back to the purchase of Sunny idea. When she saw that I was serious about Sunny she called the owner and four days later I owned the horse. I also got him very cheap. Know why? How much could you get for a stallion that no one seemed to be able to handle, much less ride well or even put shoes on? A horse that was known primarily for galloping around in a reasonably out of control fashion as well as having a disposition around other horses that often led to kicking and the like. As I considered my bargain-priced horse, I began to wonder if I really got a bargain or maybe more of a nightmare?

During the next few days, I began to ask several local trainers why Sunny was so much trouble. Since almost everybody around the area knew about the horse, it didn't take a lot of explaining. The response was almost universal; he's a stallion. "Geld that sucker and he'll be just fine" was the common response. I confess to accepting their comments without what now seems to be even reasonable argument. To blame his problems on the "stallion" aspect alone should have been questioned more, simply because there were a few people around I knew that had stallions and rode them very well. Those horses displayed very little of the behaviors Sunny was so famous for. Yet, I now feel that I *wanted* to believe it, so it would offer a solution to my troubles, and therefore did not present the logical argument I should have. After all, gelding the horse and having him become *nice* would be a simple process. I must also add another perspective to this situation of gelding or not gelding. Due to the way we currently handle most stallions, and the isolation they endure, I have no regrets about gelding Sunny at that time. He had won no world championships and had little breeding potential, even though his athletic abilities were soon to be demonstrated beyond my wildest dreams. Many people have stallions for no good reason. They should be geldings, living a very natural, social existence among other horses, and the stallion aspect should not be an issue.

The correct, macho-male response to gelding a stallion would be, "no way." And I admit to many romantic thoughts about 'riding a stallion." Just the word *Stallion* conjures up images of strength and beauty that affect the best of us. Folklore and myths about "wild stallions" and "the black stallion" and all the rest, have created such a notion that stallions are the ultimate horse. Yet even with those images in my mind, I decided to geld him, and short cut my troubles, so to speak. If that would get him to be easy to ride quicker, then so be it. I didn't plan on a breeding program, and having seen how much trouble some other stallions were at some of the events I had attended, the idea of gelding sounded like a good plan. We humans can be true masters of rationalization. So, the day after I bought Sunny, he was gelded. Having never seen the gelding process,

I was there to watch and was impressed at the simplicity of it. He wasn't as happy as I was, but I figured he'd get over it. And I'd be riding my nice, well-behaved horse, er gelding, in a week or so.

Then the phone calls began. At home. People from all around the area, especially people that boarded where Sunny was, were calling me to ask if I had really bought Sunny? I would say "yes" proudly, then they would say things like "why?" Then I would say I was going to use him in endurance rides. Then they would ask, "Then you plan to ride him?" "Yes, of course" I would confidently reply. Then they would ask, "When do you plan to ride him?" and say things like "Are you going to charge admission?" or "Can we watch?" I admit my buyers remorse was coming into full swing about now, but there was no backing out. Several people had even told me point blank that I was apparently the only sucker that would buy him.

The Saturday that I was going to ride Sunny for the first time was a beautiful day. It was the kind of day we all dream about for a summer outing of most any kind. I admit I had a few butterflies in my stomach over my impending first ride on Sunny. Actually, they felt more like pelicans. But I could not back out now. There's something about telling the entire world you are going to do something that forces you to follow through even when a large amount of procrastination seems in order. There were over thirty people standing around to watch. Sunny was moving pretty well after his surgery. In fact there seemed to be not one ounce of change to his demeanor. I kept wondering how long before this loss of testosterone would kick in. As I brought out my dressage saddle and the bridle and hung them on the hitching rail, a local trainer called me over. She was an excellent rider and had done a lot of good things with some horses I knew of, so I respected her opinion greatly. She also knew I was a novice, and I think she took pity on me, so that probably didn't hurt either. Anyway, I would happily take all the help I could get right now, so when she spoke I listened. "The minute you get on Sunny, you must not let him take control," she began. "He *WILL* test you and if you don't keep control from the get-go, things could get out of hand quickly." Somehow if this was her idea of a pep talk it was not helping my confidence. What happened to the "if you cut off his what-cha-ma-call-its he'll be a pussy cat" theory that I had bought into?

She went on, "If he tries to act up, use this and show him who's the boss." She handed me a sixteen inch crop. As I took the crop and looked over at Sunny, my nine-hundred-pound ex-stallion was rearing, kicking, snorting and stomping around his paddock as another horse was walking by. I looked back at the crop and then looked at Sunny again. I couldn't help thinking, If this little stick isn't a magic wand, I'm in a world of trouble. I hope he sees this thing and *knows* that I'm the boss when I have it in my hand. Maybe I should be sure to show it to him *before* I get on. No pressure here.

I went to get Sunny and led him out to the hitching rail. I had been walking him almost every day, for ten days, so I had completely gotten over any worries about the walking around on a lead line situation. Everyone had been amazed at how well he behaved when I was leading him around the ranch. Some of the people were already beginning to say I had "the gift." New headline, "Untrained horseman handles rogue horse." I admit I had been enjoying all the attention, but about now I was really thinking about my lack of health insurance.

I got Sunny over to the saddle and I probably spent more time than ever brushing him off. (For those of you that don't know me, anything more than one minute of brushing is a lot of time for me to spend grooming.) Then I went for the saddle. He stood there and looked at me, but never moved a foot, and I dropped the saddle in place on his back much sooner than I or anyone else expected. It had taken far longer to saddle Raj the first time I did it by myself. I fumbled around a bit, but finally got the girth fastened. Then it was bridle time. He didn't really want to put his head down and I had no idea what to do about it right then, so I stood on a mounting block. Amazing how tall a

14 3 hand horse can be when he wants to. I got the bridle on. Success. I had already gotten farther than at least a dozen people before, who were far more experienced than I. But I still had one more little item to do. I had to actually put my body in the saddle, on the horse. Wait, don't forget the crop. I put my foot into the stirrup and swung up and on. He didn't move. Not even a foot. I shuffled around a bit and got situated, awaiting the pending explosion. It didn't happen. In fact, nothing happened. He just stood there. So I just sat there. I would have been quite willing to say I "rode the horse" since I really was "on the horse" which is considered riding by most people. If you are "on" then you are "riding," right? Then the smart-ass trainer spoke up and suggested I get him to actually move. I was elated that he was *NOT MOVING*, and she wanted to interrupt that. OK, I know the game, kick em to go and pull to stop. (That was the way I rode at that point in my life, finesse and things like soft hands, leg aids, and seat were still distant concepts.) So I gave Sunny a little itsy bitsy tap with my boot. He began to walk forward, and I went too. Then I turned him left and he went left. Then right. The crowd was getting bored, as this was not what they had expected. I was actually RIDING SUNNY. I noticed I was feeling my concentration fading in and out, until someone reminded me to breathe. I think it was the trainer. Trainers tend to do that a lot, I have since learned. The resumption of breathing helped things get clearer. Sunny was walking around with me on his back and I was breathing, what could be better? Life was good.

As everyone congratulated me and meandered off to their own activities, I decided to head out on the trails. Just an easy trail ride at first, Sunny was probably still a bit sore, you know. Wouldn't want to hurt his surgery. We walked all over the ranch and then got to the main gate leading off the property. Sunny stopped. I didn't do anything to make him stop, he just stopped. This was a gate that trucks go through, and it was open so there was no obstruction to Sunny going forward. Since Sunny stopped when I wanted to go forward, I asked him to go forward in the only way I knew, I kicked him in the sides. He didn't go forward but he did start to get a bit more animated, dancing around a bit. I kicked a bit harder, but still no going forward, just more dancing around. I kicked harder yet. (I've never owned a pair of spurs. Back then I would have been dangerous had I had them. Someday I intend to get a pair.) After a couple of minutes of this increasing animation, he did something I had never experienced on a horse before; he got taller. A lot taller. All of a sudden I was looking straight ahead at his neck and I was quite a ways off the ground. At first I was confused as to what was going on. It was not very dramatic and I had no sense of danger, then I realized I was on a rearing horse. My mind instantly flashed back to my youth watching the Lone Ranger on TV. He would begin and end his show by rearing his horse Silver and yelling "Hi Ho Silver, Away," in a very deep voice. Quite impressive to a nine year old. Now here I was doing the same thing on my very own white horse (OK gray horse) and I felt like a king. I did quickly notice that my dressage saddle was severely lacking in the "things to hang onto" department. But I never came anywhere near falling off. Then I remembered that the Lone Ranger had *wanted* Silver to rear. As much as I was actually enjoying this a bit, I realized it was an unwanted behavior, and needed correction. I simply wanted Sunny to walk forward through the gate. He was telling me no and in a very definite fashion. I had to take action and take action now. I remembered the advice of the trainer and my magic wand...er I mean crop. I smacked Sunny on the shoulder and said, "Down" in the sternest voice I had. He went back to all fours, I think out of surprise more than fear or pain. I asked him to go forward again, and again he reared. Again the crop and again he went back down. After a few rather intense moments he gave in and walked through the gate. We went for our first brief trail ride. I was as happy as I could be. I had ridden the unrideable horse and survived. He had tried to resist and I had won. Maybe when you have "the gift" this training horses is not so hard after all. Life was good. [Note: I will refer to this

53

situation again in Chapter 7, and it has several very important lessons in it. Please be familiar with this incident.]

So far I had not had any great problems in my horse adventures, and I was feeling pretty good about my new hobby. True, it had become a great deal more expensive than I ever imagined, and it was a bit more complicated, what with two horses and a specific purpose of becoming an endurance rider and all. But I was enthused and really looking forward to the summer. Sunny was gelded and had been ridden. Shazi had his fifth race coming up next week, so I was a happy camper. I had gone through a difficult divorce, but was optimistic about my new endeavors with all the horse activities. My first two-and-a-half years around the horses had been eventful and eye opening, but I was still very much a novice. What I didn't know I didn't know was about to become painfully clear. I had no idea how much could go so wrong so fast. And I had no idea that the decisions I had just made about a simple hobby were to change my very life, forever. They say, "Life is what happens while you're making other plans." It's a true statement. But there is another statement that would become so etched in my mind during the next year that I now keep it on a plaque on my desk at home. It reads, "Anything that doesn't kill me, makes me stronger." I was about to get a lot stronger.

CHAPTER 4
The Struggles

We were about thirty seven miles into the fifty-mile endurance ride in Fort Collins, Colorado, and I was in a group of riders leading the way. We had pulled away from the nearest riders until they were just out of sight, which in the flat lands around Fort Collins was a good distance. We were basically on a dirt road, as straight as it could be, with a few slight rolling hills and not much else. Shazi and I were next to the leader and the others in the group were right behind us. I was having a ball. To be in the hunt to win a fifty-mile endurance ride was more than I had hoped for this soon, but it was at just thirteen miles ahead. Shazi felt strong and his heart rate was down; we were doing great. Suddenly Shazi pitched forward and almost went down. I ended up on his neck and fought to hold on as he struggled to keep from going all the way down, while the other horses darted off to the side to avoid the mayhem. We had been in an easy trot so the violence of his near fall seemed totally out of place for a simple stumble. And stumble on what? There were no holes, no big rocks, no nothing to trip over. We were on a smooth hard-packed dirt road, for heaven's sake. As he caught himself and I settled back into the saddle, he tried to go back into his trot, but something was wrong. Very wrong. He was three-legged lame. The others were yelling at me that he was hurt. In an instant I was off him and standing beside him. He was holding his left front leg up and could not put weight on it. I was horrified. In an instant we had gone from leading a race to being crippled and in serious trouble. We looked at the leg but there was no sign of any injury at all. He hobbled over to the edge of the road where he began to munch on some grass, but the left front was doing nothing. With little they could do to help, the others went on and promised to send out a vet. I stood there in shock with all the worst possible scenarios running in my mind. I kept telling myself that it couldn't be serious, he was in too good of shape and nothing had even happened before.

As other competitors came by, I had to relay the situation and hear their good wishes over and over, but I was really scared. Scared like I had not been before. It seemed like forever until a car pulled up with a vet from the camp. She came over and starting checking him out. It didn't take long for her to give me that look that we all dread. "It looks like it's broken but I can't be sure until we X-ray." Broken, how can it be broken, he wasn't doing anything stressful. "Sometimes it just takes one wrong step and these things happen. I'm going to put a splint on it to help support it, then I'll go back in and send a trailer to come get you." It took a few minutes to install the splint, and she gave him a shot for pain as well. As she drove off to get the trailer, I sat down and cried. Then I stood up and hugged Shazi, but I couldn't stop the tears. I never felt so sad and helpless in my life. I knew the story, "if they break a leg you have to shoot them." I gave Shazi a drink from my water bottle and he drank a lot. He was also quite happy to keep eating, but he was not putting *any* weight on that leg. When the truck and trailer arrived, the driver backed the trailer as close to Shazi as he could get it. Shazi still had about twenty feet to walk to get in, but it seemed like a mile. The trailer did have a ramp, so getting in would be easier than a big step up on one leg. As I asked him to walk on, he tried so hard, but each step was a big ordeal. He would have to bob his head an incredible amount just to get himself to move. He didn't seem to be in any pain standing still, but even with the splint he could put no weight on the leg. He kept trying and inching closer and closer to the trailer. He managed the ramp in a few awkward steps with great courage and, after what seemed like forever, he was in the trailer. The guy driving the trailer was real nice, but horse people always seem to show their best to help a horse in trouble. It was about thirteen miles back to camp where my truck and trailer were, and I didn't like the idea of having to take Shazi off one trailer and put him on another. The vet had said the bone was still connected, but if it shattered, we'd lose the horse for sure. The fellow driving volunteered to drop me to get my rig, but take Shazi on into Fort Collins where they just happened to have one of the best vet schools in the country. We drove slowly and carefully so as not to shake Shazi around. It was a long, dreadful thirteen miles, but finally the camp was in sight.

When we got to the camp, the word had already spread as to our predicament and everyone was offering any help possible. They had already packed up all my gear for me and loaded everything into my truck so we could head out immediately. I don't remember everything that everyone there did for us that afternoon, but they all were really wonderful, helping all they could. I didn't know the way to the vet school but the other guy did so I followed him. Also it allowed me to keep an eye on Shazi in the back of the trailer. I told the guy that if I started flashing my lights and blowing the horn, to pull over quick. I was praying that would not be necessary. I knew if Shazi went down in the trailer, it was all over. That had to be one of the longest twenty-five-mile drives of my life. If you've ever been in that sort of situation, I don't need to tell you all the things that were going through my mind. I cried and I hoped against hope that somehow he would be OK. He couldn't die. He *HAD* to be all right. He just *HAD* to.

The vet school had been called so they knew we were coming. They were very somber as we eased him off the trailer. He was such a trooper. He went wherever I asked and tried all he could without so much as the slightest fuss. There were two vets and four vet students looking him over while they got ready to do the X-rays. They worked quickly and efficiently, and in no time at all they had X-rays in hand. It was pretty obvious to them that it was the pastern bone. Broken but still connected. Even I could read that X-ray. One of the vets was touching his shoulder while looking at the leg when he turned to me and said, "You have a tough choice to make. We can operate and screw the bone together and he may survive. If he survives the surgery, and he doesn't tear the leg up after the surgery, he will walk again. He could come back almost good as new, but the odds of that are very slim. I mean very slim. I don't know what he's worth, but the surgery will cost $1500 or so, and he'll be laid up for the better part of a year. You may not even know the outcome for six months or so." I asked the only question that came to mind, "Will he suffer more through this surgery and the recovery process?" The vet replied, "No, not really, unless he can't stand the stall confinement and hurts himself. We will cast the leg, but if he goes nuts in a stall, he could tear it all apart at any time." It took less than a second for my decision, "Do it." He looked at me again and the other vet said "Are you sure you want to?" "Do it. He doesn't look like he is hurting. In his eyes he still looks like my Shazi. He hasn't quit, so I can't quit either."

The first vet looked away and then looked back to me again, as he ran his hands over Shazi's shoulder and hips. "What do you do with this horse anyway? He feels like solid muscle."

"We were training to be endurance riders," I responded, half with pride and half with fear of some forthcoming blame to bear.

He smiled a little, then said, "The bad news is he probably won't be doing any endurance rides again, but the good news is you probably saved his life. Had he not been this fit and well conditioned, his stumble could have been a real bad fall. And the fall, or at best the struggle to regain his feet after, would have severed the bone and we would not be talking about *ANY* possibilities right now."

"If he's so fit, how could this have happened?" I pleaded.

"I can't say. It's just one of those freak accidents that defy explanation. There could have been a flaw there from an old injury or it could have just happened. You are really lucky, it could have been much worse."

In fact he was right in more ways than he knew. Had we been on a more ordinary endurance ride we would have been in the mountains somewhere on some trail, not just thirteen miles down a dirt road. There would have likely been no trailer access and he would have never walked out of those trails on three legs. He could have died where it happened. We were lucky. Very lucky.

On the drive home I was torn between a glimmer of hope, and still being emotionally crushed from the day's events. Shazi would be in surgery in a day or two, depending on how the swelling went down, or something like that. They would call after it was over. I cried and I hoped. The next few days, I could think of nothing else. I racked my brain trying to think of what I should have done differently. What did I do wrong? How could I have prevented this? We humans are often so obsessed with finding a *WHY* when things go wrong that we waste an enormous amount of energy chasing questions without answers. We always seem to need a reason for something to rationalize or justify it. But unfortunately, sometimes things just happen. Accepting that is often not easy. And we tend to doubt ourselves worst of all.

A few days later I was in my office when the phone rang, and it was the vet. I struggled with answering the call. I wanted to know but was afraid of what I might hear. It had to be good news, it just had to.

"It went very well, the bone was in good shape and the screws went in like a textbook job," the vet said. "No problems at all and he should be up and around as soon as the anesthetic wears off."

I had tears in my eyes, but now they were tears of joy. We were over the first obstacle and he now had a chance. I knew he would have to stay there for a week or so for evaluation, but the only thing I could think to say was "Thank you. Thank you." And then very quickly I added, "When can I see him?"

"Tomorrow or anytime you'd like."

Those past few days had been one of the lowest points in my life. I felt shattered at seeing my friend almost destroyed by something I couldn't understand. If a horse is so fragile that a fit horse can be struck down that easy, then how could I go on riding? What would I do if something like this ever happened again? Over and over again I couldn't let go of somehow blaming myself for Shazi's crisis. I kept on asking all the same stupid questions that usually have no answers. Why Shazi? Why me? What did I do wrong? What if I hadn't gone to this ride? I finally arrived at a two-part plan of action: 1) I would do whatever was needed to nurse Shazi back to health, regardless of the time or cost; and 2) I would find him a good home and then get out of horses forever. I could not endure this pain ever again. I had loved so much the mountain riding Shazi and I had done together. I had learned so much and knew I had so much to learn, and it had been so much fun. I felt like I had found something I really, really loved to do, but the pain I was feeling was just too much. I remembered having tears at the end of the Pharlap movie* but this was real to me and it was much worse. A thousand times worse. My time with horses was over once Shazi was OK.

During the next ten days I went to see Shazi almost every day. It was over an hour's drive to the clinic, but I looked forward to each trip. Shazi was doing great and the vet students all loved him. They said he was the best patient they had and that he was always into something. I would call his name before I got to his stall and he would nicker back at me every time. Of course there were the necessary carrots. His attitude was always great, just like it had been that day riding in the snow. Soon he would be coming home to the ranch for months of rest and recuperation. Then the idea that I would soon be finding him a new home began to become real. First I would get him well, then see what to do. Then a very stark realization popped into my little brain; I had another horse. Sunny. In the recent days I had hardly ever thought of Sunny. I had not been to the ranch other than to drop off the trailer. In fact I had not done

*Pharlap was a true story about a fantastic racehorse that was killed by other horse owners because he was winning everything. You can usually rent or buy the movie in most tack stores or video rental stores.

anything with Sunny since our first semi-successful ride before the endurance ride disaster. I would have to sell Sunny too. I was not going though this type of agony again.

Bobbi understood my frustration and everything else I felt. She had lost several horses over the years, but she kept on riding. She said I would too. I said "I don't think so." Then she pointed out one small but relevant detail, "You can't sell Shazi until he's OK again, and you probably couldn't sell Sunny if your life depended on it. You were the only one dumb enough to actually want *that horse*. Who'd buy him? Where would you find another *you*? Unless you're willing to send him to the killer, you may as well face it, you're stuck with each other. Since you have to come out here to walk Shazi during his rehab, you might as well ride Sunny at the same time. If you can get him going OK under saddle, I might be able to sell him for you. But don't expect that to happen over night." At that point in time I was so tied up in knots that the incredible irony of the whole situation escaped me until later. FACT: Had I not bought Sunny the week I did, I would not have had him to deal with, and after Shazi's injury I would have gotten out of horses. By my own action, I was forced to keep riding. I had no choice. I decided to ride Sunny enough to get him salable. After all, how long could that take? Like I said before, life is what happens while you are making other plans.

My next two rides on Sunny were just the two of us (no one would even consider riding with us because they had no idea what to expect) and they were *incredible*. I mean they were good, incredible. I have had hundreds of incredible rides on Sunny over the years, but, as you will soon discover, during those first months I was riding him, most of the incredible rides we did were "incredible" because I survived. Not because they were fun. However, as if he wanted to tease me with a taste of what he could do, he was a dream on our first two outings. Maybe he was still a bit sore from his surgery, although it had not stopped him from rearing that first ride and he had had several weeks of healing by now. Maybe he was not sure about

61

me at first, so he was taking it easy with me. But for two rides he was a joy. He was only a touch smaller than Shazi, 14 3 versus 15 hands, but he was twice as agile. And a whole lot quicker. I was mentally just *going through the motions* in riding him at first, since I knew this was just a means to an end. And frankly, after the second ride, I was ready to tell Bobbi he was ready to sell. But she was out of town and I couldn't talk to her, so I ended up going to do one more ride on Sunny, just to be sure he was really ready for sale.

1. The word "ooops" can be used for many of life's problems that one does not expect to pop up when they do. My third ride on Sunny was definitely not an "ooops." 2. Many people have been in situations where they were facing great stress or really frightened, and they will speak some phrase having a religious significance such as "Oh my God!" My third ride on Sunny was not an "Oh my God" ride either. 3. Often a bad situation will get the best of even basically good people to where they feel that screaming is the appropriate action and such profane phrases as "OH S—" are likely to come out when they didn't really mean to say it. Sunny and I were not more than twenty minutes into our third ride together when I felt no choice but to go past 1 and 2 and plunge myself directly into 3 as the only appropriate response to my situation.

We left the ranch as in the previous two outings, walking at first, then trotting as he warmed up. Sunny was going along very nicely. We heard several horses approaching us from behind, but I paid little attention; Shazi and I were always around or passing other horses with no problems. As the horses passed us, Sunny got a bit more animated, and then in an instant, went from a nice little trot directly past canter (ooops), on through a very religious gallop (Oh my God) and into a "the world is coming to an end" speed (Oh S—!) that I had never felt before on horseback. We passed the other horses back in a blink as I tried desperately to slow Sunny down. I don't think so. Once past the other horses it was as if he was not looking back. I had thought at first he would slow after he passed the other horses, because that was obviously what set him off, but nooooo. He was possessed. It was quite apparent that I had lost all control. (In fact it had been an illusion that I had ever had *ANY* control of Sunny, anyway. More on that later.) Realizing it was a lost cause pulling on the reins (they might as well have been tied to a fire plug) I did the only logical thing I could think of, I screamed at the top of my lungs, "Go ahead sucker, I can ride as fast as you can run." I hoped I was right. Speaking as someone who has gone off a motorcycle at speed, many times, I must tell you *this was worse.* You see, in a motorcycle wreck you're going along doing OK then its gets terrifying for an instant (which seems like forever) but then you crash and it's over. Finish. This wasn't ending. He just kept going. And going. And going. After a few minutes of this excitement, I began to wonder if he would *EVER* slow down. I was a bit busy, dodging limbs and hanging on and praying. A lot of praying.

After awhile I began to stabilize and start to adjust to the conditions. I won't say it was fun, but I was a bit in awe of what we were doing. I had never experienced anything like that before. I even began to notice where we were. Soon I saw some familiar terrain and realized there was a turn coming up that would take us back to the ranch. I started to wonder if Sunny knew where we were (stupid me, of course he knew) and even more important, if said turn could be negotiated at anywhere near the speed we were still going. And if not, what were our options, since he was showing no sign of slowing down. When he passed the turn to the ranch, I started to wonder where in the devil he *WAS* going. But I guess horses can have brief lapses of concentration like I sometimes do because just then he realized his error and rather than slow down and go back, he just turned anyway. No trail here, just woods and bushes. Thank God for goggles, gloves, boots and a helmet. Still there was little or no reduction in speed. And other than dodging the occasional tree, we were headed pretty straight for the ranch. Maybe he had an appointment with the farrier I had forgotten about and he was trying to get us back in time. It would be good to point out to those of you not too familiar with the area between Denver and Colorado Springs, where this adventure was taking place, that the ground is definitely not flat. We were going up *AND DOWN* the Colorado Mountains at speeds I did not think possible. Obviously it *WAS* possible because I'm still here, but I didn't know that then. My education had just begun.

Eventually I saw the ranch, and as we approached, he still kept going. He may have slowed just a bit or maybe I was just getting used to the speed, but either way I had never seen anyone ride into the ranch that fast. Then, as we were nearing the tack room, he slowed down nicely and stopped. He was soaked and breathing heavily, but none the worse for wear. I jumped off Sunny like one of the cowboys in the old movies when he gallops up to the saloon, but for some reason my knees weren't working too well and I ended up on my butt in the dirt. Sunny looked at me with one of those, "What are you doing down there?" looks and calmly walked over to get a drink. Being stopped was a nice change from the previous period of very rapid movement, and I actually had thoughts of kissing the ground. But I didn't. As perplexed, angry and frustrated as I was, I knew I needed to check Sunny over and walk him out, so I grabbed the reins and started looking. He was fine. Wouldn't you know it? A horse can be left in a safe quiet stall overnight and somehow manage to get himself injured, cut up or as lame as a duck. Sunny just galloped several miles through the woods and mountains of Colorado, up and down hills, often without benefit of a trail, and he didn't have a scratch. We walked around for fifteen-twenty minutes and he was just fine. Like, "no big deal, what did you do today?" We had covered about six miles or so. In just a few minutes. Think of it as four Kentucky Derbys. With obstacles. Emotionally and physically, I was spent, and I really didn't even know quite what to think about the whole scenario. Several people had seen our entrance and came running over, thinking someone must be hurt on the trail and I was racing in to get help. "Er, uh, no. Sunny just ran away with me." Glad he didn't go someplace else.

Driving home that afternoon, (after a lengthy rest to get my knees to stop shaking) I pondered the day's events and drew several conclusions:

1) I had absolutely *NO CONTROL* when Sunny ran off.
2) It was the quickest trail ride I had ever done.
3) Sunny is *VERY* fast.
4) Sunny is *VERY* agile.
5) I can ride faster than I ever thought possible.
6) The pain from hitting a tree is directly proportional to the speed you're going.
7) Dressage saddles are very weak in the "stuff to hold on to" department.
8) Sunny now *KNEW* I had *NO CONTROL*.
9) Riding Sunny *WILL* make me a better rider, if I survive.
10) I had absolutely *NO IDEA* what had gone wrong.
11) I guess he wasn't quite ready to sell yet.

That night I couldn't sleep. My mind was racing in a dozen directions at once. I had thought I was OK with Sunny, and now this. There was no way I could sell him in this condition. I'd get sued for sure. To say I was depressed would have been an understatement, as I realized I now owned two horses, one I couldn't ride because of a broken leg and one I could ride as long as I had no expectation of where we would go. Or how fast we might get there. I had survived a dangerous incident and was grateful for that, but I was terribly confused and frustrated over what had gone so very wrong. On the other hand, I had gone faster today on a horse than I ever thought possible. I had gone up hill *and* downhill and was alive to tell the tale. I had ridden a runaway horse and not panicked… too much. And one more thing. I had felt the power of a really good horse, using his body for all it was worth. Without the inhibiting control of a human being and our limited judgment slowing him down. Sunny showed me a new dimension on the back of a horse. Granted, I was no more than a passenger but I was feeling what it was like to be at the limit of what a horse can really do. And that was a lot. What I had thought was fast was not fast. Sunny showed me what *FAST* really was. Even though I was not happy about losing control, nor did I have the slightest idea of what to do next, the feeling of sheer exhilaration at what Sunny could do was awesome. And deep inside, I was hooked.

Our next ride was not something I was looking forward to. A repeat of the previous adventure was not what I wanted and I had to really work on my fear to even go out there at all. But I had to walk Shazi, so I would ride Sunny again and see what happened. I had discussed the run away outing with a couple of trainers and they had offered various suggestions. "Keep him in a walk, no faster." "Don't leave the arena. He can only go so fast in the arena." "If you see or hear horses coming, get off." "Get a more severe bit." All in all, not a lot to work with for a novice horse trainer like me. As I saddled up, Sunny was as nice as you could imagine. He stood nicely and all went well. In fact, the entire ride of about ten miles went well. It was a Tuesday and there were no other people or horses around. We never did more than a trot. And I didn't mind that a bit. I kept waiting for the explosion, but it never came. After we got back and I was putting him away, an interesting thought crossed my mind. Maybe he was just too sore after all his galloping on the last ride to go any faster than a trot today. Ooops. I hoped for the best.

On Thursday, Bobbi was back and I outlined my experience with Sunny. She was quite somber and suggested I needed help. I assumed she meant horse training help rather than psychiatric help, but she may have meant some of both. She called a friend of hers with a lot of training experience and we talked at length. She pointed out the ineffectiveness of the mild snaffle bit I was using on Sunny, in regards to stopping a runaway horse. I already knew that. Remember, I was the one riding him. She suggested I would need a different bit and I wrote down the names she gave me. Of the three choices she gave me, she said one in particular always worked, but suggested I not use it except as a last resort. (Note: I will not mention any type of bit I used during this time frame, other than the snaffle I started with, as I refuse to encourage anyone to do what I did over the next few months.) With list in hand, I headed off to the tack store. While buying bit number one, the tack store owner made a few suggestions on other types of bits I might wish to try as well, but since I hoped I would solve all my troubles with this one, I was not interested in buying a collection. (To this day it never ceases to amaze me how often we humans want to just go buy something to solve our troubles and make us feel better. It even has a name now, Retail Therapy.) I headed back to the ranch to show Sunny my new "tool."

Over the next few months, (about eight to be exact) I rode Sunny a lot, often four-five times a week. Bit number one worked. Once. Then he seemed to ignore it and ran off again. Then he was great for several rides in various different areas. Then as if I were riding Jekyl and Hyde, I lost any semblance of control and the whole situation went in the toilet. I was a passenger again. Then back to the tack store for bit number two; much more severe than number one, and assurances from the store person that this bit was an excellent next choice, and no doubt would work better than bit number one. (By the way, this person knew the name of every single bit on the wall. It was a big wall. Called appropriately, *the bit wall*. And since she knew the names of all those bits, she *MUST* be knowledgeable about solving my problems. During a subsequent visit to the store I asked that same person what she rode. With great enthusiasm, she said she hoped to have a horse someday. Oh yea? Ooops. Be careful whose advice you take.) Much to my surprise, bit number two did work. Once. I was beginning to see a pattern here. There were a few successful rides and the distances were lengthening too as Sunny got more and more in shape. I defined the "successful" rides as any ride without a runaway. On the rides without a runaway, I had a horse of athletic ability that seemed without limit. Not to say his athletic ability was any less when he was running away with me, I was just less able to appreciate it very much.

After bit number three, we tried a mechanical hackamore (children, do not try this at home.) and it worked off and on for a while. Then he ran off again. Usually it was in response to other horses, but occasionally we were just going along and he got too fast and "checked out" mentally. Maybe I was riding "Psycho Horse." There were some great rides between the runaways, but the runaways were getting longer since we were farther and farther from home. And he was getting more and more fit. The duration of the runaway was determined by Sunny's energy level at the time and our distance from home. Sometimes he would even stop the runaway *before* he got home, but not often. On a couple of rides he ran away with me, and I did get him stopped, then later in the same ride he ran away with me again. All in all we had forty-one or forty-three runaways during about eight months. The variable in that number is whether you count two runaways in the same ride as one or two. I was keeping a journal on both of my horses to keep track of our conditioning progress as well as to offer my surviving family members an insight into my obviously strong lack of judgment prior to my demise. On Sunny's rides the entries were done as much to log any progress in gaining control as with any regard of increased fitness. Often my comments from that period were not fit to print in this book. There was one significant change to Sunny's behavior as the result of the various bits being used on him. During the early runaways, he ran like a normal horse, head stretched out in front. Now when he ran away with me, his chin would be up in the air. Shaking his head sideways. When that behavior started, I kept wondering how he could see where he was going with his head like that?

The trainer's solution to that new additional problem was to add a tie-down to our equipment roster. It did keep his head down. Until he broke it. Then I got tie-down number two. This was getting expensive and tacking up was getting more complicated.

Believe it or not, I actually took Sunny to a few endurance rides after about six months of conditioning. None of the rides were any fun at all. I spent all the time, and I mean *ALL THE TIME*, trying to hold him back, and not doing very well at it either. He seldom even finished the event as he would spend so much energy fighting with me to go fast, that two-thirds of the way into the ride he would just quit. Exhausted. Once I got so frustrated at trying to hold him back, I just let him run. He actually went over thirty miles (the first two legs of the race, including a vet check) only to turn up slightly lame at the last vet check and get pulled. He was fine the next day and showed no sign of any trouble from the race. I, on the other hand, felt like I had been through a war. And lost. On the good side, I was developing a great set of trapezius muscles from all the pulling on the reins. I was also becoming a much better rider, but I need to quantify the phrase "better rider" for you. I was not becoming a "schooled rider" as one gets from quality instruction, but I was learning to stay on an out-of-control horse going over any kind of ground. As one means of keeping Sunny slowed down on the conditioning rides, I would look for the worst possible terrain to take him over. Steep down hills and steep up hills were a favorite. Rocky terrain was also good. Really tight trails that switched back and forth a lot in very dense woods worked well too. In hindsight I wonder if that was such a great idea at all. Taking a runaway horse over *REALLY BAD TERRAIN*. Probably not brilliant on my part, but it was definitely exciting. We (Sunny and I) were also not very popular with the other people at the ranch as far as a "fun to ride with" evaluation would go. The reality of the situation was that I had adapted to Sunny, and learned to cope with his out- of-control behavior. He had incredible potential, but I was not able to use any of it effectively, because I had little or no control of him in many situations.

Today I often see people, in less dramatic, but equally dangerous situations with their horses, and like I did with Sunny, they adapt to the horse because they don't know what else to do. They think they can't change it because with *their level of knowledge* and the *type of help* they have been getting, they *haven't* changed it. They accept that the past equals the future, without even realizing it. And for all of you reading this and wondering why I kept going, remember this defining concept: Human beings are the only species on the planet that will do the same thing over and over, and expect something different to happen. If you keep on doing what you've been doing, you *WILL* keep on getting what you've been getting. This is true of your job, your personal relationships and it's true in dealing with horses. At that time of my life, I still didn't know what I didn't know, so I was not even asking the right questions, keeping the solution way beyond my grasp. After trying one or maybe two bits, I should have realized that since the bit was not working *the bit was not the solution to my problem.* But my lack of understanding of the horse in general, unaided by the equal lack of understanding on the part of most trainers I sought help from, was perpetuating the very problem I sought to solve. Also, do you remember when I initially asked the trainers what made Sunny such a problem, and they had all said, "Cut off his what-cha-ma-call-its and he'll be just fine?" What happened to that theory? As a gelding he was just as much trouble as he was a stallion. I now knew that gelding him didn't help, and that the bits weren't helping, so at least I knew two things that did not work. (NOTE: Although it is true that gelding a stallion later in life is less likely to change aggressive male behavior patterns, than it would have if it had been done earlier, in Sunny's case, I doubt the result would have been dramatic even then. I have seen it proven repeatedly, that proper training and interaction is far more effective in controlling stallion behavior than gelding the horse. But as with gelding, the training solution is most effective when started early.)

You may have guessed that my problems with Sunny became a major focus of my life during this period and even pushed my plan to get out of horses aside. Temporarily. I had been walking Shazi on a regular basis and he was healing just fine. Eventually, as the months passed, he was turned out and he could trot and canter like a pro again. I was ecstatic and watching him run around during those weeks would often bring tears of happiness to my eyes. I knew I had done the right thing and the vet bills and months of worry seemed far away and less important. In the years that followed as I became involved in working with injured horses all over the U.S., there were many situations where a horse had to be put down due to some critical problem. I often remembered my crisis with Shazi and that helped me understand and empathize with the feelings those people were going through with their horses. I am never one to easily give in to the loss of life, as some would say, since "it's just a horse." On the contrary, I feel the life of each horse is important and we should take more care than we sometimes do.

Riding Shazi was a nice break from Sunny and I even had thoughts of trying to compete on him again, but after a few trail rides, I decided against it. Any injury that occurs usually does not heal to the same strength as that area had been prior to the injury. (This will be discussed at length in Chapter 8 – The Physical Horse). Since I could never forgive myself if anything ever happened to Shazi now that I knew he had a previous injury, I had to let him go. Bobbi came to the rescue as usual and found a young couple that wanted a good trail horse for short, normal Sunday rides. (Not everyone goes on twenty-thirty mile horseback excursions all the time.) About ten months after the injury, their vet gave Shazi a clean bill of health, as had my vet, and Shazi had a new home. It was really sad to let him go, and I found myself thinking I should keep him forever so I was sure he would be OK. (From time to time I see people everywhere display that same attitude about horses, and even though it is usually very well meaning, I came to understand later how truly arrogant of me it was. How could I think that *I* was the only person that would take care of a horse? Without *me* he would not have a good life? We need to take care when we sell a horse that the next owner has sincerely good intentions for the horse, and that the horse is reasonable for the new owner's needs. Bobbi sells a lot of horses, and she often refuses to sell a particular horse to someone when she feels it would be bad for the horse or the owner. She helped me understand the reality and the humanity needed in selling horses. And I thank her for that along with the many other lessons she taught me.) Shazi seemed to like the young couple, and they really loved him from the first ride. After all, what's not to love about Shazi? Now I had sold my second horse and as with Raj before, he had taught me a lot and changed my life even further. Bye Shazi, and thank you for everything.

On the other hand, Sunny was taking a toll on me in more ways than one. He was often not fun to ride, but almost always exciting. I liked excitement, but I also wanted to *ENJOY* my riding. And I was not enjoying this. The frustration had run its course and I was feeling very spent. When I put Sunny away after a particularly tough ride one day, he had blood on the side of his mouth from the bit. It had happened a couple of times before, and things were not getting any better. At that point I decided I had had enough and said, "No more." I put Sunny away for the last time. I had to align myself to letting Sunny go, even if it meant putting him down, before I got seriously hurt. It was a testament to his athletic ability that we had never taken a bad crash during all the past months of out-of-control riding. I was out-of-control regarding his mind, but he was never out of control of his body. Truly an awesome horse. Considering the severity of the terrain we had gone over, and the speed we had used in going over that terrain, I was probably lucky to be alive. No one but me would ride him on the trails, obviously. He was still considered a rogue, of sorts. And my friends were constantly warning me about getting hurt. I think the most common comment was, "Oh, Dan? Yea, he's crazy." I had hired several trainers to work with us and a couple of them even rode him in the arena. Nothing had produced any results. I *thought* I understood why I couldn't figure this problem out; I was a novice. But nobody else was doing any better. And they were supposed to be the experts. For almost two months, I didn't ride at all while I struggled mentally and emotionally with my dilemma.

I went and saw Sunny a few times, but the whole situation was more than I could deal with at that time. Often I would just sit with him until the tears filled my eyes and I had to go. Those visits, seeing this beautiful creature with so much potential, which might not even survive, was as difficult a time as I can remember.

But during those two months something happened that had been happening all along, but until now, I hadn't realized it. Over the past months when I had an especially rough day on Sunny, I would go home depressed, and scribble furiously in my journal, but somehow, in a few days I was eager to go back out and try again. Why? I tended to forget the bad and remember the good. Probably because the good was as intensely good as the bad was intensely bad. When I was away from Sunny, I missed him, and the thrills and pleasure I got from what we did together. Somehow after two months off his back, with the very sad visits and no riding, I realized it all didn't seem so bad anymore. I knew it really was bad, there was no doubt in my mind of that, but I believe the time had taken the edge off, so to speak. That was why I kept getting back on Sunny all those months before. People say I'm stubborn. I like to think I'm persistent. I decided I would give it one more try, but not just doing more of the same that I had thoroughly proved wasn't working. There had to be something different to do that I was missing. There had to be someone, somewhere that could figure this dilemma out and save Sunny. I had no idea what to do, but I was going to do something. And although I still didn't know what I didn't know, I did know that Sunny's life was at stake. He would get one more chance, and I was determined to make it count.

CHAPTER 5

Awakening, The Journey Begins

The timing could not have been better for the phone call. My friend said there was a famous trainer coming to a nearby town to give a clinic, and it was said he could "fix" any horse. She said he worked with all kinds of "problem" horses as well as training young horses and the like. It was some sort of a "round pen clinic," whatever that was, but it sounded different, and I knew I needed different because I had now, finally figured out that *normal* was not working with Sunny. That's where I needed to take Sunny. (Isn't it funny how often someone from out of town, or maybe another country is always a bigger expert than a local just because they are from someplace else?) I agreed to give it a try. And for four hundred dollars, it had better be good. Horse stuff is seldom cheap but sometimes we think it's better just because it's more expensive. Sunny and I were going to our first clinic. I was still looking for "the answer" and I hoped to find it at the clinic. "The Answer" would turn out to be a lot more involved than the simple "fix" I was hoping for.

Sunny always went in the trailer very well, and he was pretty easy to handle on the ground in general, so the trip to the clinic was a piece of cake. I unloaded and tied Sunny to the trailer. Then with great expectations I set out to see what was what. I ended up at the "round pen" with about seventy-five others that seemed to be grouped in two distinct factions; desperate neophytes like myself, and previous clinic attendees here to learn more from their guru. The spread was about seventy-thirty. You would have had no trouble telling which group I was in, but I didn't care, I was here for help and I knew it. But then to my shock, this "cowboy" walked into the round pen and started talking. A *COWBOY*? Nobody told me that the clinician was a cowboy. He had the big buckle, the hat, the chaps, and even the little round tin in his back pocket. He was definitely not a city cowboy; he looked like the real thing. He talked like it too. Not that he wasn't intelligent, in fact he was *VERY* intelligent, he just didn't use a lot of words in most of his sentences. Now I was definitely *NOT* a cowboy. Dressage saddles, red and black riding tights, and fanny packs with water bottles are very good for riding horses, but they are absolutely *NOT COWBOY*. I had also seen a lot of what I thought were cowboys, (really just people with western clothes and horses), who were *VERY* rough with horses. In fact the word "cowboy" was considered by some to be a verb, meaning a very negative way to handle a horse. I remembered thinking to myself, If he starts beating on Sunny, we're outta' here. I had a lot to learn, I just didn't realize yet how much of it had more to do with myself, than it did with horses. Learning is a complicated process that can be easily contaminated by the attitudes of the student and teacher. I almost lost out on an incredible opportunity because of my attitudes and negativity. Fortunately, I was so dumb about horses compared to the trainer, that I was easily impressed and won over. Unfortunately I still see people come to clinics and bring with them so much attitude, that it's almost impossible to get to them. More on this later in the chapter on Psychology.

During the first day, I saw the trainer/cowboy put horse after horse in the round pen. He'd rope the horse, then do some stuff I didn't understand, pulling the horse around on the rope, or running the horse back and forth around the round pen. The veteran clinic-goers were all nodding in approval and the rest of us were just watching whatever it was we were watching – many of us with far too much skepticism and not enough open- mindedness. It can be hard to accept what you don't understand. But one strange thing did begin to happen; all the horses began to change. They began to pay attention to the trainer and they began to become more responsive as well. When it came Sunny's turn, I was really nervous. He did *NOT* want to cooperate. Surprise, surprise. But after awhile, he did start to change. It took longer than the others, but it did happen. After awhile he was being as nice and responsive as the other horses, and then the trainer said I could come get him out now. Step one is done. I had been watching every move they made with great intensity and yet I had no idea what step one was. And now it's over.

I wasn't sure what had just happened but it was pretty neat. I didn't have a clue *HOW* it happened, but I was impressed. And every single horse, both young and old, seemed to change, no exceptions. Some took almost no time, and some took longer. Sunny was the longest. The trainer had even said something like, "You got your work cut out for you with this guy." I was also very curious as to what the devil did that "run around the round pen" stuff have to do with solving my problem of Sunny running away with me? Which is why I brought him in the first place. Running was what he did too much of already. Day one ended and I had not been on the horse at all. Oh well, it was a four-day clinic so I assumed we'd get to the riding part soon enough. During the next few days I saw a lot of interesting things, and did begin to learn how much I didn't know, but I admit to being more frustrated than educated. I could tell that whatever was being done was far more complicated than I was understanding. That was another place where I was wrong. It was really far more "simple" and that's why I didn't understand it.

Finally after several days in the round pen, we were all going to ride around this big outdoor arena, and the goal was to work on something called a "soft feel." I really didn't understand it but it had something to do with "not" pulling on the reins most of the time, then pulling a little and then letting go. Or something like that. Like I said, I didn't understand, but I was willing to give it a try. With about thirty-five of us on horseback, many on very green horses, we were to walk around the arena with a "loose rein." No contact. I was surprised at the number of people having trouble with that. Sunny did "walk" very well. And we made several uneventful trips around the

76

big arena. Then we were asked to trot on a "loose rein." Things got more exciting for some of the people as the speed picked up, but Sunny could trot with the best of them, so we were still OK. Then came the request I was dreading, "Canter your horses on a loose rein." It took all I could do to *NOT* grab a tight rein while I asked Sunny to canter. Believe me, it was one of those, "I know I'm gonna' die, but if you say loose rein, I'll do it" things.

I think Sunny was in shock at not having me pulling on his mouth, because he actually did a few strides, cantering on a loose rein, before he left. I went with him. We were now galloping, flat out around a very big arena full of all kinds of people on all kinds of horses. Going in all kinds of directions. They were parting like the Red Sea as the guy on the out-of-control gray horse galloped through. That was me. The trainer was mounted on his wonderfully trained, perfectly behaved, totally controllable horse, watching. He saw my situation and yelled, "Pull his head around to the inside. Do a one-rein-stop!" He had talked about the one-rein-stop a bit, but I had never done it and I wasn't sure exactly what he meant. However, he was the one on the behaving horse and I was the one on the totally out-of-control horse, so I figured his suggestion outweighed anything I was likely to come up with at this time. Sooooo.... I pulled Sunny's head around to the inside as hard and as far as I could, and hoped for the best. I was now on a runaway horse with his head turned to the side, galloping through a bunch of neophytes on green horses. And I paid $400 for this experience. Eventually Sunny slowed down and went back to walking. Two people came over and asked me if I would ride their horses that were acting up after I finished training Sunny. It hadn't felt like I was doing as much "training" on Sunny as I had been "hanging on for dear life." But if it appeared that I had been "training" Sunny to them, I'll take it. I don't know if they admired the fact that I could ride well enough to stay on Sunny throughout that crisis, or if they just wanted to get Sunny out of the arena so we would not be galloping through the middle of all of them again. I said, "Thanks, no I'll stay on Sunny. We need the practice." Besides most of them didn't know how easy that little venture really was for Sunny and me. In the woods for the past months, we'd gone further than that and none of the trees even *tried* to move out of our way. Sunny probably enjoyed seeing obstacles dodge *him* for a change. We tried a few more times, but never did get Sunny to canter. Several people suggested I should let him go till he tires out. I smiled politely at that one.

By the end of the four days, I was exhausted. I could not control Sunny any better than I had before, so on one hand I was very disappointed. However, I had seen a true horseman do things with all sorts of horses, including Sunny, and he never hurt them, or seemed to be overly forceful at all. And they seemed to almost enjoy it, and truly *understand* him. I didn't, but the horses did. *I could not do what he had done, but I could see that I needed to learn how to do it.* And I don't mean to infer that the trainer was not trying to teach me and the other neophytes. He was. But he didn't understand that what he did so naturally and easily, appeared so foreign to me and many of the others. I couldn't see what was right in front of my face, and he couldn't explain it so that I could. We had a communication problem. I was too quick to blame his lack of discussion, and sometimes cynical answers to questions, as an excuse for me not learning more. Back then I was, as many others still are, not open enough to let go of what I had been used to, and take in something so different and new. Years later, when I was asked to teach what I was now doing with horses, I remembered these experiences in my life, and drew upon them to help me become more effective in getting others to more quickly accept and understand what had been so difficult for me and taken so long. The key that I was missing was the *understanding*. Not just understanding the trainer, but understanding the very nature of what was going on between the horse and the person in the round pen. Many people have attended round pen clinics and learned techniques to copy, while never really understanding the horse and what is going on for him during an appropriate round pen session. I say "appropriate" because many round pen trainers rely mostly on fatigue to get the submission from a horse, and that demonstrates that *they* do not understand the process either. If you first understand the horse more completely, and the *why* of what you are supposed to do in a round pen, then you will act out of conviction, rather than simply go through some rote motions with little sincerity on your part. That may sound trite to you now, but believe me, a horse can sense your emotions and intent as easily as you could tell I have on a red shirt. Because of what *is* going on between you and the horse in the round pen, if you simply go through the motions, you will accomplish nothing. And you simply cannot have any conviction or belief about something if you don't understand it first. Hence the reason you must understand the process first, before you try to make it happen.

I had found out at the clinic that the trainer had learned all of this round pen stuff from an older trainer who was supposed to be even better at working with the horses than the younger guy. I decided to go see the master. He was doing a clinic in another state a few weeks later, so off I went. I had to fly there this time, so Sunny stayed home. He didn't mind, but he said he would miss galloping through all the other horses. Sunny has a great sense of humor. Another four days, another $400 and I had now done two round pen clinics. As an observer at the second clinic I now saw things I had missed at the first clinic – kinda' like going to see a movie the second time. Also, I observed a phenomenon in watching the *people*, which I still see to this day in clinics and workshops of all kinds. When you bring your horse to the clinic, you tend to be so concerned about how your horse will look and do in the clinic, as well as caring for your horse, that it distracts you from your ability to focus on the clinic itself. It's true you learn by *doing*, but as I said before, until you *understand,* you should not attempt to *do.* That observation helped me design the format for the workshops I teach today.

So far I had learned several things from a comparison of my two-clinic career in round pen training: the "master" was a bit better with the horses than the first trainer. Not a lot, but a bit. After all, he had twenty or so years more experience. The "master" was much rougher on the people than his protégé. In fact he openly said during the clinic, "I'm not here for you, I'm here for your horse." I understood his point, but if you don't get to the *people that own and ride the horses*, how do you help their horses? I still didn't understand the round pen much, and the "soft feel" bit was not working for me, but I kept coming back to what these cowboys could do with the horses. It seemed like magic. Watching the students look mostly so crude, (except those few veteran students that had it figured out somewhat) while these round pen trainers looked so effortless, efficient and most important, *connected with the horse*, had me hooked. Now if I could just learn how to *do* it.

I was now fully convinced that I needed to learn all about this round pen training stuff, so I set off to the tack store to buy some books on the subject. And tapes. And videos. And surprisingly the tack store person was *VERY* negative when I mentioned the trainers I had seen. She said a friend of hers had attended a round pen clinic and her horse was so abused and exhausted he almost died. Cost her hundreds for the vet bills, and all in all it was a horrible situation. She warned me to be really careful with *those round pen people*. Mind you, she didn't know the name of the person doing the clinic with the catastrophic outcome, but he did use a round pen. And now she was very adamant about not liking *any* round pen training. Whoa. I didn't expect that. How quick we are to judge a group by the action of an individual. I thought I was on the road to true enlightenment and now I'm hearing that the round pen is a dangerous weapon for damaging horses. True, one lady fell off her horse at the second clinic and broke her wrist, but stuff happens. And I hadn't seen any horse abuse. Still, the comments made me think. Throughout the next few years I heard that same negativity expressed so many times by so many people. I have also seen numerous people, calling themselves round pen trainers, abuse and literally destroy horses in the round pen – validating all that negativity. Like any tool, be it a round pen, a car or a gun, it is the *person* using it and their intent combined with ability that determines the results of the use of the tool. A car driven by a drunk driver can be unnecessarily deadly, and a round pen misused is no different. Those negative perceptions regarding round pen training, generated by inept people calling themselves trainers, is the primary reason I do not refer to myself as a round pen trainer. It would turn off too many people that I could otherwise possibly help before I ever got the chance to try.

Soon I was forming a list of some of the most well-known round pen trainers around. Each a bit different, and some having attained wealth and celebrity status beyond reason. I began to read their books and watch their videos. Over and over and over again. The beauty of videos. And I discovered a somewhat universal and interesting fact about round pen videos; in most cases it was a real accomplishment if I could just *stay awake through it*, much less learn anything. This is not necessarily a criticism of the trainers (although some of them were pretty poor), but more a comment on the subtleties of the method and its difficulty in translating into normal human thinking by the medium of TV. It just doesn't click without a really good explanation. But the more I studied, the more questions I developed. I went to more clinics, everywhere. I saw all kinds of demonstrations. I bought more tapes and more books. I spent a small fortune – in both time *and* money. In fact, I could have taken the money I spent and *BOUGHT* a really well-trained horse…or three, for what I spent on learning. I all too often see many people taking that approach; if this horse doesn't work out, sell it and go buy another one that will. Never mind that it may have been our ignorance that kept the horse from working out in the first place. That approach would have seemed to be the easier way out for me, but more important, I would have still been the same uninformed horse lover as I started. And that would have been my loss.

Bit by bit (again, no pun intended) I began to figure out what was going on in the round pen. At least the techniques and mechanics involved. But the lack of communication skills on the part of many of the clinicians was still keeping me from the *understanding* I really needed. Many could *demonstrate techniques*, but they were not *teaching understanding*. I had been a corporate trainer and motivational speaker during a recent part of my life, so I had been trained to be aware of the mental interaction that goes on when someone is learning. It is a complex situation. Such things as the attitudes and background of the student can play a big part in the receptivity of the student to new ideas as well as what they respond to. The emotional state of the student has an incredible impact on her ability to learn and just retain information, much less apply it. In any heightened emotional state you are likely to mentally "anchor" yourself to the wrong information, creating more trouble later on. Most learning involves a step by step progression of ideas, organized in a fashion that takes the student through a logical process. For instance, in math we start by teaching numbers and counting, then addition and subtraction, then multiplication and so on; eventually getting to geometry, calculus, etc. Without the basic understanding of the numbers and how they work, all future work would be useless. Weaken any step in the progression and the later work will fall apart. Worse yet, skip the fundamentals, try starting with algebra and see how well things go. Additionally, if you are trying to learn something less cut and dried than math, something that touches your emotions as well as involves a real change in behavior from what you consider normal, you had better develop an *understanding* of the *whys* involved. Without the understanding you will not do anything with true conviction. And that lack of conviction on your part will diminish your effectiveness dramatically. In fact, many times a teacher needs to be very adept at understanding this learning process in order to get the student to change old behaviors before they can be replaced with the new ones. Even when the old behaviors are *not working*, we will hold on to them desperately. Often, challenging old patterns of behavior with understanding is the best way to begin to break down those ineffective behaviors. Humans resist change with a passion. But change is what learning is all about.

As I went from trainer to trainer, I saw one man that could articulate things so I could understand a bit more. He was Pat Parelli. He was also a cowboy, but a very articulate cowboy. Sometimes it was almost as if I was trying to put together a jigsaw puzzle, and bit by bit the pieces were starting to fit. If ever so slowly. Pat's explanations and his book made more difference than anything I had seen, perhaps because I had seen and done so much before I got to Pat, but I know I was in a better place mentally when I did see him. I really think it was his ability to help me understand the process that was so important to getting me going in the right direction. I must openly tell you that I learned a lot from many people, *I am still learning today and will continue to learn*. But unlike many of the contemporary clinicians, I believe you should see everyone you can, rather than find a guru and go down any singular, limiting path. If you find someone you can understand and relate to, then learn from him. But don't ever feel that another clinician with different ideas is not worth a visit since you've found "the way." I have been to clinics where all I learned was that I would never ever do what they did with the horse, and that was still learning. If I learn one good thing in a class, then it was worthwhile and I am happy. Sometimes I learned nothing, but simply had things I already knew reminded and reinforced. That's OK too. There are some clinicians I see as dangerous and fraudulent in their methods and I will never mention, much less endorse those people. But the people like Monty Foreman (not to be confused with Monty Roberts), Pat Parelli, Buck Branaman, Ray Hunt, Dave Seay, Damon Wills and Tom Dorrance have contributed a lot to the horses and their owners. I do not agree with all of everything they each may do, teach or sell, but you need to see as much as you can to find out what works best for

YOU. They would be worth your time. They each helped me, and they have my enduring gratitude for that.

During the past months of my "educational journey" I had attempted to work Sunny in the round pen a few times. It didn't go well or last very long. Mainly because I didn't know what I was doing. Going though a bunch of mechanical steps like run him around this way, then turn him and run him the other way proved an exercise in futility. But now I was beginning to feel I had some grasp of the idea and I was ready to exert a serious effort. For the next six weeks all I did with Sunny was done in the round pen. First I only played with him at liberty.

> ITEM- Notice I used the phrase "played with him" rather than "worked him"? The words you use define your attitude, and often even your very character. Choose your descriptions carefully as they can at least set the mood. The question you ask is the beginning of the answer. Often a single word can so change the intent presented by the question that it affects the outcome. I'll give you an example. When a horse is acting up, it is common to hear someone say, "What's wrong with that horse?" It's the same question we use on each other when we don't like what's happening with us. Suppose you change a word in that question and tried, "What's troubling that horse?" Very different feeling behind that question, is it not? Imagine if someone were asking that question of you. The first question is very confrontational and offers little room for a non-defensive response. The second would tend to better open a dialog and offer possibilities. And there is usually very little *wrong* with most horses that a change on our part would not eliminate.

Then I saddled him, but didn't ride him. Then I played with him at liberty with another horse in the pen too. Then I used three horses in the pen together. Then I rode him in the pen, walking only. Then trotting. No canter. I'm not saying this progression was ideal, since I would do a lot of it differently now that I have more experience. I made so many mistakes it would take another book to list them all. But I was learning at the same time I was trying to help Sunny. It was like putting a novice rider on an untrained horse. Potential disaster. It really helps if at least *one* of the parties knows something. A novice rider can learn faster on a trained horse, just as a veteran rider can teach a green horse. Because I was unsure of myself, I simply did something and then waited to see what happened. If it seemed productive, I did it some more. If it didn't work, I then had the added stress of trying to decide if it didn't work because I did it wrong, or my timing was poor, or because it was a bad choice of what to do. And don't get nervous because I'm not detailing here in this chapter exactly what I did do. The "How To" chapter will cover the process completely for you. Suffice it to say that everything I did was an experiment. Some days I felt like a master, some days I felt like a fool. I could sense a lot of resistance from Sunny in the beginning, but it began to break down rather quickly. He also began to pay attention to me with a certain intensity. He was *really* watching me, not just noticing where I was as he walked all over me. We worked on basics more than anything technical: things like standing still; standing still with me sitting on him; sometimes for ten minutes at a time. That was a goal I had. His previous record for standing still while mounted was 1.5 seconds. We also worked on standing to be mounted. Early in my efforts with Sunny, I had become very proficient in getting on a moving horse. Simply because once my foot hit a stirrup, we were under way. Do you notice how I had been adapting to him up until now. We worked on walking around the pen while the two other horses wandered around the same pen, loose. That didn't go well the first few tries. But the first time I rode him and he ignored the other horses, I *knew* I was succeeding. I knew it.

I was getting a lot of teasing from people asking if Sunny was going to be ridden indoors from now on. Since it had been months since we had gone out on a trail, I think a lot of people thought I had lost my nerve. Some even consoled me, saying I had every right not to take him out again after all I'd been through. As difficult as that time was, I was determined to continue as planned. People had often called me a daredevil all my life, long before horses. But I never considered excess bravery to be a reasonable substitute for intelligence. Yes, I enjoyed thrills. To me, living a boring life without passion would be the ultimate waste. But I had no desire to die, much less even get hurt. I was never "into" pain. In all of the car racing, motorcycle racing, skydiving and horse activities I've been involved in, I only have a broken collarbone and broken toe to show for it. I don't enjoy pain in any way. I will happily agree that there is always a degree of luck in all we do. And I will *never* turn down the option to be lucky. But thinking and using your head is more dependable than relying on luck alone. I was not afraid to ride Sunny again, but I would not get on until I thought the time was right. I had already proved I could do this horse stuff, all wrong. Now I had to try to get it right. I was not ready to leave the pen yet, so I would not do it.

One thing about having a very limited amount of knowledge on a subject; you don't need as much time to do all you know. Sunny and I spent a lot of time in the round pen looking at each other while I tried to figure out what the heck to do next. My "tool box" of horse training techniques was not overflowing with options. As time went on, I felt better and better about Sunny. Other people would ride by or maybe even have problems with their horses right next to where I was riding Sunny in the pen, and he would pay them absolutely no mind. At times they distracted *me* more than him. What a change. So one day, without any plan, I decided today we were going for a trail ride. The mountains were still there. The trails were still there. Sunny and I needed to be there too. Oh, by the way, I forgot to mention one little item. During all this time riding Sunny in the round pen, what do you think I had chosen to use for a bit? Wrong. During the first clinic I had described my runaway problem with Sunny to the trainer and asked what bit I *should* be using. His response was short and to the point. "Don't matter. If you'd train your horse, you could ride him with a string around his nose." OK, that helps a lot, I thought at the time. But again, he was right. I had proved the bit wasn't the problem, since I changed bits and accomplished *NOTHING*. The next chapter will explain why he was right, but for now I will tell you I had been riding Sunny in the round pen in a halter only. No bit.

The gate to the round pen was swung open by a cautious onlooker. I was sitting on Sunny and had been for several minutes. And we stayed still for several more minutes with the gate open. It was a test. We passed. We then started to walk out of the pen and head for the trails. Walking. Suddenly a couple of people seeing us leaving, called out rather frantically, so I stopped Sunny and turned to them. "First big ride out with Sunny and you already forgot something. Your bit," they offered. "Thanks, but this is what we ride in now," I replied, then headed off again. They ran to catch us and shouted desperately, "You can't go up there with no bit after all the times he's run away with you. You'll get killed!" Now, I appreciated their concern, but I want you to think about what they said and the insanity of it. For eight months Sunny had run away with me, using every severe bit I could get in his mouth. How much *worse* could he run away with me, now that there was *no* bit? I had absolutely *NO CONTROL* with the bits, so how much less control is there than *NO CONTROL*. Do you see the point? They were shaking their heads as I rode off into the mountains, on Sunny, with the halter. No bit.

No, it wasn't a great ride. Not the fairy tale ending like some stupid Hollywood movie. Not like the beautiful, snowy ride on Shazi that opened my eyes to really being with your horse. But it was perhaps even a bigger success. I tried to get Sunny to just walk and trot only, for the whole ride. Time and time again he tried to run off with me. But time and time again I stopped him. Something I had *never* been able to do before.

87

Never! He would bolt forward and within a few steps we were stopped. And I was able to accomplish that no small task with the halter. No bit. I was ecstatic! It wasn't real pretty, but it was working. We were out for almost two hours and I had no idea that they were already getting mounted to come looking for us when we came back. The word had spread that we had gone out with the halter, and everybody just knew we had run off some cliff somewhere. When they saw I was not only still on, but rather happy, and walking in, they were speechless. So was I. I remember someone saying that they knew I had the "gift" from the beginning, and this proved it. I smiled. I knew I was not gifted. Fortunate, maybe. I had gone through a lot of pain, study and hard work for what just happened, but I was just now starting to realize how *little* I really knew. The important part is that before I didn't know what I didn't know. Now I *knew* what I didn't know, which would allow me to get on with learning it. That may sound like a lot of semantics, but it isn't. It's a fundamental of human thinking that limits each of us more often than we realize. This book is about horses, but it is also about us. People.

Over the next few months I rode Sunny a lot and he never successfully ran away with me again. That is fact. And I rode him in the halter almost all the time. I did occasionally ride him with a mild snaffle bit. Nothing else. I continued to play with him in the round pen almost every time before I took him out for a ride. Only for a couple of minutes, but it was not a step I felt comfortable to skip. One of the rewards was that often people would ride up to us on the trail and after a minute, notice my well-behaved horse and ask, "Is that Sunny you're riding?" "Yep." I would casually reply. "That's Sunny? Boy he sure is different." "Yep." I was starting to sound like a cowboy.

But the other thing that also began to happen was people began to ask me to help them with their horse problems. One "fixed" horse and now I was considered an expert. I have often said "results speak loudly." Sometimes they *shout!* I had effected major changes to a not very well-liked horse, but I hardly felt like an expert.

The idea of being able to ride some other horses did appeal to me, so as time went on I began to ride horses for other people and train them. Actually I should say re-train them. I had no skills in creating a dressage horse, or barrel racer or show winner. What I was doing was taking unwanted behaviors, like runaways or horses that rear, and eliminating that behavior. (I'll discuss this re-training at length in the next chapter along with the reality of what I had and had not done with Sunny.) I was also doing a bit of conditioning work for people; riding their horses to get them more in shape for endurance riding. The Colorado Mountains were excellent for that. I was also riding horses that Bobbi had for sale to keep them fresh and manageable. Every so often she would get in a horse that was a bit of a handful. She was always saving this horse or that horse from some lousy situation. And sometimes the horses had some "baggage" in the behavior department. And she was always looking for horses with real endurance potential. At one point she had bought a couple of horses from a ranch somewhere and told me I could buy one of them if I wanted, for resale. She suggested I could ride it, do a little training so it was good on the trails then she'd help me sell it and make some money. Sounded good. So far the words "riding horses" and "making money" had been diametrically opposed in my life. I agreed to her offer. I saw the horse's papers and he sounded nice. I didn't know a lot about breeding, or blood lines and the like, but Bobbi did and I trusted her judgment. This was a four-year-old (almost five) gray Arab gelding, fifteen hands and very well built. Gee, Raj was a gray gelding. Shazi was a gray gelding. Sunny is gray and now a gelding. Sounds like my kinda' horse. He would arrive in a week or so.

When Bobbi called and said I should come look at the horse, I got nervous. Why do I need to look at the horse? I knew the shipper was due today, but I didn't expect a call like that. Needless to say I headed for the ranch with all sorts of things running through my mind. Don't over react, I kept telling myself. When I arrived at the ranch, Bobbi directed me to a paddock that had a horse in it and indicated, "That one's yours." Well, he was gray. He was an Arabian. He was a gelding. And his withers were about fifteen hands off the ground. But... he was missing something. At least two hundred pounds or more. He was *really* skinny. He was friendly and happy to be around people. He had big, soft eyes and appeared to be as sweet a horse as anyone could want. But he was *VERY* underweight and looked pretty bad. With his skeleton so exposed, the straightness of his legs was easy to see. So was every other bone in his body. His name was Cisco but I immediately started calling him Bob. "Bob" was an acronym for "bag of bones." He was. I had to decide if I would keep him because if I was going to back out, it was now or never. I had every right to back out, but I wondered what would happen to him if I refused the sale. I liked his personality right from the start, but I really wanted a strong trail horse, not a physical disaster. I needed to know more about him if I were going to take the chance on getting him fit and hoping he would sell. As luck would have it, I decided to take him for a short ride around the ranch just to see how he was under saddle. (I always thought "under saddle" was a funny thing to say. It makes sense and I have used it, but now that I ride bareback a lot, I don't say it often. Instead I say "under me." Seems more accurate to describe what I'm really concerned with.) I even felt guilty about just putting the saddle on him because of the way he looked; so I told myself "if he has even the slightest hint of trouble or doesn't want to go, I'll get right off and walk him back."

He showed no sign of trouble with the installation of saddle or bridle. He also stood quite nicely to be mounted and when I asked him to walk off he did just that. Walk off. Up to now I had developed a procedure for every new horse I rode, which included a bit of time playing with the horse at liberty in the round pen *before* I ever got on them. I still do that to this day. I didn't with Bob because he looked so thin and weak and I was afraid *ANY* laps around the round pen could have sapped whatever strength he may have had. As we started our little ride around the ranch, he came to life and was paying great attention to everything we passed. Obviously it was a brand new environment for him, yet he wasn't at all bothered by the new surroundings, he was just taking it all in. He was relaxed and seemed fine. After a few minutes to warm up and stretch his legs he appeared to be OK, so we started to trot. Surprisingly he was quite eager to go. In a very few strides his trot began to extend and he felt absolutely awesome. I kept asking myself, Where did *this* come from, he looks like he should be barely moving yet he was covering ground like a pro! He even did a bit of cantering and it was just as good as the trot. I probably over-reacted to his movement since I almost expected him to fall over rather than move at all, but he did have a great trot and a long stride. OK, I'm keeping this horse. Easy to ride, great disposition, and he can really move. Maybe I'll do endurance after all. Bobbi was pleased that he was OK, and the horses she got were also all right, just thin. We would feed him all he wanted and get him back in shape. Wow, if he goes this well out of shape what will he be like when he's fit? Good question.

Shortly after I got Bob, I mean Cisgo, Sunny came up lame. I hadn't ridden him for several days and he must have done something in the pasture, because Bobbi called and said he was off in the right front. I buy a new horse and the old horse gets hurt. This was a déja vue that scared the dickens out of me. All the past anxiety about Shazi came back with more vivid clarity than I wanted to experience. Fortunately the lameness was not serious, but if we hadn't caught it when we did it would have been. His primary problem was a tendon, but it was not bowed, just quite sore. There was also some inflammation in the knee and ankle. He must have been running around chasing another horse or something and taken a fall. We never really know what all goes on out in the pasture when we aren't watching, do we? Since I knew he loved to chase other horses and play with them along the fence line I was not surprised. Shortly after he was gelded, he was turned out in a pasture with several mares and geldings and it went fairly well. Unfortunately the vet recommended I keep him in a stall for a while and not ride or work him for four to six months, maybe longer. I was so relieved to find out he was going to be all right, I didn't care about the time off. Whatever he needed was OK. My only two concerns were how well would he come back and how much of the behavioral improvement would I lose during months of not riding and training? Time would tell. At least now I had time for Bob, er Cisgo.

I didn't ride Cisgo at all for five weeks. I wanted to see his ribs disappear before we began any riding. And his hips and all the other bones he had sticking out all over his body. He ate and relaxed in the pasture, and fattened up very well. He got along well with the other horses and just acted like he had lived there forever. I rode several horses for Bobbi as well as horses for other people, and walked Sunny on a lead line as often as possible. When I began to ride Cisgo it was all walking and easy trails at first. No rough terrain, no steep mountains, and NO speed. He felt good from the beginning and was a joy to ride. Always willing but never hard to control. All in all he was an absolute pleasure. His color was almost a dirty gray, but he was blossoming into a very impressive horse. He was a wonderful reminder of how much pleasure riding a good horse can be. There were no bad habits other than standing too close, like he wanted to be in your lap. As time went on, we had many great rides together and began to cover longer and longer distances. I was starting him slower than Sunny, because he was younger and not at all fit in the beginning. Constant care and using the heart monitor proved to be great assets in bringing him along safely. In any conditioning program, there is the need to push the limits of the athlete, be it horse or human in small incremental steps. But pushing enough to build without breaking anything down is the key to successful conditioning. Cisgo responded to my efforts by becoming stronger and more fit with every ride. He had turned five by now, so I knew he could soon do his first endurance rides. (One of the best rules in endurance riding is that horses cannot compete in fifty or hundred mile races until they are five years old. This eliminates much of the "young horse breakdowns" so common in other equine sports.) My only real concern was that I was having trouble getting Cisgo's papers from the previous owners. The papers increased the value of any Arabian, and since he was a good horse, I wanted to have the documentation on his background for reference as well as value. I had repeatedly tried to complete the deal with Cisgo's previous owners (I was not going to make the final payment without the registration papers they said he had.) but there was always some excuse. Finally the papers were lost in the mail. They would order duplicates. Bobbi had copies of his papers so we knew they existed. No big deal, just another aggravation.

Several months into Cisgo's conditioning we did a ride that is worth a mention here. It was a significant experience, one that would help me greatly in an endurance ride later on another horse. Bobbi had hosted an endurance ride at her ranch and I had helped mark the trail. For those of you that may have never had the opportunity to have to mark a one hundred mile trail, it is a serious task. It takes several people and usually horses, jeeps and motorcycles. Jeeps or four-wheel drives can mark dirt road sections of the ride very quickly. Dirt bikes can cover trail sections faster than the average horse, as well as measure the mileage needed. It is also important to ride the trail on horseback to be sure of the difficulty of that terrain for the horses. A trail that's too dangerous is not fun. In order to mark the trail, you need to tie a colored ribbon every so often to a tree or fence or whatever is available, so people riding in the event can find their way. We also use paper plates with arrows drawn in magic marker, as well as lime dust poured on the ground to indicate turns and the like. Some people use few ribbons, making it more difficult, but Bobbi and I always agreed that the task at hand should be the ride, not desperately avoiding getting lost. We put up lots of ribbons. Since the ride was mostly in the National Forest, immediately after the ride we had to *TAKE DOWN* a hundred miles of ribbons. Even though we used ribbons that were biodegradable, The National Forest Service said they still had to come down. I never minded an excuse for a good ride. So two days after the endurance ride, Bobbi, a friend of ours and I took off to get the last remaining ribbons.

I was trying to hurry things along as it was getting late, but Bobbi and her friend were not in the same hurry I was. It was summer in Colorado and it doesn't get dark until 8:30 or 9:00, so we had a lot of time. But it *does* eventually get dark. We took off about 1 p.m. It was a nice ride; we'd go a ways then find some ribbons and alternate taking them down. Kind of leapfrogging each other, and it was going very well. On one stretch of road, the ribbons had been put up by a jeep driver, who had tied the ribbons while standing on top of the roll bar of his jeep. Quite a bit higher than a seated horseback rider could reach. Bobbi was a bit upset, since the Park Service people wanted the ribbons down *now* and it was Bobbi's responsibility. We were a long way from the ranch, so we were facing another trip out to get these last few ribbons in a truck or something tall. We really needed to get the ribbons now. "No problem," I said, "I'll just stand on the saddle and I think I can reach them." Short guys always like reaching high things. It happens so rarely. Sounded easy enough. I'd seen cowboys stand on their saddles on TV. Bobbi reminded me that most TV cowboys don't ride young Arabian horses and use dressage saddles. On TV they also use *very trained horses,* not four-year-olds with a few weeks of riding experience. I figured we'd never know till I tried, so up I went. If you've never tried standing totally vertical on the saddle while your horse is standing free, reaching up for all your five-foot-eight can reach, and trying to untie a knot in a ribbon, it is a different experience. (Kids, don't try this at home.) Cisgo stood like a statue and all the ribbons came down as planned. Everyone considered it a big deal, except Cisgo. It was a great little experience, but that's not why I am relating the story of this ride.

As we were heading home, it began to sink in that it was getting late. Real late. We would not be home until well after dark. Now to any good endurance rider, a little ride after dark is just another way to have fun on horseback. But most of my evening rides had been on pretty summer moonlit evenings. In addition I always carried a flashlight and light sticks when I expected to be out late. This time we were not prepared at all. Often in the mountains a moonlit night can be quite bright and you may actually see very well. I had ridden many times on these bright, moonlit evenings, and had no trouble seeing enough to be very comfortable. However, tonight there was no moon. Dark was about to mean *DARK*, not just the reduced light of the moon. You know, *BLACK*. Can't-see-your-hand-in-front-of-your-face dark. Also worth mentioning, and most concerning to my fellow riders, was the terrain we would end up on during the last few *hours* of our adventure. The trail home wandered through a lot of dense forest and along numerous steep mountain trails; some alongside cliffs as well as up and down some very narrow rocky paths. These trails could be nerve racking to many less adventurous riders – *in the daylight*. In total darkness they were potentially dangerous. The third member of our team was not a very brave rider at that time, due to a lack of experience in this kind of riding. She was actually a very good rider, but anyone out of their element can become afraid quite easily. Bobbi was a *very experienced* rider, with decades of riding under her belt. She had also survived all that riding by not being too adventurous. Although I heard she was quite a wild rider in her younger days, at this point in her life she liked safe, easy, fun rides, so rocky cliffs in the dark were not on her list of planned outings. Yet, here we were. We had few choices. No phones. No short cuts. Any alternate routes would have added hours and hours to the trip, probably requiring a trailer to come get us eventually in the wee hours of the morning. It was cooler than we expected, and like I said, *very dark*. If you've never been in the woods on a moonless night, you may have trouble imagining what *DARK* is. Go in a closet and close the door; close your eyes, and put a towel over your face. Now you get it. I was riding Cisgo, a gray horse and Bobbi kept saying she couldn't see him or me and we were right in front of her. Heck, I couldn't see *HIM and I was ON him*. I had also not ridden him in the dark like this before so I was hoping he would be OK with the dark. Da, remember Dan, horses live in the dark every night. They even eat during the night without depending on the light in the refrigerator coming on. It was 9:00 p.m. and we were at least three hours from home. The worst of the trails were ahead. Imagine riding a horse for three hours with your eyes closed. In the mountains.

I admit I was concerned, but not overly concerned. I remembered reading that horses see very well at night. When we read things in print, we believe they're true. (Nowadays we also believe *anything* they say on TV, but that's a whole other issue.) Fortunately for us that thing about the horse's vision was valid. They *must* be able to see well at night, they run around in the dark all the time. And I had long since learned from riding Sunny when he was running away with me all those months, that he knew where to put his feet going over rough terrain. Yet I was not too comfortable right now, and I was very worried about my fellow adventurers. They were really nervous and each ray of light lost during sundown had increased the anxiety. Once immersed in total darkness, we kept talking to each other to keep track of where each was. I kept being surprised by branches hitting my face. I'm not sure why I was so surprised since we were riding through the forest. The reason the branches didn't usually hit me in the face was because when I saw them coming, I could duck or push them out of the way. Key phrase here is *"saw them coming."* I sat low and tucked my chin down towards my chest, to let the helmet hit them first. But the most dramatic observations for me were the changes in my riding due to my loss of vision. When you ride, most of us ride with our eyes open, (except during moments of extreme fear) and we are directing the horse where to go. We are planning ahead or at least prepared for each change of direction because we see where we're going. Take away your vision and you don't know in advance when the horse is changing direction. (Sometimes you don't know anyway!) If you're riding under normal conditions and the horse suddenly turns left, it surprises you and it can be a problem, but you see it happening the instant it begins to happen. And you adjust accordingly. In the dark that night, *EVERY CHANGE IN DIRECTION* was a surprise. Not only left and right changes, but on those mountain trails, up and down changes were even more unsettling. We'd be walking along a fairly level path, then it would turn left and drop down very steeply. All we'd feel was the horse dropping away and to the left *after it began to happen.* The people behind me had it a bit easier as they would at least hear my horse changing direction, but that was not much warning either. We were riding *behind the movement of the horse* instead of *with the movement of the horse.* Add to that the fact that most horses tend to want to hurry home, especially if they are late for dinner. So the horses kept trying to trot rather than walk. I also wanted to trot just to get home sooner. My two fellow adventurers were voting for "walk only" as the gait of choice. A lot of the ride home we were trotting since the other two had a limited amount of control and none of us wanted to have any great struggles with our horses here on the side of a sheer cliff in the pitch black dark. You can understand that, can't you?

As we went along (and remember, this lasted several HOURS) a very strange change began to occur for me. I began to let go of my fear and turn my well-being over to Cisgo. My entire perspective on the ride began to change. I *had* to trust him, because I had no way to control the situation. We humans always want to be in control because we think we know it all. Sometimes we don't know it all. Lose your sight in the mountains of Colorado on horseback, and you find out how little control you really have. I cannot begin to tell you how much those few hours on that one ride affected me, but it was profound, to say the least. I was feeling things I had never felt, and sorting it all out would further change me forever.

This book and my workshops are all about teaching people how to control your horse. But this situation underlines a key aspect of what I teach about control; never try to control things you can't control. Control what you can, but you must learn the difference between what you can control and what you cannot. In other words, knowing when to let go. Sometimes letting go is the best choice. I had to let go of my fears and give up any attempt to stay in control of a situation I had absolutely no control over. I had to trust Cisgo. Were I to try to control or steer him on those trails, do you understand how I could have gotten us killed? My judgment in those conditions was poor at best. Most of the time I didn't know exactly which way was up. He could not only see better than I, but he knew where we were and where we were going. And he didn't miss a step the entire trip. Conversely, the third person in our caravan initially kept trying to guide the horse and she unknowingly got the horse off trail and he went down on his knees three times before she stopped steering and let him alone. Eventually I closed my eyes as I rode along and that actually helped. I stopped trying to *see,* so it became easier to accept not being able to see. I let myself go and I began to just *feel.* And I started moving *with* the horse. I began to *feel* him beneath me like never before. I sat low and deep in the saddle, put my chin on my chest and hooked my thumbs under the breast collar for security. And rode the horse. It was another awesome experience. In fact after about an hour of this I began to laugh and giggle. I felt so connected and so totally one with the horse that it was magic. I was also totally dependent on him for my well-being, as I had never let myself be before. I *had* been totally dependent on Sunny when he was running away with me, but I could still see then and make my own reactive decisions. Now I could do nothing but feel. And trust a horse to take care of us both. At that moment I realized what *the horses must feel with us.* Since they are totally dependent on us for their well being all the time, they must trust us. We determine where they live, what they eat, what they do, and virtually every aspect of their existence. I suddenly felt a great responsibility as a horse owner. I would never take owning or riding a horse lightly again. And I would work on learning to be better at knowing when to let go.

It probably goes without saying that my two fellow riders thought I had cracked up when they distinctly heard laughter from their leader on the gray horse they couldn't see. I tried to explain, but they were in a different place mentally at that time and my attempts at explaining the pleasure I was experiencing were not well received. Due to the darkness, we had little idea of where we were even though we had ridden that trail a hundred times. In the dark it was so different. At first the time had seemed to drag on for me, and I'm sure it did for the others throughout the night. Yet the last hour and a half or so seemed like minutes. Interesting how our attitude and state of mind affects our perception of time. Once we saw the lights of the ranch below, and we knew we were safe, there was a great shout of relief from my two friends behind me. I was almost sad it was ending. I felt so good on the last hour or hour and a half of that ride that I cannot accurately express it. Although we arrived safely back at the ranch about midnight, I didn't settle down and get to sleep for hours. The folks at the ranch were considering sending out a search party for us, but it was too dark. And there was too much area to search. Everyone was relieved and all ended well. For us all, it was a ride to remember. For my two friends, it was a ride to recall as a dangerous adventure, survived by good fortune and not to be tried again. For me, it was simply awesome. Thanks, Cisgo.

Once again, Bobbi called me at work and that usually meant a problem. "Dan, I got a new horse in and I'd like you to take her for a ride," she offered. It's never quite that simple when someone wants me to ride their horse. I was informed that Bobbi bought this beautiful five-year-old bay Arabian mare from an auction. She was great the first day but then got hard to handle after that. (I guess the drugs wore off.) A couple of people including a trainer tried to ride the horse but didn't get anywhere except dirty. They had shod the horse but that simple process had taken hours, even with a farrier, a vet and several helpers all doing their best. Bobbi was worried about this one. I said OK, I was coming down to the ranch today anyhow. When I arrived Bobbi took me over to the paddock where this beautiful little 14 3 hand mare was standing. She had great breeding, and was very correct in conformation. Bobbi bought her very cheap. Why does a beautiful, pure-bred Arabian with great lineage sell really cheap at auction? There is *always* a reason. She had big eyes, but they were definitely not soft. She was wired. Bobbi had already talked to a previous trainer for the horse and he said they wanted to put her down a year earlier as they thought she was nuts. Couldn't do anything with her. She had been bred to be raced on the track, but ended up going from barn to barn with no success. Anytime a very correct horse goes from barn to barn I get very nervous. Bobbi said she was so nice at the auction it seemed like a real waste to let her go. Drugs.

I went in her paddock, and the look in her eyes was not good. She was really scared and it took about five minutes just to catch her. Then we headed off to the round pen. She was very bothered by everything, and her only response to any action by me was to run and run. And run. In about an hour I had her saddled, but she wasn't happy about it. I went slowly, and patiently, letting her move around a lot. And boy could she move. It was like watching a nine-hundred-pound cat. Instant movement. Any direction. No control. Emotionally she was a basket case. In another few minutes I was on her, but really unsure of my judgment about that move. We rode around the pen and she was responsive, more accurately said, too responsive. Anything I did got a dramatic reaction. I kept trying to tone down every cue and movement to get her to settle but the changes were slight. Once I was able to point her as I needed, someone opened the gate and we headed up the mountain. Bobbi watched with great concern. The ranch bordered the National Forest, and about a hundred yards out a trail started up the side of a fifteen-hundred foot climb. It was a great place to get a horse in shape. Or to get yourself in shape if you had the where-with-all to hike or jog up the trail. The logic in riding her *up* the mountain was that it took a lot of energy just to go up the mountain, so any initial runaway would be short lived. I was counting on that, because I had never ridden a horse that felt so close to an explosion for so long. I had ridden wired horses before, but they always eventually calmed down. Not Kasty. Every muscle in her body was tight and I had little connection with her mind. In other words – she was dangerous. Had I known then what I know now I would not have gotten on her that day. We went four or five miles and she never did settle down much. I was trying to balance doing just enough to keep her somewhat manageable, without doing too much so as to make her freak out and go ballistic. You've heard the expression "walking a tightrope?" During the whole ride I felt power and quickness that rivaled Sunny on his best day. She was awesome to say the least. If this energy and power ever got channeled, she could be great. As we rode back into the ranch Bobbi was waiting and looking us over as we got closer. She was pleased to see I was still on, and did not appear to have come off. "How was she?" she asked. "Awesome," I responded, "but not an easy horse to ride." There I go with those understatements again. Since she still looked ready to go off at any second, Bobbi quickly added, "Good, you ride her a few times and see how she does."

That was my introduction to Kasty. No one told me in advance that she had never been on a trail before, which could explain why she was really looking at everything on the mountain. She had been ridden a bunch, but usually at an out-of-control-gallop. Another déja vue. She had never been ridden in the mountains and never in the woods. Great, several firsts in one day. And she was very hard to catch and handle in general, continually spooking at everything and anything. Several questions began to run through my mind. Who would want a horse like this? What makes horses like this? And, can they be changed? I always did like a challenge. Since I was the only one that could ride Kasty at that time, Bobbi had me focus on her for a few weeks. We did a lot of round pen time to work on her mind with seven trail rides mixed in. In short order, she became easier to handle on the ground, but the first hour on her back each time out was a challenge. She made Cisgo seem like a dream. She made Sunny feel predictable. The *old* Sunny. On the seventh trail ride, I was riding with Bobbi, who was on her main endurance horse at the time, preparing for a three day, one-hundred-fifty mile event. Fifty miles a day for three days straight. I was planning to take Cisgo, but we would only do the first and last day because he was new at it and I wanted to make sure he had a good time and no stress. Bobbi saw Kasty happily trotting down the trail, easily keeping up with her best endurance horse and thought she looked great. She did. Bobbi suggested we take Kasty to do the second day of the event that Cisgo wasn't doing. I said OK. Kasty's eighth trail ride would be an easy fifty-mile outing. We were doing slow, twenty-mile rides with her, and she was already solid muscle when she had arrived from her race-training background, so an easy, slow fifty would be good for her. And after all, there was space in the trailer.

The first day on Cisgo was a blast. We finished thirtieth out of about sixty riders, so I was happy. He performed like a charm and was his usual pleasure to ride. He had experienced no physical problems, although at the slow pace we traveled, I really hadn't expected any. I had not given much thought to riding Kasty on the middle day, as I was mostly concerned with Cisgo. Then I saw the map of the second day's ride. It started in a beautiful picturesque canyon and zigzagged back and forth, crossing a small river about fifteen or sixteen times during an eight-mile stretch. That, in and of itself, did not seem to be a problem, until Bobbi asked me if I'd ever taken Kasty through water. Oooops. No, I don't ever remember taking her through any rivers. "Does she like water?" Bobbi persisted. After all it was *her* horse. During my initial rides on Kasty I had been concerned with keeping her going safely and trying to get her to relax. I had not been looking for any challenges for her yet. "She doesn't like puddles, but I don't know about rivers," I volunteered. "I guess I'll find out if she likes rivers tomorrow."

The next morning I had to take Kasty to be vet checked before the ride and she was a bit nervous about all the commotion. Let me rephrase that. Kasty was going nuts on the end of a rope as I walked her to the vet. The dawn hours preceding a ride can be a bit chaotic and it's something that new horses have to get used to. When Kasty bit the vet before she even got started with the exam, I knew we were in trouble. Kasty had never bitten me or even done anything aggressive to anyone that I was aware of. The vet had been a bit pushy and hurried, and suggested I calm her down and come back later. I walked her around a bit, then took her to a different vet. Good move, Dan. She passed the check and we mounted up in the nick of time. As we started out I suggested Bobbi not leave us if Kasty refused at the river, since it was her horse. She agreed.

We were running about eighth in a group of ten horses when the first crossing was reached. Horse after horse splashed on across until Kasty got to the water. She stopped and looked at the river with those big eyes even bigger then ever.

All the other horses crossed until it was just Kasty and me left on the near side. Bobbi was on the other side coaxing Kasty, to no avail. I kept her pointed at the water and after a minute or so she lunged across, clearing the six to seven foot stream by a mile. One down, fifteen to go. At least she did it. The next crossing produced the same halt, except she only stopped a few seconds then lunged again. Boy can she jump! As the ride progressed, each crossing got progressively better, until she would not even slow up, but trot on through the water and would actually scoop up a drink as she went. For the rest of the day it was a pleasant, easy ride, except the place where we were cantering in single file through a very tight overgrown trail. A limb caught Kasty's right rein where it clipped on the bit and the rein came off in my hand. When Bobbi saw the rein come off she yelled a warning but there was really nothing I could do then. I just rode on with the one remaining rein, until we came out of the bush and then I reached up and clipped it back on the bit as we cantered along. By the end of the day our slow pace had proved a good move since a lot of horses had been pulled due to going too fast too early and the heat took its toll on many horses. Kasty finished nineteenth and had hardly broken a sweat. She looked like she could go another fifty and was still full of energy. Bobbi's enthusiasm for her new endurance prospect was growing rapidly.

Over the next few months I took Kasty to a few other rides for Bobbi, and she did very well. She was never real relaxed at first, but the calmer I was, the quicker she'd settle down. Bobbi had several other people try to ride her in hopes of buying her, but the results were not good. Kasty would get nervous and the rider would get nervous, then Kasty checked out. Mentally. End of demo ride. No sale. Finally after much pressure from me for her to ride her own horse, Bobbi took Kasty out once to see for herself what she was like. Bobbi called me at work the minute she got back. You know what that means. "This is the fastest, most unstoppable horse I've ever ridden. And I don't ever want to ride her again," was her commentary on her adventure with Kasty. Then came the plan. Bobbi is very good at coming up with a plan. "Since you like her so well and you can ride her, why don't you trade me Cisgo for her? I can sell Cisgo to a friend of mine who needs a good solid horse that anybody can ride, and you can race Kasty." Then came the kicker. "If you don't take her, I can only sell her as a brood mare, but if that doesn't work, her future does not look good." Bobbi had heard from the horse's previous trainers and handlers and they had wanted her put down rather than go to the auction since they were afraid somebody would get hurt. I thought about it overnight with mixed emotions. I really liked her power and speed. She was a rocket compared to Cisgo. But Cisgo had proved to be a great all around horse. He could be ridden by anyone and he would probably be able to compete successfully in any endeavor desired. He could do anything for anybody. And that's what decided it. Cisgo was OK, and he didn't need me. Kasty did. So, in an exhibition of very questionable logic, I traded a perfect, wonderful, anyone can ride gelding for a mare that had been only ridden successfully by one nut. Me. We did the deal and Kasty became mine while Cisgo went to a good home in California. But, there was one more detail to the story. After I signed Cisgo over to Bobbi, she finally got his papers. I had yet to get them at this time and when they arrived Bobbi called again. "Guess how old your horse is?" she asked. "What do you mean? He's five," I said. "Not according to his papers, he's really only four now, he was three when he arrived here. We've been competing on a four-year-old who was supposed to be five," she said. It was true. Since I had been riding him easy there was no harm done, but that year difference could have been a disaster under other conditions. Thank goodness we were conservative with him and all went well.

It is interesting that all my activities in the horse world had brought me to a place where I was the proud owner of two

Kasty and Dan during an early endurance ride in Colorado.

105

horses that nobody else wanted. Sunny, another gray gelding in the Sumerel tradition of gray geldings; and the newest entry (and severe break with tradition) Kasty, a beautiful bay mare. There was more than one occasion when I stopped to ponder the logic that permitted me to end up with these two horses. I rationalized that the Shazis and the Cisgos of the world would fit in anywhere. The Sunnys and the Kastys are the ones that need help. Besides, I figured they could make me a better horse-man. I was right on all counts.

By this time Sunny was ready to start conditioning again and his leg was fine. Kasty was already quite fit and ready to go, if I could just hang on. I had continued to learn more and more by round penning many different horses, so my skills in that area were increasing. But I had just sold my automotive business and was looking to change careers. My life style was about to change and rearrange everything. Twenty years in various forms of the automotive industry, as well as racing cars and motorcycles, had tired me of that arena. I wanted to do something different. I guess a lot of middle-aged people go through those feelings. I had actually told some friends that I thought I wanted to work with horses as a profession. Most of my horse friends laughed at the idea of me starting a business in the horse world. I was also given the normal advice about not changing a successful career at "my age." But I really wanted to do something in the horse world. Then, just by chance, I was invited to ride a horse belonging to a man I met during the three-day ride where Kasty learned about rivers. He invited me to ride his horse in a race called the Race of Champions. It was a pretty big deal in those days, so I decided to take the opportunity. Besides, the horse was a gray gelding. While there at the race, I saw this thing called a BioScan. It was used on horses to find precisely where problems existed, instead of guessing. It could also help correct many of the problems it found. (I will outline the BioScan in the chapter on physical problems.) After a lot of talking with BioScan's developer, I decided to go into the horse business with BioScan. I had found my horse business and it would allow me to travel and help horses like I never dreamed possible. During the next few years I traveled seventy-five thousand to a hundred thousand miles a year for BioScan, all over the U.S. I had the good fortune to be working with all different breeds and all different disciplines of horses. I could be at a barrel race one day and at an Arabian show barn the next. From the racetracks to dressage arena, I got to see and work with them all. I got to drive a trotter on the Springfield Mile. I got to ride a top reigning horse. I even got to ride a Grand Prix Dressage horse. (He was much smarter than I at what we were trying to do and it was a very humbling experience. The experience gave me a great appreciation for upper level riders and upper level horses.) To date I have used the BioScan on over two thousand horses, not to mention hundreds of dogs and cats. But during all that traveling and seeing all those horses, a rather amazing situation began to occur over and over. Someone would be having a behavior problem with their horse and I could see in a blink why it was happening. They were doing things all wrong. The horse was upset, they were upset, and it was going nowhere fast. I would offer to help, and I got to play with the horse – usually out of frustration or sometimes just the old "if you think you can do better, go ahead." And the horse would change. Then the people would ask, "What in the world did you just do?" Usually just after they watched me do it. One lady was so shocked at the change in her horse, she asked me to come back the next day and teach what I did. I tried to shrug it off but she persisted. I tried to refer to a couple of the trainers I had worked with, but she said she had already worked with them and still didn't understand what I just did. There's that word again: understand. Finally she offered me a large sum of money to teach her how to do what she just saw me do. Not being a stupid person, I met with her the next day and in a few hours she had totally changed her way of handling her horses. She took me aside and told me she had been around horses all her life and had never seen anything like what I had taught her that day. She said I needed to be showing this to other people

107

and that would help a lot of horses. That was four years ago. She started me to thinking about taking what I had learned about horses and combining it with what I had done as a corporate trainer to develop a better way of teaching it. Since then I have taught and lectured across the U.S. and Australia and so much has happened so fast, I still can't believe it. That's the story of how I got into the horse business. Much the same as the way I got into horses in the first place. By accident.

I called this chapter "The Awakening, A Journey Begins" because to me that is just what my time with the horses has been. In a few short years since the day I first bought Raj, through all the experiences I have shared with you here, as well as many more I couldn't list, I have had many things presented to me by fate, by luck and most of all by many great horses and people. Those things have taught me and changed me into a different person than I was when this adventure started, and the adventure is far from over. Now that you have read about the events that brought me to where I am today, I hope to share with you the specifics of what I have learned from it all. The understanding I will share with you in the next chapter will define many aspects of the stories you just read. Much of that understanding I did not grasp at the time of the individual incidents, but only later did it become clear as the parts to the puzzle began to fit. The horse/human relationship is so very complex, but yet so incredible when it works the way it can. It is a relationship that I have come to understand through study, observation and most of all, actually playing with hundreds and hundreds of horses around the world. It is the horses that have taught me the most, and I continue to learn from them. Obviously it took a vast array of circumstances to let me be in the places I was at the time in order to experience what I have experienced. But perhaps the most valuable asset that allowed me to get to where I am was my awareness that *I knew so little about horses going in*. That open-mindedness allowed me to question the *normal* when others of greater experience accepted it willingly.

One simple situation that occurred just after I got Raj for Lisa, and we were looking for a second horse, made such an impression on me I have never forgotten it. We were at a multi-million dollar horse facility looking at horses to buy. The proud owner brought out a gorgeous Arabian stallion and began to "set him up" as is done in the show world to display the horse's beauty. While the horse was standing, the owner kept popping a small whip in his face to keep his eyes wide and to keep him taut. While the owner proudly went through his routine, I began to cringe in disbelief. I turned to Lisa and told her that even though I knew he was the big-shot owner and he was the one with all the ribbons and trophies all over his walls, I would *never* do that to any horse of mine. I knew nothing about showing horses, but my heart told me I didn't like what I was seeing. And *normal or not*, I could not accept it. That was a minor example and the man was not even hurting the horse. But he was also not considering the horse's perspective on the situation. He didn't see anything wrong in his actions, yet had I done it to him, he may have thought otherwise.

I'm asking you to not accept the *normal*. But unless you have other choices, the *normal* will hang on forever. Now I'd like to offer you choices.

CHAPTER 6
Control, Communication, & Alpha

I know this will sound very simplistic at first, but every aspect of this book and all the lectures I do focus entirely on "Control." Specifically, controlling the horse. Because the horse is so big and we are so small, we need to *develop the ability to control the horse*. We all know this at some level, (perhaps all too often out of simple self preservation) but nonetheless the *normal* approach many of us take has some serious problems. Those problems often arise because we never took the time to evaluate the many complexities of the task we are facing. In fact most of us never took the time to even *define the task at all*. You might relate this to starting out in your car on a trip before you ever decide where you are going. Or even *WHY* you are going. You would never consider doing that, yet we get a horse, realize that we need to be in control, and start some illogical, inconsistent group of interactions with no planning, focus or understanding of the "trip" we've begun. Mostly we just do what everybody else is doing because "that is the way it's done." We want a quick fix with immediate gratification – often at the expense of the horse. Before we start discussing any techniques or methods of controlling the horse, let's try to understand what *exactly* is it that we are trying to control in the first place.

The primary goal of controlling your horse would be safety. That would have to include not only your safety but also the safety of the horse. Few horse owners have *never* been hurt in some fashion by a horse. That's an eye-opening revelation. Most of us have experienced first hand the power and force that a horse can generate. Not to mention the incredible speed with which they can generate that force. They can be all done moving before we knew they were going to move in the first place.

And we're lying there in a bloody puddle on the ground wondering what went wrong. Do the math, they weigh 1,000 pounds or more, we weigh about 150. When handling your horse becomes a contact sport, we lose. They can move faster than we can even begin to move. Again we lose. They are far more aware of their environment, so they notice things that we fail to see, which can set them in motion. It is so easy for us to get hurt when handling a horse. If they weren't so good-natured it would be a lot worse. Without control of our horses, we are at risk. Our safety usually depends on us being in control. Think about this; if you get on your horse, do you *know* you can stop him? Do you *know* you can turn him if needed? Do you *know* he will go when asked, but only as fast or slow as you want? Too often the answers are vague at best but frequently they are just plain no. If I offered you a car that had inconsistent brakes, steering that only worked sometimes and a throttle that could stick wide open at the worst possible time, would you drive it home? Of course not. Yet you would get on the back of a horse with those same guidelines in place, and think nothing of it. The one primary difference is that the car has no brain, it only responds to what we do. (And look how much trouble we have in staying safe in a machine that we *do have control over*.) The horse is capable of independent thought. He may have an agenda that does not equate with yours. And then what do you do? Instinctively you know the instant you have lost control; that's when you panic. Yet all too often even though you thought you had control before you lost it, *you really never had control in the first place.*

The horse's safety also depends on us being in control. If you look at the environment the horse lived in for fifty million years before we came into their lives, it was very different from the environment we thrust them into. The average "horse facility" (as we call them) is about as far from anything a horse would build if he were in control, as the man in the moon. Horses like open spaces so they can see the predators coming. They like lots of space to move around in. They like lots of grass and water, and maybe some shade trees. A facility designed by a horse would never include tractors, flashing lights, speakers that squeal or scream out loud music, plastic bags, slippery floors, tiny cubicles with no windows, dusty buildings with poor ventilation, or the myriad of other things we see in every horse property around. And most importantly, fifty million years of evolution prepared the horse for an environment very unlike what he finds himself thrust into today. For fifty million years they developed the means to survive in their *natural environment*. Now they find themselves in a very *unnatural environment*. Their ability to adapt seems almost endless, but we must realize it is our responsibility to see to their safety in this environment we put them in. We brought them into this environment and now we control their lives. Keeping them safe and at ease is the least we can do for them. Any time you put a horse in a situation where he becomes afraid and freaks out, you and he are likely to get hurt. In those situations, just saying "You're OK, you're OK, settle down," while you are as tense as can be, is not going to save the day. And the reality is that if you haven't done your homework with the horse *prior* to the crisis, there may not be much you *can* do at that point. Bottom line, we need to be more in control to be safe.

Now let's get into defining control. What is it exactly, that we are trying to control in the first place? If we ever get hurt by a horse, do you realize it is always the result of some movement of some part of his body. Sound too simple? Can a horse hurt you if he didn't move? Be it kicking, rearing, stepping on your foot, biting, running away with you, bucking you off, slamming you against the stall wall, and on and on, he simply *has* to move his body to get you hurt. So from a point of safety, controlling the movement of the horse's body is the critical fundamental. Taking it one step further, controlling the movement of the horse's body equates to two possible activities; either you are trying to get the horse's body *to move* in some particular fashion, or you want to keep his body *from moving* in some unwanted fashion. Make it move or keep it from moving. That's all that matters. With those two simple steps in place, you have just made your horse hobby a whole lot safer.

In fact, we can take this same concept a bit further for those of you that compete on your horses. And most of you do compete. Whether you are involved in showing, barrel racing, dressage, jumping, roping, racing, driving, or whatever sport you do, the outcome of that competition is determined by who has the best *control* of their horse. True, there is a degree of luck in all sports, and we cannot eliminate the variations in judging where that comes into play, but is it not true that winning is all about control? You may be riding the best dressage horse there, but if you can't get him to do what he needs to do when he needs to do it, you lose. And that is a demonstration of a *lack of control* costing you a win. A lesser rider with a lesser horse can beat a better rider if they demonstrate more control on one particular day. Pick any sport and you will see it is all about control. What are all those hundreds of lessons you took, as well as hundreds of hours and thousands of dollars you spent, all about? Gaining control in order to compete to win. And, as you get higher and higher in you levels of competition, think about this: the control of minute details may have little to do with safety, but it can mean the difference in fame and fortune, or disappointment. For example, in the 1996 Olympic games, Isabell Werth won two gold medals in dressage – without question, one of the premier sports in the horse world. Who was fourth behind Isabell at that Olympics? You probably don't know. And that's a shame because I doubt you would call the person who was fourth a failure. How would you feel if you were fourth at the Olympics? I'd say anyone who made it to the Olympics was pretty spectacular and probably deserving of much credit. But the point is, that on that day, at those Olympics, Isabell had more control and got her horse to do a better job than anyone else. And the fame she attained was due to her ability to control her horse. The more control you have, the safer you are and the more successful you will be as well.

We said control is about getting the horse's body to either move or not move, at our discretion. What happens when it goes wrong? Whether you are trying to get the horse to move, and he won't, or he's moving and you can't get him to stop or change, you are confronted by the actions of his body as the problem. I often see people in a horse's stall when the horse leans against the person and the person starts pushing back against the horse. The person is confronted by the movement of the horse's body, so the person reacts against the body. We forcefully go after his body to solve our movement problem, since it was the body that presented the problem in the first place. And that is our primary mistake. We went after the result, not the cause. It is understandable that we resort to force when the body of the horse is doing something we don't want. It's the body we are confronting. But what is it that controls the body of the horse? What is the *source* of our problem? The manifestation of the problem is the movement of the body but the source of the problem is the *mind* of the horse. If the mind of the horse says "run," the feet are moving. If the mind says "stand," the feet are still. You know how heavy the foot of a horse can be when you ask him to pick one up and he just looks at you. If he's standing on *your foot,* it's even worse. Yet, let him decide to pick it up and the foot becomes as light as a feather. What changed? His mind cooperated with you, and the movement problem ceased to exist. If we learn to always go after the mind, or at least the attitudes in that mind controlling its decisions, we become far more effective in influencing and hence controlling the horse. But there's more.

When faced with getting a horse to do something, we usually rely on some piece of equipment, (bit, spur, crop, tie down, etc.) which can apply a force or pressure to some part of the horse. Did you ever think about what most equipment does *to* the horse? Most equipment is creating a degree of pressure and even pain. True, most equipment can be used well or used abusively, so I am not saying never use a bit, or crop or spur. But have you ever looked at all the bits in the average tack store?

114

How many of those would you like in *your* mouth while someone with heavy hands cranked on the reins? Don't you think we're talking about pain here? I have seen horses with raw flesh where they have been spurred repeatedly. I have seen horses with bloody notches cut in their nose from a chain being used as a tie down. And the list goes on. If you get right down to it, most of the time the use of equipment is telling the horse, "If you don't do what I want, I can hurt you." How's that for an offer you can't refuse? How would *you* respond if I made you that offer? Probably not well.

The irony of it all is that the above scenario is also not usu-ally very successful. Yet we keep doing it over and over because it's *normal*, but is it effective much less appropriate? If the first severe bit had worked on Sunny, I would not have needed the others. But it *didn't* work, and subsequent bits inflicting more and more pain *didn't work either*. By using equipment or force to hurt the horse in order to gain a response, we are starting a *physical struggle* to solve a *mental problem*. Starting a physical struggle with an animal much larger than we are just doesn't seem too bright. Moreover, we are creating a resistance in the horse every time we hurt him that will tend to accumulate and show up later when we least want it. He may submit at the moment we use the equipment, but do you think he likes it?

I don't want to be misunderstood about what I have outlined above and my feelings about using equipment on a horse. I am categorically *NOT AGAINST* using equipment on a horse in general. It is necessary for many training steps, and many forms of *specific task training* could not be accomplished without using equipment. But it is my belief that equipment should be used as a means of *communication* rather than *punishment*. Since we cannot use complex sentences to explain to our horse what exactly we need, we have to get him to understand what we want by touch. If the attitude of the horse is submissive (that will be explained later), then when we ask for something he will try. If he tries and we reward, he will try again, perhaps harder. Eventually he will give us exactly what we need. So how can we ask for specific actions that we can't describe verbally to the horse? We touch him. We use equipment to apply a soft but firm *pressure* to some place on the horse in hopes that he will *yield* to that pressure and provide us the movement we wanted. A leg pressure to the left side of the horse should get the horse to yield away from that pressure and move to the right. We are developing a tactile form of communication with our horse. Equipment is a vital part of that communication and can be used effectively and benevolently to enlist specific responses with no pain involved. It is the excessive amount of force or pressure created by the incorrect application of equipment, or the absolute pain created by unnecessary types of equipment, that I am vehemently opposed to. If the horse cannot be ridden in a mild snaffle bit, no other bit is appropriate. If the horse does not respond to a gentle spur on his side, then the solution is not more and harder spurring. It may be that he does not understand the cue or communication. It may be that his attitude is still very resistant and needs help there. It may even be that the problem is with the *rider* and the use of the spur was vague or confusing. Heaven forbid that the poor response from the horse could possibly be the result of our error. In which case, the solution to the problem would be an increase of our knowledge and skill levels, not further torture of the horse.

I personally do not use much equipment on my horses for a variety of reasons:

1) I have been able to accomplish most of what I need from my horses without it. It often tended to get in the way.

2) I do not usually require extremely complex actions from my horses, so very specific tools have gone unneeded. In fact, now that I am engaged in mostly riding bareback and beginning to pursue the bridleless/bareback approach, my body is the primary communication tool I am using. Sunny seems to be enjoying it as well.

3) I like things simple, so more and more equipment seems undesirable to me. To me a horse is at his best running free with nothing man-made on him, so I have no desire to cover up his unique beauty with other stuff. The American Indians didn't use a lot of stuff on their horses and they did OK.

4) I still don't know how to use many of the things I see in most tack stores, and even as I learn about them more and more, I find little desire, much less need to employ them.

Use whatever equipment you need for your particular sport or discipline, but evaluate it from the horse's point of view as well as the convenience it offers. Use it to communicate and not to punish. And use as little as you can.

Since we mentioned communication, this is a good time to discuss that topic. It is a serious problem for most people with horses and I spend a great deal of time in my workshops on it. Heck, it's a big problem for most relationships between people and we're the same species. No wonder we don't do too well with it with our horses. It is also a major factor in discussing control. Since we said control is about directing the movement or limiting the movement of the horse's body, how can we affect that control if we can't communicate our wishes to the horse? The three-step approach I teach to working with horses is Understanding, Communication and Training. Most people are heavy into the last one, yet have few skills in the first two. No wonder there is so much of a struggle between horses and people. Communication is a fundamental we take for granted. We talk to our horses all the time, but we do very little communicating. Let me explain.

If I were writing this book in a foreign language, such as Chinese, you would probably not be here right now. You wouldn't "get it." Not because you were stupid, nor because it had little value, but simply because you and I were not able to communicate. I understand that if I want to communicate with *you*, I have to go to you in a language that *you* understand.

117

English. And I can effect that communication with you either verbally or in writing, but the language must be English. We know our horses can't read, yet we assume they can understand us verbally. It's a trap we fall into for several reasons. Often we say something to our horse and we get the wanted response. We assume he understood our language when, in fact, it was nothing more than a conditioned response. That is really what word commands with horses are all about. For example, if you get a horse to back up a step, and you say the words "back up" during his step, and then repeat that process several times, in short order when you say "back up" the horse will provide the action he associated with the word. (Providing he is willing; in other words his attitude is submissive. We'll explain this oh-so-important aspect later.) Had you done the process with the phrase "fitz gribick" he would back up when you said "fitz gribick" just as well. He does not use English as a language, but he learns through associations, and he's a master at it.

Now we get to the real issue of communication problems between people and horses: you *think* all your talking has meaning to your horse. It doesn't. It is *normal* to think your horse is listening and understanding your words. That is unfortunately an incorrect assumption, and the ramifications of the assumption create other problems that are ongoing. Let's discuss several aspects of this *supposed* verbal communication.

First of all, horses are prey animals, which tend to be quiet by nature. Predators spend their lives going after prey animals for food. Prey animals spend their lives trying to avoid becoming lunch for some predator. Horses and other prey animals have survived within that system for fifty million years and it is an integral part of their very being. You never hear a loud deer, or loud rabbit or other prey animal. Most of a horse's day is quiet because they don't want to attract the predators to their location. They prefer to go unnoticed. If they are making noise they are less likely to hear and hence be warned of the approaching predator. Did you ever notice how your horses tend to get

118

bothered and nervous when it's windy? The reasons are mainly due to the fact that the sound of the wind tends to hide other sounds that can alert the prey animals to approaching predators and danger. Add to that the fact that prey animals are good at detecting motion visibly, and use their sight to look for movement that could indicate the possibility of an approaching predator. When the wind is blowing it gets noisy, and all the trees, grasses, and everything else around the horse is moving, making the predators approach much more difficult to detect, either audibly or visually. Hence, from fifty million years of experience, the horse knows he is more vulnerable when it's windy and he gets nervous.

Another aspect of the problems we humans have with our tendency to rely on verbal communication with our horses relates to the natural tendencies for horses (and people) to ignore sounds that are constant or at least ongoing. You have no doubt had the experience of being around someone who talks incessantly. It is common for you to tend to "tune out" that chatter and very shortly you are there, but you really hear little or nothing of what is being said. I'm sure you did that with certain teachers when you were in school, didn't you? Horses do the same thing. They adjust to your constant chatter and "tune you out," basically ignoring the *noise* you are making until it changes dramatically, drawing their attention back to you. In other words, you have to shout to be heard by a horse standing one foot away. If you want your words to have meaning, they must be used more sparingly. Even more fundamental than that is the basic concept that horses are completely versed in non-verbal communication. Horses do have social communication by sound, but that is a very small part of their natural communication process. For the most part, horses are quiet.

Yet being quiet does not mean there is no communication going on. Horses can communicate with great specificity and yet make no sound. Their primary communication is by *reading body language and movement*. And the advantages to this form of communication are incredible. For instance, did you

119

ever watch a herd of deer or horses running across an open space? They seem to move as one, yet there is no leader screaming out, "Get ready, we're all gonna' turn left at the next tree!" That simply wouldn't work. Things are happening way too fast. But by developing the ability to "read" the movements and body language of the other horses, the members of the herd just watch the horses ahead and react instantly to what they see. The result is that the herd seems to move as one. To take it one step further, watch a flock of birds flying together. They move in a three dimensional arena, not just two dimensions, and they demonstrate the same harmony of movement, flying as one. We humans have become so addicted to relying on verbal communication that we have given up much of our own mental awareness and ability to "read" that same kind of body language in others. Many of the classes I have attended for my corporate training and motivational work discussed "reading" the other person's body language to help you become more effective in negotiations or teaching. We can all take lessons in this area from our horses. You see, the more you watch how the horses do it (read the body language) the more advance notice you can perceive of impending actions. In other words, when you get really good at it, you can tell what is going to happen *before* it happens. It is a very common occurrence in my workshops for someone to be handling a horse while the class and I are observing and coaching, and I will point out that the horse is about to do so-and-so. To the amazement of the group, the horse almost always does just that. They think I'm psychic or I have "the gift," but it was really just a matter of reading what the body language of the horse was telling me. And, because of the way the workshops are conducted, by the end of the day, many of the students are able to do the same thing.

The subtleties of this kind of communication are such that, if you are not made aware of them in detail, as well as have them pointed out to you *as they happen*, you can miss it entirely. There is also another major stumbling block that interferes with humans learning this skill, and it is covered in my workshops by a very different but very effective approach. The key to communicating with your horse is for *you to learn his language* before you attempt to try to get him to understand yours. (Just as I said I couldn't teach you in Chinese, I had to go to you in your language, English.) And the first step for you in learning his language is for you to begin to listen to him. And the biggest problem for you to be able to listen to him is for you to shut up.

You can't listen if you are talking. And we humans are always talking. Especially around our horses. I challenge you to go into any horse facility and stay out of sight and just listen to the verbal diarrhea, which constantly exudes from people standing next to a perfectly nice horse. "Stand still. Be a good boy. Don't do that. Come on I said don't do that. Let go of the rope. Let go of the rope. Back up just a little bit. Come on you can do it. It's OK. I'm OK. You're OK. Ouch. Don't step on my foot you know better than that. Come on get off my foot. Whoa, stand still, whoa, stand still…" During all of this "verbal expression" on the part of the human, the horse is likely just meandering around on the end of his rope, paying only slight attention to the human at any time. Sort of sounds like the horse isn't really listening, doesn't it? You'd tune it out too if you were the horse. As I said earlier, you think you're communicating with your horse when in fact you're just rambling on to yourself. With no effect on the horse.

Also I think it is important at this point to define *communication*. One definition in the dictionary describes communication as "the exchange of information." Where in the verbal outpouring listed above was there any exchange going on? There was none. Did you ever attempt to have a conversation with someone who never shut up? How did you feel? How effective was that communication? Bingo. A major focus during my workshops is on communication from *horses to people*. It is that step, so often overlooked, that has helped my students become more effective using the round pen and all the other techniques I teach. Getting people to be quiet is the first step in getting them to *listen to their horse*. Back in kindergarten or first grade, the teacher told you, "Be quiet and stop talking. You cannot listen to me and learn if you keep talking."

Well, we need to learn from our horses and, in most cases, they have been trying to "talk" to us as best they can, but we have been turning a deaf ear. How can we possibly know what they need us to do in training if we are so unwilling to listen to what they have to say and what they show us? They will usually tell us what they need, if we will only learn to listen. But we listen to our horses with our eyes, not our ears. And that is another adjustment required from us. As we play with the different horses during my workshops, I am repeatedly saying, "Watch the horse, watch the horse." And by pointing out, "Do you see his ears? Did you see how he turned to his left? Watch his right front foot," etc. The people begin to see how much information is available to us by learning the horse's language. Body language.

Before we get more into trying to use the horse's body language, there is another dimension to the horse we need to understand better; how his vision works and how it affects his thinking. A different pattern, but with similar relationships (vision versus thinking) occurs within predators like us and can be a barrier to understanding. The horse can see in two different directions at one time and therefore keep a good lookout for approaching predators. He has very little binocular vision (depth perception), except straight ahead. His focus is done more by changing which part of his eye he looks out of than by refocusing the eye itself, as we do. Head high, he is focused on distant things. Head low, he is focused on things that are close. Our primary concern is the two eyes looking in two directions at once, part of his vision and how that affects the workings of his mind. Consider this, you can only see one scene at a time, so you have one TV screen playing in your mind at any given time. If you could see in two directions at once, two different scenes, you would have to watch *two separate TV screens all the time*. Occasionally they would overlap when you looked forward. How confusing could that be? Suppose you focused on something going on to your left then something dramatic happened on your right? Could that cause you to be startled? And spook? You bet. Think how this complicates the information processing within the horse. He can look all around himself, yet doesn't focus well without changing his head position. Certain places are blind spots to him, such as right in front of his head. Ever see a horse pull back quickly when you came at his head straight on with a halter or something? Now you understand why. Even more important is what I call "lack of transfer." Due to his mind having to process his visual input from two separate "TV screens" his mind is divided, left to right. In most cases if you teach a horse something from the left, he does not relate it to his right at all. You must teach it over, to the right side of his brain before it becomes "universal" to the horse. That is why you can mount your horse from his left and it's no problem. Then one day try it from the right and he blows up. To him it was a totally foreign experience and he was frightened by it. In the round pen you will need to remember this important point as you evaluate the horse from both sides equally. He doesn't see as you do nor even relate the information he takes in as you do. So he responds differently than you. And you need to consider *his* perspective as you interact with him.

Another aspect to learning the language of the horse is developing the ability to *express yourself* in their language. If you have ever tried to learn another language, you know that often you begin to *understand* before you become well versed in expressing yourself in the new language. That is normal when learning a verbal language, and learning the body language of the horse is no different. It is also quite common for someone in a foreign land to continue talking in their native language even though the people they are trying to communicate with have no understanding. The longer we continue to try to use the old language, the longer it will take for us to embrace the new language and become proficient with it. I was fortunate to discover this very important concept in my work with the horses.

As I began to teach, I soon saw that I needed a way to break people's old patterns of behavior (talking to the horse with little effect) if I would have any chance of installing a new pattern of behavior (using the horse's language). I have also repeatedly talked of how people resist change. So my task of getting people to shut up and begin to listen to their horse has been a real challenge. The solution I came up with proved to not only work for this situation, but to be very empowering to the student in other ways as well. In my workshops the students are not allowed to talk to the horse at any time. I have duct tape if needed.

By taking away something that most people rely on constantly with horses, talking, several things occur immediately. They feel uncomfortable; they have lost a crutch they were very attached to. It was a crutch of little value but they don't realize that yet. In that state of being a bit uncomfortable, they are looking for help. They need something to replace their missing crutch. Sometimes the degree of discomfort in some people will approach desperation. The fact that this feeling of discomfort often occurs when the student is going into a round pen with forty people watching as they attempt to do something they have never done before, with a horse they may be having problems with, can add to the degree of discomfort. Then, when the student is *mentally willing to accept coaching,* I can get her to do things with the horse they would have argued about otherwise. And then, when they get the horse to change and respond, doing what I suggested, they feel success and they know it works. It is also true that in this state, people become far more "aware" of the horse than is usual for them. They begin to notice and pay attention to things they have never even seen before. And as I coach them (I do not harass or belittle people in my workshops as I feel it is a poor training tool. I prefer to coach people through their learning), into reading the horse's language and then using their body to influence the horse (expressing yourself in the horse's language), the student begins to develop the ability to *communicate* with the horse as never before. It is this ability to express one's self in the horse's language that becomes so eye opening to the student. They begin to be able to understand how little it takes in body movement for them to influence the horse's behavior. They start to realize how much they have done in the past while handling horses that the horse was reading as communication, yet they had no idea their movements ever mattered. They begin to understand how in past situations a horse may have done something that the person could not justify, yet now they realize it was their action or movement that caused the horse's response in the first place. And we often blame the horse for doing exactly what our body language told him to do. Be careful what you say in a language you don't understand. It may mean something your really didn't want to say. Remember this, if what you say with words is not matching what you are saying with your body language, the horse will follow the body language and ignore the words. For example, if you say to your horse, "It's OK, relax, you're OK." While you are scared stiff and every muscle in your body is tight, your body language is NOT saying he's OK, it's saying we're in trouble, and he is not likely to calm down when your body language is telling him that. You've been there, I know it.

It is both interesting and rewarding to watch people go through this process in the round pen. They think initially that they have been training the horse to get the responses they have achieved. The horses often start out nervous and even wired and then they calm down and become attentive, responsive and softer. Often they display a dramatic change in a short period of time. In point of fact, the people have actually done virtually no training. They have simply been communicating. The process they just went through was all about language and communication, not training, and it is very important for you to understand the differences. We use the term "training" to encompass everything we do around horses. And although it is true that horses are watching and learning every second you are around them, I don't consider that training. I tend to separate training from communication in that training relates to task actions, such as dressage work, show training for specific gaits, etc. Communication is a necessary part of training, but only a part. On the other hand, *communication helps establish the relationship needed before any training can begin.* As an example I would suggest you look at the human concept of dating – especially from a woman's point of view. There needs to be a relationship established before anything else can go on. If a strange guy walked up and grabbed you and gave you a big kiss, you would most likely go ballistic. He may have even been a good-looking guy, but that alone would not have been enough to skip the part about establishing the relationship first. (I know, some of you women are asking, "Well, how good looking was he?" knowing that may have affected your response in the above scenario. We won't go there.) That same guy could have introduced himself, *started a conversation* with you to establish a relationship, and the rest of the story would have been quite different. Why do we introduce ourselves and shake hands when we meet new people to start the relationship? Introductions start the relationship. Then we *communicate* to establish the *nature* of that relationship. Anytime you meet someone new, you evaluate that person by what they say, and what you observe about them during that early stage of your relationship. You then apply your values and beliefs to determine how you will approach a relationship with them. If you don't like what you see or what they do, you will develop resistance to that individual. If on the other hand they exhibit similar beliefs and values to yours, you will respond in a much more receptive fashion to them. That concept of establishing a relationship is quite simply what the round pen interactions are all about. But we need to understand one more major difference between humans and horses, before we can attempt to apply any of this to a horse.

In the wild we have said that horses survive by being incredibly aware of their surroundings and avoiding becoming lunch to some predator. Nature provides animals with a very honest but not very forgiving system to live within. A mistake in the wild is often rewarded by death. That does tend to weed out the weak and injured and even the dumb ones, perpetuating a stronger and better species. Understanding the serious nature of their environment, horses do not take their daily activities lightly. And the primary daily activity for every horse is survival. And make no mistake, the few thousand years we have been playing with them has not erased all those *millions of years* of evolving their behavior.

One major aspect of the social behavior within the horse's herd is the establishing of the hierarchy, or pecking order. You can demonstrate this quite simply and observe its importance with any group of horses you see. Whenever a new horse enters a herd, or if you just put one horse in with another horse it does not know, the first action they embark on will be to approach each other. They will be alert and very poised. They are introducing themselves and, most importantly, evaluating the other horse. Evaluating for what? For character. You see, in that herd of two horses, one of them will become the leader, or Alpha horse. And they know they need to establish that leadership position as quickly as possible. Why? Because they never know when a threat may appear and they will need to act as a herd or organized group, not frightened independent individuals, if they are to survive. Instinctively they know that the horse with the most character, not necessarily the biggest or strongest horse, must be in charge, because that horse will make the best decisions and ensure their best chance for survival. So they approach each other and posture and see who backs down first. They may even kick at each other or jump around, acting quite menacing, yet rarely is there any serious contact made. I often hear people express great concern for horses hurting each other in the pasture and then arguing the position I just offered on posturing. They aren't totally wrong – they just missed a couple of important points. There are two main reasons horses in the wild don't hurt each other often, where the same casual mixing of horses is far more dangerous with *domestic horses*. First, in the wild, horses grow up together and learn to socialize better than domestic horses. No one separates the colts from the fillies in the wild. In fact, in any herd of wild horses, how many geldings are there? NONE. God doesn't make geldings, people do. We aren't as good at teaching socialization to the horses as He is. Second, the wild horses do not live in the synthetic confines we force horses into. In other words, if two horses really don't get along in the wild, one can run away. When kept in small paddocks we remove that option from our horse's choices. If they can't get away, they will get hurt sometimes. We even do the same thing to ourselves. Look at the crowding in any major inner city environment and notice the violence and crime generated by that cramming together of too many people in too little space. Why do people in the city dream of having a place in the country?

Now I know a lot of you are saying you've seen the stories on the nature channel about the wild stallions fighting to the death and all that. And it is true that fights over sex can get pretty rough sometimes, occasionally resulting in death. We humans are supposed to be civilized (whatever that means today) as well as the most intelligent species on the planet and we sure don't do a great job of controlling our sexual drives. How can we criticize the horses? But the reality of the horse world is this. If you think they are so brutal and would kill each other off so much when mixed together, how did they survive for fifty million years? They didn't kill each other off, and they survived quite nicely. Without our help.

How does all this herd behavior relate to you and controlling your horse? Quite simply it relates to *leverage*. Ever watch the herd leader in your horse's herd and how the other horses treat him or her? Yes, it is often a "her." The horses standing by the water trough will quickly and politely part like the Red Sea whenever the herd leader approaches for a drink. And if you are still not convinced about the horse's ability to communicate, study the body language of the leader or alpha horse, and watch the response from the other horses and you will see it. If any particular horse doesn't yield to the alpha quickly enough, the alpha will make it very clear that he needs to move and show some respect. NOW. And believe me, it will happen. The respect given the alpha relates to the survival of the herd during a threat. For example, in the wild, if a member of the herd spots a predator in the distance, he will "point" out the threat to the herd. Since his feet are busy holding up the front of his body, he "points" with his nose as he raises his head high to get a good view. What happens next is specific and critical to the survival of the herd. Everyone will immediately look to the alpha to decide what to do. How do they know where alpha is? They *ALWAYS* know where alpha is. If the alpha moves, there will not be a horse in the herd that doesn't know it – unless it is an enormous herd which will have several sub-groups and sub-alphas making up a chain of command. But every horse will keep an eye on his alpha. His life may depend on it.

At this point in the crisis, the alpha will evaluate the threat and decide the best course of action. Let's say there are twenty horses being stalked by one or two wolves. The alpha may decide to get everyone in a circle, rear ends out, and if the wolves approach, the horses will kick them into the next county. Or, there could be a pack of fifteen to twenty wolves, which would change the dynamics of the situation greatly. The alpha may decide that the herd needs to beat feet *NOW* or somebody is going to die today. Alpha will decide the course of action, and if that means run, alpha will determine which direction to go and when it's safe to stop. The only variation to this scenario would be if the predators had separated a horse from the herd. That horse would realize he screwed up and is on his own. He would also realize he is about to die, and he would run for his life. As I said, mistakes can be fatal.

If the alpha said, "we're going this way" but Herbie, horse number twenty on the pecking order, thought that direction would be scary and he wanted to go a different way, would not stand off to the side and go where *he* wanted. He would instantly follow the leader with every ounce of his strength, without question. His life would depend on it. Such is the *leverage given to the alpha by the horses in his herd.* And that brings us back to you. I said earlier that we need leverage to control the horse because he's so big and we're so little. The leverage most people rely on is the use of force or inflicting pain, most often by the application of excessive equipment. I also said that I feel the use of pain creates a resistance in the mind of the horse, which I find unacceptable. The leverage I prefer to use is the *leverage of respect.* The leverage of respect is *given* to the alpha by the other horses because he or she demonstrated the character that *earned* such respect; the same leverage that lets the alpha horse instantly control an entire herd of horses in a life and death panic situation with no force or equipment required. To me, that's leverage. It's more powerful than any piece of equipment could ever provide. It will remain viable during times of stress, where most equipment loses all value if the horse panics. Being alpha cannot be forced or taken, it must be won and earned. And it comes from the mind of the horse, only. Remember we said the mind of the horse runs the body of the horse. Control the mind and you control the body. Win the respect of the horse by becoming his alpha and you will enjoy a *willing submissiveness* like most horse people never get to appreciate. Fundamentally speaking, you are becoming alpha to the horse in order to influence his attitude about you. You will also get to enjoy a few side benefits of this process that offer great value.

Horses only pay attention to what they feel is important. Ever felt like your horse was not paying any attention to you at all? Like his pasture mates or dinner or a strange noise had him totally focused somewhere else? And can you remember that at that moment when you lost his attention, whether you were on his back or on the ground, you also felt like you really had *no control* of the horse, and he was about to do something you didn't like? It happens all the time. One of the most profound facts I have come to understand about working with horses is that if you can keep their attention, that one action alone will solve most of your horse behavior problems. Period. If you lose their attention, you *have* lost control. They will only pay attention to what *they* think is important, and if that isn't you, then they are telling you that *you are not very important to them*. And that means the only leverage you have to rely on is whatever you can do to their body in an effort to control the movement you know is coming, but you really don't want. Pretty weak. (We will talk a lot about getting and keeping the horse's attention in the How-To chapter.) By learning to pay attention to what the horse is paying attention to, you will develop the ability to control your horse in situations that would have left you helpless before. But again, we are still talking about understanding and communication here, not training.

Another benefit of becoming alpha to your horse is going to solve a problem common to most horse people; being crowded or even stepped on when handling the horse from the ground. Do you remember my mention of the horses standing at the water trough, and the alpha approaching for a drink? Then the horses simply open up and let the alpha through, with plenty of space I might add. That is because the personal space of an alpha always takes precedence over the personal space of the lesser horse. Alpha can move into your space but you don't dare move into alpha's unless invited in. This concept of personal space is easy to understand and it is critical in learning to work with horses, especially when they are at liberty (loose and free). I refer to personal space as your bubble. We will describe how to employ this concept in detail in the How-To chapter but for now you need to know how it helps. Once you begin to become alpha to your horse, he will dramatically change his view of your space. He will be careful that he does not infringe on your bubble unless you ask him in. AND, he will yield his space to you whenever you encroach into his bubble. He will do this out of *respect* for you and without any *cue* from you in most situations. And the more alpha you become, the better it will get. He will become *softer* around you and much easier to handle, as well as becoming more attentive to your every move. If you turn to leave, he will try to follow. If you walk into his space, he will softly back up until you let him stop. All this will occur because you have earned his respect, and without you depending on any equipment or force or food. He will also come to you in the pasture and not run away when you turn him loose. All in all, it can totally change the nature of your relationship with your horse. And it will happen so quickly it will amaze you.

We need to go over a few more points about becoming alpha to your horse. First, it is a process, not an event. You can be somewhat alpha to your horse today and be a lot stronger alpha in a week or two. Alpha progresses in degrees. Since it is earned rather than taken, it can improve with time and practice. But it will change your effectiveness with your horse almost immediately. The main problem most people have with becoming alpha is that they are not consistent in their actions around their horse. If you act like an alpha in the round pen you need to act like an alpha *out of the round pen* also. Alphas are *ALWAYS CONSISTENT*. We humans tend to get lazy and relax our awareness around our horses. We ask them to behave sometimes but let things slide other times. We see that as being *lenient* while the horse sees it as being *inconsistent*. Being inconsistent around a horse makes you appear unpredictable to the horse and horses don't feel comfortable around anything unpredictable. Being inconsistent around your horse will make him more nervous, tense and overall less able to relax. Also less trusting of you. There are enough things in the world that can get your horse wired, keeping him from settling down; you shouldn't be one of them. By learning to become more consistent with your horse you will become a stable, dependable aspect of his life and therefore someone he gravitates to as a source of reassurance and security. Have you ever seen someone handling a horse where the horse was getting more and more wired until it actually blew up and the owner lost all control? I see this occurrence all too often. An uptight, nervous horse is dangerous where a calm, relaxed horse is a dream. Anyone can get a horse wired, but how many people can really get the wired horse to calm down and relax again? Becoming alpha to your horse is the first step in developing that ability. The key is improving your consistency.

Along with consistency, I'll give you two other words to keep foremost in your thoughts when working with your horse, *patience* and *persistence*. I think patience goes without saying, yet many of us have trouble being patient with our horses. The more you understand the horse's perspective, the more you will be able to patiently deal with his issues. When you fail to understand why he's doing what he's doing, when it seems so illogical to you, your patience will grow shorter and shorter. That will hinder your effectiveness with the horse. The same lack of understanding of the horse can challenge your persistence as well. To keep at something will be much easier if you have faith in its correctness and that it will work in the end. I was persistent in continuing to ride Sunny, while changing bit after bit and having no success. But I wasn't being very smart. And it was a period of horrific emotional and physical struggles for me, and Sunny. Once I learned a different way of dealing with Sunny I still faced a long period of getting him to come around. The difference was that then I knew I was going in the right direction and I could succeed. The slowness of my initial progress in the round pen was of little stress to me because of my new awareness. My realization that I was attempting something I had not done before (I was learning as I went), allowed me to be patient with myself as well as the horse. Knowing I was going to make mistakes with this new approach, and understanding it to be a process, not an event, took most of the stress out of it for me. I'm not saying it was always a piece of cake, it wasn't. But it was a heck of a lot easier than all those months on a run-away-horse. And the result was far more impressive as well.

It is also frequently misunderstood whether horses can have more than one alpha and does alpha transfer from one person to another. In any herd there is a pretty specific chain of command not unlike the military. Why? Because if the alpha horse were to be separated from the herd or killed, the herd must go on. There must be a new leader to take over in such a case. In a herd of twenty horses, there is one horse that has nineteen alphas. With that in mind, I tell people that each person should become alpha to every horse they are around. I become alpha to every horse I handle – some more than others, depending on time available, but I am always the alpha. You must be too. As you become more adept at the way the system works, it will become easier and easier for you to implement becoming alpha with new horses. You will develop a demeanor or manner about you that says, "I am a leader." Not like the arrogance of a bully, but more a confidence in yourself that the horses will read in a blink.

As to the transferring of alpha to other people, it just doesn't work that way. There can be some benefit if a horse had six people in a row that all became his alpha and treated him well. The next person who approached the horse may have it a bit easier if the horse assumed from experience that most people are alphas; but rest assured, if that next person did not *behave* as an alpha, the horse would change his opinion in no time flat. Every horse will test you, some more than others. It is always easier to be alpha to a horse if you start the relationship with that horse that way. I can usually become alpha to a horse much faster than his owner can, for two main reasons; the horse has no prior history with me so he doesn't know what I'm like until I interact with him now. Secondly, I've done this with hundreds of horses for many years, and I'm experienced at it. The horse knows the owner as probably not being an alpha so this behavior is a change to him. The owner is also usually trying this type of approach for the first time and will definitely make mistakes with it. There is often a third factor that is more subtle but sometimes of great importance; the owner's impression of the horse as being a problem. In other words if you have been around your horse for three years and he's been a problem for three years, you see him as a problem. That's why I often work with the owner's horse briefly at first. I say it is to evaluate the horse and demonstrate the procedure, when in fact I need to have the owner see his horse being good with me, so the *owner* will let go of his impression of the *problem horse*. When the owner sees the horse behaving well, he will shift his perspective about the horse and that will aid his effectiveness in the procedure. In short, each horse develops his opinion of each person based on the way each person treats that horse. Not unlike the way you evaluate each person you meet, based on how that person treats you. At least I would hope that's the way you work.

One last important point in understanding the concept of alpha. I often hear people say, "I don't need to do this because my horse already comes to me and follows me around." Then I watch the person with the horse and the horse is walking all over the owner, not respecting the owner's space but *is* following her around. This scenario is all too common and it shows me several things. The person is not alpha to the horse. The person has little control over the horse. The person and the horse need help. And, *the horse likes the person.* Don't confuse being liked by your horse with having his respect. They are totally different. The alpha horse in the herd has horses that he likes and will hang around with. If you feed your horse carrots and treats, and groom him, and take him for outings he likes, he will enjoy all that and like you for it. He will most likely come running when you show up because he wants the treats. He may also walk right over you with little concern because, since you are under him in his pecking order, he is expecting *you* to move out of the way like any smart horse in the herd would do. To become his alpha you will have to earn his respect, but he will also learn to like you as well. He will begin to feel that he needs to be with you rather than coming to you just for the treat. I call it the "grandma syndrome." Many grandparents spoil the grandkids by always bringing them something. The kids like the toys and associate grandma with getting toys. I'm not saying it's bad for grandmas to spoil kids. It's a lot of fun. But the relationship should be more than that. It's kind of like trying to buy friends. Not too dependable when the chips are down.

CHAPTER 7
Horsy Psychology

Before we get into the 'How-To' chapter and send you off to play with your horses, we need to go a bit further in the understanding department. A lot of the things I talk about regarding horses seem illogical to people. That's because it is. It's based on what's logical to the horse and our logic becomes irrelevant. We are trying to attempt to communicate with and influence a creature that is quite different from ourselves. Our approach, in order to be most effective, needs to proceed with his perspective in mind. We need to put our attitudes and perceptions aside and focus on his feelings and needs first and foremost. To do that effectively, we need to truly understand how much our perceptions and our attitudes influence and control our behavior. There are many sayings that present this idea, but simply put, "what we think determines what we are." It is unquestioned that our thoughts guide us, but I've worked with many people who were seriously in trouble in certain aspects of their lives because their mistaken beliefs or attitudes directed their actions in a negative way. I have been guilty of this in my life and so have you. Your perspective is based in your attitudes and beliefs, which evolved from your experiences. The attitudes we all carry around about horses were created by some often bizarre and unrealistic programming done to us by a variety of sources – just as I accepted the advice from the trainers who told me to geld Sunny and then change to a more severe bit to slow him down, because they were the experts. I then adopted their position as reality due to the credibility we give "experts." They were also employing "normal" beliefs and procedures. I now know they were wrong. Not wrong as in evil, but wrong as in misunderstanding. Their beliefs and expert opinions are still very "normal" in most of the horse world.

They are also still very wrong. Those trainers are not wrong because they were bad or mean people. They are frequently nice people doing what they thought best. But their attitudes were based on incorrect assumptions about the horse that contaminated the validity of their actions. Let me share a story with you to help you understand my point.

Imagine yourself riding home on a train or subway after a hard day at work. You're tired, as are most of the other commuters on the train. It's crowded and packed like a typical Friday afternoon commuter train would be. At the last stop before a long run to your town, a man gets on the train and sits right next to you. He has four kids with him and the kids are a bit rowdy. In fact, they are running up and down the aisle and bumping into people and in general making a real fuss. Their yelling, and playing continues to grow louder and more disturbing. The father appears to pay no concern to their behavior and simply sits still. The oldest kid is nine or ten and the youngest is about five. The yelling and running is escalating and really beginning to bother you and the other passengers. At one point two of the kids actually bump into an older lady and knock her package from her hands. Still the father says nothing. You feel your anger increasing as you think this situation should be handled and the children need to be told to settle down. Other people are mumbling to themselves and the kids are showing no sign of slowing down. Finally you turn to the man next to you and state in no uncertain tone, " Sir, can't you see that your children are behaving like animals? They are upsetting the other commuters and almost hurt that older lady. Would you please ask them to behave and sit down." His stare breaks as he turns to focus on your comments. Everyone is looking at him now and he turns to you and speaks in a soft almost quivering voice. "I'm very sorry. I wasn't thinking. They are really good children. Children, children, stop misbehaving and come sit down." Again he turns to you and says in an almost whispering voice obviously directed away from the kids, "Please forgive me, but I just left the hospital and their mother died this afternoon. I have been trying to think of how I can tell them their mother is gone, and I wasn't watching them. Please excuse us." The children are coming back to him and the car is now silent. How do you feel? Did your attitude toward the man change with a sentence or two he said? Was your perception of the situation valid or did you really not have an accurate understanding of the whole picture? Do you get the point? Any perceptions or attitudes you have affect your actions. Yet if those attitudes are not based in fact and reality they will contaminate the effectiveness of your actions. Before we can be truly effective with our horses, we must first evaluate those areas within ourselves that will inhibit what we do. We must align our attitudes about our horses with the horse's reality, even if that means doing what seems illogical to us.

Another area that can obstruct our effectiveness with our horses is our tendency to prejudge too much, the use of *good* and *bad* in defining behavior in the horse. I try to not use the words good and bad to describe a horse's behavior. Not that it would be incorrect to say a horse that kicks is bad, or a horse that rears is bad. But it is not an optimum choice of words. A horse may display a behavior that you don't like and it may even be dangerous, such as kicking. Yet a horse only does what he thinks is best for him at that moment. From his perspective, a kick was a reasonable action for that situation. I see very little of what you might call evil or mean in horses. Remember this fact: horses never do something for nothing. They only do something because of something. If we are facing a behavior we don't want, we need to eliminate whatever caused that behavior as a means of eliminating it, rather than just punishing the horse, which is often more routed in getting even than in correcting the behavior. And every time you call the horse bad, you are affecting your demeanor in a negative fashion and often creating an antagonistic situation. Let me give you another way to see this. I said earlier that the words you choose have an impact on the way you judge a situation as well as the way others react to you in that situation. Often when a horse is acting up, you will hear people saying things like, "What's wrong with that horse?" A typical question. We even use the same question on each other within personal relationships. Ever been in an argument and said that to your friend or even your spouse? "What's wrong with you?" The question itself tends to create a confrontational environment, doesn't it? Suppose you changed one word in that question that would totally restructure the effect of the question on you and the other party? Suppose you asked, "What's troubling you?" Any difference? Do you feel how that simple change gave you more empathy and made you less judgmental? Do you see how it took the confrontation out of it for the other party? A confrontation is sometimes needed, but most often not. Confronting a friend or spouse is seldom as productive as offering a helpful inquiry. Starting a confrontation with your horse is just plain stupid. And when your tone or terminology is confrontational, your horse will react to it that way. So I try to refer to behavior I don't want in the horse as unacceptable or unwanted, rather than bad. I've worked with many horses that I had been warned about how "bad" the horse was only to find the horse to be very nice with me. If the horse is "good" with me, and "bad" with the owner, is it a "bad" horse? I think not. As I said, a horse never does something for nothing, it only does something because of something. In this case the "bad" behavior of the horse was a response to actions on the part of the owner, just as the "good" behavior was a reaction to my actions with the horse. If the term bad needs to be applied, apply it where it is most appropriate, not to the horse.

Now seems like an appropriate time to discuss discipline, as I have yet to allude to that area at all. I often say that what I try to get people to do with their horses is to become more wise in the ways of the horse and thus be less dependent on force or equipment for retaining control. I rarely strike a horse because it is rarely necessary. But I want to be clear on the fact that in my opinion there are times when striking a horse is an appropriate action. I am not against striking a horse. It should not be ruled out in the tools you use to control your horse, but it is a rarity, a last resort. Not the first choice as many people consider it. If we take a minute to *define our goal* when disciplining a horse, it will give us a better perspective on when we may need to strike a horse and the ramifications of that act.

When most people hit a horse, it is for revenge and out of anger. That has nothing to do with discipline. That is simply an exhibition of a human flaw. Discipline should be an act, which causes the recipient to rethink his last behavior and initiate a different approach when a similar situation arises again. In other words to think, "I'm not gonna' do that again." To cause a horse to rethink his actions and eliminate an unwanted behavior we must first understand what a horse wants in life. Quite simply put, he wants to avoid pain and be comfortable. His needs are very simple and quite defined, unlike the many involved and complex things needed to keep us happy: new cars, color TVs, jewelry, etc. A horse can be quite happy just standing still, experiencing no discomfort. If you doubt that, try observing horses for hours on end. Their "daytimers" have consistently similar entries day after day – "eat a little, then stand around. Go potty. Stand around. Walk over there and stand there awhile. Get a drink, then walk back over here," etc. A horse perpetually seeks the state of being comfortable. Thus, rewarding a horse does not require food, or petting and, of course, not words. Most humans reward horses by applying human values. I'm not saying a horse won't like a treat or a carrot. I'm not saying he won't like a nice gentle rub. (He will not like being slapped on the neck, as many people must think he does. Horses never strike another horse to show affection. They rub. I have a rule for you about slapping a horse as a reward; never slap a horse for praise any harder than you would like to be slapped in your face.) I'm not even saying he would not like to hear a gentle voice to soothe him emotionally. Verbal praise is vital with a human child, but the human child is far different from the horse. Words to the horse are unnecessary. They are also less effective than what is natural to him; let him be comfortable. Relying on the treat/carrot idea is even more weak as you may not

141

always have access to food, thereby eliminating that possibility. If that was your leverage with the horse then what happens when you have no treats to bribe with? Remember the popular song a few years back that had everyone singing, "Don't worry, be happy!" That could be a horse's theme song.

If just hanging out being OK is all a horse needs for a reward, then any act of discipline would involve the opposite; excess activity without purpose. As you will learn in the next chapter, when I am playing with a horse, I simply make him move to get control of him or discipline him for an unwanted behavior. To reward him I simply leave him alone; let him relax and do nothing. You are probably thinking this is much too simplistic to be effective, but you will appreciate its effectiveness very soon. Since getting the horse to move in the first place may require some "leverage" as he may not want to move, many people are quick to hit the horse. They say, "go" and he says, "I don't want to," so they respond by hitting the horse to get the action they asked for. It may get the response wanted, the horse is now moving, but it was usually unnecessary. The "leverage" I prefer to use is *animation*. Horses tend to withdraw from movement they don't understand. I use a wand with a plastic bag attached to the end, or my arms waving about, or a lead line being shaken, or any other animated movement I can generate as my "leverage" to get the horse to move, rather than hitting him. If that animation fails then I might hit him, but I only hit a horse on *three occasions last year.* And I worked with a lot of problem horses. Not only do I not like to hit horses, but I firmly believe that the more physical violence you use on a horse, the less connected the horse and you can become. I want to be as connected with the horse as I possibly can without the hindrance of those problems to overcome. I've worked with many horses that have been beaten and either hate men, or are severely head shy, etc. If you saw how fast they come around with this simple change in approach philosophy, you would be amazed. I am. Horses can forgive so easily. If only we were so noble.

So what am I saying here about discipline? I'll be specific. If a horse tries to bite me, I'll have no problem slapping him in the mouth. If he kicks me I would be willing to kick him right back. And if it were so bad that he were rearing and striking, then I would feel no guilt at swinging a lead line around and around and tapping his nose with it, if that's what I had to do to get him to back off. I have done all on various occasions. But let's be clear on what was going on in these situations. The horse does something that is unacceptable and probably dangerous to me, like trying to bite. I become as animated as I can and I slap his mouth or nose. He backs off. He gave in, I made my point. Do you think I hurt him? Get real. Horses do worse to each other in play every day than we could hope to generate from our little bodies. More important, the amount of pain is not what matters, it is the *mental impact on the horse* that our action made that counts. Discipline is a mental procedure, not a physical one. Never forget that. I don't want to hurt him but I want him to think he's going to die. If you really hurt him you may be initiating a *physical struggle* and you could get a *physical response* based on self preservation from him. If you make a mental impression but there's little or no pain, then he's thinking, not hurting. And that is what you want. Really.

One other aspect to discipline and just handling horses in general that I feel is the most important and most misunderstood aspect of the whole game is *TIMING*. The timing of your actions around your horse is usually more important than the nature of the action. Again if we look at the way the horse thinks, he lives in the moment. Unlike you and me, he is thinking about now. We can be thinking about things like last night's party or what we want to do at work, or many other unrelated things *during our riding lesson*. The horse is thinking about now. Prey animals have to live in the moment so as to heighten their awareness of their environment. That's how they stayed alive in the wild for fifty million years. That's how they are able to notice every little thing that we are often so oblivious to. They notice everything. Drop you off in a jungle somewhere and see how quickly you become more adept at living in the moment. The side effect of this "living in the moment" is that a horse can only relate to a given situation or action for about *two and a half or three seconds*. After that time he is in the next "moment" and does not connect with the previous event. In other words, if he kicks you and you fall down and then get up slowly, brushing yourself off, and eventually get around to punishing the horse eight-ten seconds later, *he doesn't relate your violence towards him to his act of his kicking you, hence your discipline has no effect.* No, that's not exactly right. He will not associate your violence towards him to his kicking, but he will associate your violence towards him *to you*. With no meaning behind your action that he can perceive, you hurt him for no reason, by his way of thinking. That's not discipline, it's abuse. So if you can't respond to an unwanted behavior from your horse in three seconds or less, then you must let it go. Know that the behavior *WILL OCCUR AGAIN*, and use that knowledge to take appropriate action to correct it. How? By setting up the situation where the horse will repeat the behavior, only this time you are ready and you react *not within three seconds, but AS the horse initiates the unwanted act.* That is true discipline for the horse based on correct timing, and that approach can correct unwanted behaviors so fast it is incredible. It will require thinking and timing on your part, but the results are staggering. Optimum discipline occurs *as the unwanted act happens*. That creates the best effect. Response discipline occurs *immediately after* the unwanted act happens. Less effective than optimum discipline, but still very effective. Any other response to an unwanted act is just revenge and abuse with only negative associations.

One more point while we're discussing this "living in the moment" idea and how it affects the horse's thinking. Since they live in the moment and notice just about everything around them, one of the things they are continually noticing is *you*. They see every little detail and movement you initiate (except when they have placed your importance well *BELOW* them in their pecking order, so now they know you're *NOT IMPOR-TANT* and they mostly ignore you). Using their way of thinking as a guideline (horses never do something for nothing, they only do something because of something, hence everything horses do has purpose), *they assume that everything we do, we meant to do for a reason also.* They interpret everything we do to be intended and meaningful, while much of our actions around the horse have little intent on our part. Talk about miscommunication! How many times have you done something around your horse that he noticed and responded to, yet *you didn't even realize you did it?* As you become more aware of your horse you will also become much more aware of yourself.

If you are to develop the ability to employ this idea of becoming alpha to your horse as a means of establishing an effective and benevolent relationship with him, then your understanding of the "process" needs to go a bit deeper. I keep referring to the "process" of becoming alpha, and stating it is a "process" rather than an event. Let me explain. We humans like things like light switches; we flip it on, it works, we flip it off, it stops and leaves us alone. Very simple. We unfortunately like to apply similar "event" type procedures such as flipping a switch, to get results in more complex situations. The horse runs away with me, so I change the bit. The switch is flipped, crisis over. We want one single immediate "event" (or action) to change a situation that was the result of an ongoing "process" or series of many interrelated events. It is not like that at all. Being alpha is about establishing a position in a relationship. Relationships take time to develop and evolve if they are to survive and prosper. You don't develop a life-long, best friend relationship in a minute or two. Feelings like trust, respect, confidence, and even love take repeated reinforcing experiences with that person in order to provide any foundation for the relationship. Since people change, a person that was once a friend may now not be as close due to changes in interest or even changes in values. As you experience different behaviors presented by the friend, your values about those behaviors may change the nature of your relationship with that person. Such is life.

The relationship between horses is similar and equally dynamic. Any group or herd of horses thrust together will have interaction within the group, allowing each horse to establish his place or relationship within the herd. One will become the leader and the rest become members of lesser standing and hence less "alpha." If, over time, the initial leader does not continue to display the character that garnered that alpha position, he will be replaced by another horse that does. During his "reign" as alpha, he will be tested repeatedly by the others to make sure he is still the right horse to follow. Those tests will be very slight at first and often go unnoticed by people observing the interaction. Yet if even the slightest test went unchallenged by the alpha, there would soon follow a stronger more aggressive test and a weakening of the leader's position. Someday, even the strongest alpha horse will become too old and weaken. His failure to adequately respond to testing would facilitate his loss of position. He will be replaced by a younger, stronger and more appropriate alpha at that time. The original alpha would progress down the pecking order and become less significant to the herd.

How does all this help you? Simple. You need to understand that you can be a little bit alpha right now, very quickly. That can be accomplished in usually an hour or so with most horses, and immediately improve your relationship with your horse. It will offer you a leverage to control your horse and a means of keeping his attention on you like never before. Sometimes the change is so dramatic that the person is lulled into a false sense of power and well being that they lose track of reality – meaning, don't let a taste of greatness go to your head. The process is just beginning. The relationship is not "set" yet, it's just initiated. To truly be alpha to your horse you must *continually present yourself as an alpha.* Remember the word consistency? To be perceived as an alpha by your horse you must *become* an alpha. Years ago a TV actor did a commercial for some medicine and used a line that became famous, "I'm not a doctor but I play one on TV…." You cannot simply "play at being an alpha." Initially you may do that as you teach yourself *HOW* to be an alpha to your horse, but as time goes on you must become one. That is how you develop the "presence" around horses I referred to earlier. You become an alpha.

The first key to becoming an alpha is to understand the horse and you're working on that now. You're reading this book. The next step is increasing your awareness of things that are happening around you and use your new-found understanding (knowledge) to react appropriately. A common example is something I see all the time: a person is handling a horse and the horse swings his head into the person's space, perhaps even hitting the person. I recently worked with a lady who had a broken finger from that exact situation. Anytime a horse willingly moves into your space with his body, or swings his head into your space, he is telling you "he does not see you as alpha." That would *never* occur in the pasture to an alpha. If the horse just met you and bumped you with his head, it would be considered a test. But if you don't respond to the test, you *are accepting and in fact endorsing the behavior he exhibited.* You told him in very clear terms, "You are alpha, and I'll get out of your way." Important fact to remember: any behavior you do not respond to and stop, you are endorsing from the horse. In the example above, a slight brush with his head will quickly evolve into a total disregard for your space and you in general. He will walk all over you with no concern at all. Fortunately most horses are not mean, so they will usually not do anything to deliberately hurt you. Some will, but not most. Unfortunately if the horse steps on your foot and breaks it, or swings his head into your space and knocks you off your feet, breaking your nose in the process, the fact that he didn't *MEAN* to hurt you is of little compensation. As I said over and over, they are too big and we are too little; we must be in control.

This testing will continue for as long as you and the horse are around each other. You may get tested every month or so, or it may be more regular than that. Sunny continues to test me every few weeks. But know this. The more alpha you become, in other words the more quickly and specifically you respond to each test, the stronger your image to your horse becomes and the less often and less dramatic each test will become. Which again throws the burden of awareness back on you. You must stay aware that that little brush of his head was no accident; it was a meaningful test of your authority and resolve. And you must respond appropriately. (I will define appropriate response in the How-To chapter.) Sunny's testing of me is so subtle and even cute, that I actually welcome his little exercises. I can almost see the look in his eyes, like he's thinking: Are you really still my alpha or could I get a little control back? That look will be followed by a very slight nudge of his head if I'm on the ground or perhaps a flip of his head with an unrequested turn or change of speed if I'm on his back. Remember his forty three unrequested changes of speed and direction earlier on? I do.

Those were on a much grander scale than any recent test. Also, did you notice the difference in my attitude about his "tests?" Now they are fun and no trouble. I see the process as a game to play, not a war to win. What changed? Is Sunny not the same horse he was then? He is. He could very easily become the same runaway he was then. The difference is me and what I learned. And then most important, how I changed. The problem was never the horse in the first place. It was the people around the horse. And that is the case with almost every horse I see. Suffice it to say that being alpha to your horse is not a contract, but an ongoing relationship you must work on in an ongoing fashion if it is to provide the *magic* it can. For you both.

Next, let's take a philosophical look at the idea of controlling the horse, the initial step needed, and establishing our mental position about that step. We discussed the fact that when we talk about control we are talking about controlling the movement of the horse's body. The usual starting point with most people is to try to minimize the horse's movement by tying or

148

restricting it in some way; most often involving some type of equipment. We want to teach the horse to be still when we tell him to be still. But is that what restriction and confinement are teaching a horse? Not really. In fact, the very nature of the horse, entrenched by fifty million years of practice, makes the horse want to *resist* any form of confinement. You may get the horse to submit to being tied, it happens all the time. But his underlying instinct is telling him to get loose, or at least that he would be safer if he were loose. How often do you see a horse get loose, then he is off on his way and hard to catch? His evolution taught him when he's trapped, he's in danger. When he is free to run, he is safe. Mobility is his security blanket. He feels safe and comfortable when he is loose. So think of it this way; when the first thing you do with a horse is to restrict his movement, you are starting off by taking away the main thing that makes him feel safe. You take away his security blanket and expect him to be calm, still and cooperative. He doesn't even know you yet and you expect him to trust you implicitly by giving up his main weapon against danger. Great way to start a relationship. Let me suggest an alternative approach that sounds totally illogical to you but is much better for the horse.

The first step I use to gain control of a horse is to turn him loose. I know you think I really lost it on this one, but stay with me a minute. Also, there is a qualifier to the "turn him loose" part; I mean turn him loose in a round pen. An arena can be made to work if there is no round pen, but as you'll soon understand, you really do need a round pen. Really. If you turn the horse loose in a pasture, say thirty acres, he will most likely just leave. And you can't stop him. Many of you have experienced this phenomenon when you try to catch your horse in his pasture and he says, "I don't think so." Their legs are substantially more effective than ours. And they know it. So we are looking for a compromise. When I first meet a horse I would like to *give* him the one thing that will make him most comfortable, his freedom. I want him to have the ability to move. But not too far. And I don't want him to be "coaxed" into stopping by the enclosure either.

149

What I mean by that is that if he is moving down a straight wall or fence in an arena and he runs into a ninety-degree corner, he may stop. Assuming I am asking him to move (which I will be doing) I have let the enclosure create an action in the horse contrary to what I was asking for. Not good. Hence the round pen: no corners. He gets his freedom and the ability to move, but I have a safe, controllable space in which to supervise that movement. A win-win situation. And it's small enough to prohibit him leaving my proximity to avoid me. All in all, the round pen is a controlled environment that sets up the playing field, giving me the advantage.

Many of you are probably wondering how I'm going to exert any control over the horse when he is free to run about. Since you think of control as being affected by something you put on his body, you consider a free running horse as beyond your control. Until you get that lead line hooked on him, you think you have no control and he can still get away. The two important realities of this situation are: 1) you had more control than you think before you hooked on the lead, and 2) he could still get away *AFTER YOU HOOKED ON THE LEAD.* Since I consider control as the influence I exert on his mind, which works from within his body to control it, there is a great philosophical difference between our attitudes here. Since your attitudes direct your actions, we need to make some changes there. Another reality to consider is that you can have great influence on a loose horse if you understand how to apply the tool you use to generate that influence. We discussed it briefly earlier and the tool is pressure. Not physical pressure but mental pressure. Remember the bubble? The horse's personal space? Let's take a minute to really understand what this is all about.

The bubble is the immediate space around you that you consider private to you. It has been described many ways, but suffice it to say it is dynamic and changing, not static. It is that point at which anything approaching you is judged by you and quantified as to its threat value based on *your value system.* The point where you say, "Don't get any closer." As an example, suppose you were on an elevator, by yourself (assuming you are not claustrophobic), the doors close and up you go. A couple of floors up, the elevator stops, the doors open and there stands a very large man. He's about 280 pounds and wearing shorts, a tank top and sandals. He's very hairy, except on his head, and there is an unlit cigar hanging from his mouth. He is quite sweaty and rather dirty on one side. He apparently hasn't shaved in a few days either. As he got on the elevator, would you: a) move towards him, b) back into a corner to get as far away as possible or c) get completely off the darn elevator regardless of the floor? You probably said c. But why? And if you chose b, was it a big elevator or a tiny one? Probably a big one or c would have won out. If you chose b, how close could he have gotten before you would have become uncomfortable? Before you would have gotten vocal? Before you would have been terrified? And why? Because of your bubble.

Now I have to tell you that this guy is really a very wonderful grandfather who has spent all morning building a tree-house for his grandkids who love him deeply. He is a church deacon and been married to the same lady for twenty-six years and has three grown children that are all well-adjusted members of society. And eight grandkids. How do you feel about your actions in the elevator? I admit I was setting you up a bit, but do you realize that your judgments in the elevator were based on your observations, combined with your experience and your values? And that determines the size of your bubble at any given moment in any situation. And it is constantly changing. Suppose we go back in your elevator and the doors open and Tom Cruise steps in? (Assuming you're a female. If you're a guy, feel free to substitute any lady you find quite attractive.) Would you choose a, b, or c now? How big would your bubble be with that person? Or did it just pop altogether? Get my point? Our values and perceptions determine our bubble. But there is one more lesson to think about here. Suppose on the elevator, the guy was good looking, but not a face you knew? How would that affect your bubble? Depending on looks or first impression too much could be a real problem. Is a small horse less dangerous than a big one? No. Was the good-looking guy you liked on the elevator Ted Bundy?

So how do you use this bubble concept on the horse? As you have experienced many times, when anyone gets too close, if they hit your bubble, you will "feel" a pressure from their presence. The closer they get, the more the pressure you feel. If a small poodle ran at you, you would feel less pressure than if a large Doberman ran at you, because you'd have bigger bubble for the Doberman. The presence of the bubble is what allows you to put pressure on a horse without touching him. Most people do not consciously think about the bubble. They also often overlook another basic yet important fundamental in handling horses; *horses learn* from the *removal of pressure*. But you can't very well *remove* pressure until after you have *applied* it. Unfortunately most people believe horses learn from applying pressure so they pay little attention to releasing it. Later we'll deal more with releasing pressure and timing. For now suffice it to say that the horse will respond to pressure on his bubble. Being aware of the horse's bubble and using it to apply and then release pressure is the way you influence a horse that's free. If he's free and loose the only pressure you can use is the pressure you will put on his bubble and you may do that from thirty feet away.

You can apply pressure to his bubble and begin to interact with the horse so as to cause him to move, hence controlling his movement. (Initiating movement from a still horse is a form of controlling movement.) What can you do to "apply" this pressure to a horse that may be thirty feet away from you? Move. (We'll go over the specifics in the How-To chapter.) You are going to move and create animation in order to get the horse to move off, away from you. Every time you move and cause him to initiate a responding movement, you are controlling him. Simple movements at first, such as, "go that way." Since earlier I talked about "control the things you can and don't try to control what you can't," it is understandable when I say that at first the movements you get the horse to do will be very general. You can't go in a round pen with a strange, loose horse and ask him to bow and expect it to happen. For many reasons. As the horse becomes more responsive you will be able to get very, very specific movements. The horse is loose and you are controlling him.

As you and the horse begin this process, several very important things start to happen. You take charge. (It's kind of an alpha thing.) The horse begins to keep an eye on you as he is trying to figure you out. He is starting to pay attention to where you are and what you are doing. You begin to watch what *HE* is paying attention to, and if it's *NOT YOU* then you create some animation commanding his attention back to you. Now he is *really learning* to pay attention to you almost constantly. He initially *responds* to you, which soon evolves into *submitting* to you. Which is establishing your alpha position in his herd. As you are able to control him more and more specifically from a distance, your power seems more impressive to him. By not hitting or hurting him, there is no resistance being created by your actions. (I must clarify that statement since there may be great resistance in the horse even before you begin with him. I am asking you to differentiate between *dealing* with the resistance he has, versus doing things that are *creating* new resistance in him.) As the interaction continues, you will utilize a tactic I call "Do and Then Don't Do," which is helpful to both you and the horse. Do and Then Don't Do is intended to overcome the human tendencies to be far too proactive when handling horses. It also works incredibly well at calming down an excited horse and lets the horse have a chance to "digest" what just transpired. It also provides you a break from doing anything, which will allow you time to evaluate what the horse just did in response to what you just did, and plan what you want to do next. What a concept. Rather than just continually going after the horse with a series of unending demands, based in vague purpose, suppose we do something, then stop doing and see what the horse does, and then plan what would be the best next step based on what we saw. A logical process that allows us to adjust as we go and consider the horse constantly.

The idea of evaluating a horse is always discussed by horse people, yet it is often done from a somewhat contaminated position. Evaluating the horse is done to see what you have to work with. But to *really know* what the horse is like you need to go back to the first step I use in controlling the horse – turn him loose. Ever notice that some horses are a bit fussy when they're loose, but as soon as you get the halter on, or lead line on the halter, they settle right down? Did you doubt the horse could tell the difference between tied and free? Do you think that the horse has any different attitudes when tied versus free? Many horses are dramatically different when tied versus loose. Are kids any different when the teacher leaves the classroom? When I handle a horse I want to know what is *really* going on in the horse's mind, not what he has been conditioned to display. The differences are sometimes like black and white.

Remember this: what he really *feels* is what you will have to deal with, someday if not now. If you never give him the opportunity to express what he really feels you may not be riding the horse you think you are. Ever hear anyone say, "He was always such a great horse, then suddenly he did so-and-so. And we had no idea where *THAT* came from!"? "That" had been there all along, but they never looked for it. When you turn a horse loose and apply pressure, you will get all the "thats" in the horse to show up. But you will get them to show up in an environment where you can effectively deal with them. Often they show up a little bit at a time, kind of in stages as the horse goes through what I call "un-layering" or "peeling the onion." It may go like this: On the surface the horse seems OK. Then he gets real aggressive. Then gets OK again. Then even more aggressive. You are working your way into the horse, level by level, breaking down all the baggage that has been built up in the horse over past years of crisis and poor handling. Not unlike when a person goes in for therapy and the psychiatrist asks him to talk about his childhood. Sometimes it gets painful and very stressful. Yet the end result can be a release of pain and tension, which has burdened the patient for decades. Horses deal with stress and trauma all the time, yet the overly confined environment we force them into deprives them of their primary release tool, movement. They can't get it out of their system so to speak, so it lingers and festers inside. And it will show up when you least expect it. Liberty work with horses is the most natural way I have seen to free a horse of his stress and allow him to relax. Really relax. This often accounts for why some horses change dramatically from almost unmanageable to soft and responsive after a few days or weeks of effective round pen handling. And it's always safer than fighting with a horse on a rope.

At some point in the round pen process, something significant will happen in the horse's mind. He will decide that maybe, just maybe you are an alpha and he would be better off in your herd than on his own. At that point he will *choose* to join you. He will do it in a soft, almost polite fashion, asking for your acceptance. You will see a definite change in his eye and a lowering of his head. He is relaxing since now that he has a herd leader, a lot of responsibility has been lifted off of him. He will follow you willingly *without cue*, and pay attention to you eagerly. He will yield his space to you when you approach and move when you apply even the slightest pressure (not even touching him). It is the most incredible of moments for a person with a horse. I have experienced it hundreds and hundreds of times and the magic of it never fails to touch me inside. For some of the worst-case horses, it is probably the first time they have ever been at ease around a person. But you must understand, the moment when this horse first decides to join your "herd" and give himself up to you, is not the end result; it is a beginning. It is the beginning of a different kind of relationship with the horse. A relationship where he becomes a willing partner rather than a forced slave. His willingness to be submissive to you will be greater than any force could create. And his comfort level within the situation will be the strongest aspect of your bond together. It will be the beginning of a relationship where the rules were established by his world, not yours. By aligning yourself with his way of understanding, you have given the horse an incredible gift, a leader he can relate to. It is not the *NORMAL* way most people relate to a horse. Too bad. You already know how I feel about a lot of *normal* horse practices. I hope to change some of that.

When you get to this point with the horse (and many people are quite surprised at how quickly it happens), you will have a new means of disciplining the horse that is awesome in its effectiveness and side benefits. To best explain it to you we must go back to the nature of herd life during the fifty million years (are you getting tired of hearing that phrase yet?) before we decided to take over their lives. Safety was in the herd and a horse learned that from his first experiences with mom. The horse most likely to die today is the horse that is weak, or injured, or does something dumb. If a threat appears, the weak or injured are not likely to be able to keep up and therefore get separated from the herd. And most likely the rest of the herd, (the safe ones) will get to watch the victim be caught by the predators. The dumb ones will let themselves get separated from the herd and the rest of the herd will watch them get caught as well. The underlying rule for every horse will be, "Stay in the herd. To get off on your own will be fatal." There is one more line to that rule: "The closer you are to the herd leader, the safer you are." Why? Because predators aren't dumb. You'll never see a lion or a pack of wolves say, "Let's go try to kill that great big, extremely strong, very fast, toughest horse in the herd." That type of a struggle would be much more risky for the predator. And a lion with his teeth kicked out is as good as dead. A weak or injured horse would die running. A strong, tough, fit horse would die fighting, and that's not a fight the lion wants. So the fit horse would live. Consider that point: the wild animal predator doesn't want to start a struggle with a fit horse if he can avoid it. Is there something about you I don't know that makes you a better match for a fit horse in a struggle than a lion or wolf? I think not. Me either. As I said, starting a physical struggle with a horse is stupid. Only humans consider it a normal option.

This helps you with your horse because once you become his alpha, he will gravitate to you of his own free will. You become his best option for being safe. He will associate you with being safe, and *choose* to follow and stay with you. At first this connection may be weak or inconsistent, but as you continue the *process*, the effect will become better and better. Although I don't recommend you take your horse out all the time without a halter and lead on him, due to the surprises and risks you may encounter, I have often taken my horses out with nothing on them at all. Several of the pictures in my display at various shows include pictures of Sunny standing loose on a rock or running through some trees in the Colorado mountains. With nothing on him. Many people don't even notice, but often someone will ask how we got those shots that appear to show a free running horse in the woods. The answer: we turned him loose and took pictures as I walked around the woods with him following. Sometimes I ran, sometimes I stood still. And he actually wandered off a short distance several times, but all I had to do to get him back was to *run away from him*. He didn't want me to get too far away, so he came running. Again I stress, this is not *normal* in the horse world today. If he chooses to be with you on his own, your lead becomes incidental. I still halter him almost all the time as a safety back-up for what I call the "unknown crisis." You know what I mean. Something unexpected always happens when you have a horse with you. Be prepared, but be smart.

The other means of disciplining the horse I referred to is your ability to take advantage of the horse feeling most safe when near you. If he does anything you deem inappropriate, you simply send him away from you where he doesn't want to be. And you don't let him come back until you feel he got the message. Mares use this technique to educate and control the young horses all the time. It is part of the socialization process of all young horses as they grow up and learn the workings of the herd. If a horse acts up, it will be sent off, away from the others and forced to stay there awhile. Once alone, he knows he's in trouble and will be eager to get humble and be allowed back in where it's safe. You can use the same approach. You can even add to that, get the horse to move around a bit when he's away from you, and experience the double aggravation of being away from the herd and moving with no purpose as well. He will come back to you more polite and submissive than when he left. Often when people see me utilize this tool they will get very perplexed and ask, "Why is the horse trying to come in to you since you just got very animated and sent him off?" Now you know. Remember this tool and use it. Your horse will understand even if no one else watching does.

So how do we sum up this discussion of the psychology of the horse? Perhaps it would be most easily explained from the horse's point of view.

"Let me have as much freedom as possible as I find confinement unnatural and unnerving. Be aware of my nature and don't expect me to be that which I cannot. I will *give* you control of me if you show you are worthy of being my leader. Once I see I can trust and understand you, I will be happy to follow your lead. Be consistent in how you treat me and don't hurt me. I will respect your space and do my best not to hurt you in any way. If you continue to act in this fashion, my bond with you will grow stronger and stronger, with no ultimate limit. I will be your friend and play with you as often as you like. And I will carry you through fire, should you ask. I am your horse."

Perfect Union

Come little man let me take you for a ride,
You of such great intellect but oh so short of stride,
You carry on and boast and brag of all that you have done,
Let me show you my world and what a horse does just for fun.
It's not a world that you can have by building some machine,

The way I move, my grace and speed has crept into your dreams,
You watch and marvel when I run at what I love to do,
Come share my passion for my world as I share that world with
   you.

I'll take you through the forest with such speed you'll know
   the fear,
When people do with horses, what horses love so dear,
To run just to run, feel the wind against your face,
To run because you love it, not to get to some new place.

I'll share with you my power, my world of strength and speed,
You'll feel what I feel as we become one, and conquer each
   new deed,
For all you ask I'll give my best, my heart knows no other way,
For I am a horse full of spirit and pride and you are in my world
   today.

So ask me to run and I'll take you along, we'll go where you
   can't go alone,
But care for me well as we are a team and you need me to get
   you back home,
As with any team when we are together, we do more than each
   could as one,
So trust we must build, each in the other, for we share something more than just fun.

I'm not a machine but a creature of flesh you must learn to
   respect and to know,
For it's not just my world I'm sharing with you, but my heart
   and even my soul.
Two beings so different yet so drawn together, so perfect when
   union is known,
A man and a horse like no other creatures, become one in a
   world of their own.

159

Dan and Sunny today in Virginia. Photo by Susan Sexton.

CHAPTER 8

How To

SECTION 1 – THE ROUND PEN

Now we have a pretty good understanding of the horse's world and his reality. It is quite unlike our world, and it is important that we accept that. A large portion of what we have discussed so far is to let us understand that the horse makes choices about everything based on *his* value system. We must be willing to *allow* him to make those choices without our judging him as stupid or silly, simply because the choices were not what we thought best. Even when a horse does something we disapprove of, it was usually the right choice for the circumstances based on his value system. Accepting that single fact can help you become less judgmental and therefore more fair in how you deal with the behaviors your horse presents. It will also help you to understand how you can change the behaviors you don't want by applying the horse's value system in your approach. This may at times be difficult, as you will do things that seem illogical on the surface. The utter simplicity of the approach described in this chapter will seem foreign to you and often off the point. Yet you will see it work over and over as you begin to play with your horse and see the changes appear. Some of you will accept this all quite quickly, and for others of you (who are more like I was in the beginning) it will be more of a struggle. As I've said before, be patient with yourself, as well as the horse.

So far everything we have discussed was directed towards getting our mind-set to where it needed to be. Preparing us, if you will, for what we are about to *DO*. Before we start you should be sure you understand the following guidelines.

1) We will start from square one and develop a relationship with our horse. Even if you have had your horse for years, you must go back to the basics.

ITEM: I recently had a call from a prominent dressage trainer overseas that had attended one of my workshops and had begun to use what I suggested with her horses. She had owned and ridden this particular horse for years and won on him many times. He was her top horse. As she began to play with him using the approach you are about to learn, he showed large amounts of resistance that she was quite surprised at – to the point where it actually became a bit more effort than she anticipated and she thought it might not be working. She even took my advice and didn't ride the horse for over two months while she tried to restructure their relationship. To use her words, "At some point there was a change in the horse. He became more responsive to me, yet it was in a different way of being responsive. He was responsive and relaxed, but still very aware of me. But it was not until I got on to ride him after all that time off that I began to truly appreciate the change. His attitude was better, but also his body was softer and more fluid. Everything bothered him less than before. And most dramatic was that the time I expected I would need to "bring him back" from so long out of training, was almost nothing. He is now performing at a level far above where he left off before. And I find it hard to believe that a horse I was so proud of before, could be even that much better now. He is a different horse."

2) We will then begin to influence his behavior in a fashion that is as natural to him as possible within our limitations.

3) Our communication with him will be such that he can understand us, and we will try to stay aware of all he is trying to communicate to us.

4) Discipline will be specific and fair, and never out of anger on our part.
5) We will always give him time to figure out what's being asked of him.
6) We will act in such a way as to let us *both* enjoy the process.

CAUTION: **Please do not put a horse in the round pen and attempt any of the procedures in this chapter until you have read and are comfortable with the *ENTIRE CHAPTER*. This could be considered the "instruction manual" for your horse. You must read *ALL* the instructions before you try anything.**

OK, here's what you need to start. A round pen. A knowledgeable handler can do some of what we are going to do in the round pen, without the round pen. I occasionally have had to handle problem horses without the benefit of a round pen, and I can usually accomplish what I need. I don't like it, but I can do it. It is usually much harder and slower. I have found it to be *INCREDIBLY MORE DIFFICULT* and *MUCH LESS SAFE* to attempt to *LEARN* to do any of this work without a round pen. You can buy one, build one, rent access to one or whatever, but it is an invaluable tool, as you will soon see. You can even use a square pen if you rope off the corners, making it an octagon. There are also a lot of variations in round pens and their theory, so let's discuss that right now. Some of the Round Pen Trainers, as they tend to be called (more by the public than by any of them), are in favor of walled, solid wood pens. This keeps the horse from seeing any distractions, hence making it easier to get him to focus on you. A true concept, yet I disagree with the application. I try to get the horse to pay attention to me from the first minute I enter the pen, and although it would be easier to accomplish that with no distractions, most of us don't ride our horses alone in a room. At some point you will have to take the horse out into the real world where there will be *lots of distractions*. I prefer to teach the horse to pay attention to me while there are distractions all around from the very beginning.

In fact, if there are no distractions present, I will often go get some and bring them into the area where the pen is. Distractions can be anything from a barking dog to a plastic tarp blowing around, to a tractor, to the always distracting, nearby horses. I don't want a horse to be paying attention to me because I am the only living thing in sight; I want him paying attention to me no matter *what* is around. Short term, the walled pen is easier, but long term easier isn't better.

So I recommend tubular, rail type pens where the horse is free to see out. For my workshops the rail pens are much better for the added benefit that the attendees can see the horse as well. It should be at least five feet high, preferably higher. Seven feet is perfect but few pens are that high, and most of you can do just fine with a bit over five. There is also a big variation in the quality of round pens and that brings up several safety issues. Anything that protrudes into the pen such as bolts, flat edges of metal, pins, etc. can do a lot of damage if a horse hits it. And rest assured the horse *will hit it*. They will bump it and test it and find anything that could cut them in the process. So be sure there is nothing that isn't round on the inside of your pen. Also, the place where the panels connect together should get pretty close together so if the horse rears up he can't come down with a leg wedged between the panels. That could be a broken leg in a blink. The bigger the gap between panels the greater the risk. Another safety tip is to install a panel of boards such as half-inch or thicker wood along the bottom of the pen, all around the inside a couple of feet high. This will do two things. It will keep the horse from getting his leg through the rails if he were to slip and fall. It will also allow dirt to bank up around the base of the pen giving the horse better traction. I rarely see round pens that come with any paneling like this, but it can be easily fabricated. Be sure you attach it so there is nothing sticking in where the horse could scrape himself on the attachment bolts.

The pen needs to be fifty to sixty feet in diameter, and that is a pretty specific dimension. It could be bigger, and bigger

 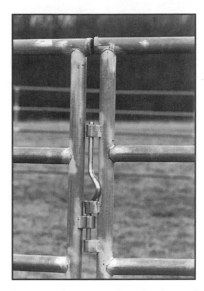

This is an excellent round pen. The panels are 6 feet high and there is almost no gap where they meet. The heavy-gauge connecting pins are easy to use and do not fall out to get lost. And the gate is tall enough to ride under safely. Photos by Susan Sexton.

is a bit better for doing a lot of riding in the pen, especially on larger horses. One place I lived recently had an indoor fifty-five foot pen and an outdoor seventy-six foot pen. I did a lot of advanced work and riding in the outdoor pen and it was great. But ground work, especially on a new horse will require a lot more movement from you in a pen over sixty feet. If you want to skip going to the health club and doing the aerobics class, just use a big round pen. Playing with a horse in a large pen will get you to sweat, I guarantee it. A pen under fifty feet can be dangerous. Remember our discussion about the bubble and pressure on the bubble? Remember the part about horses learning from the removal of pressure, not the pressure itself? In a round pen too small and a horse with a big bubble, you will not be able to take the pressure off and the horse can get out of control if you aren't careful. Best suggestion, stay around the sixty-foot size. You are better off and so is the horse.

Also be sure to check out the gate if you are buying a ready-made pen. Be sure it is not too narrow, and that the overhead rail you go under is high enough if you are riding the horse. I don't care for double-wide gates as they can create risk when you have several horses in the pen and want to remove just one. They are also heavy to move and carry. The gate is usually the weakest part of the pen and first to bend if the horse hits it, so check it out carefully. Be sure the latch is easy to work *with one hand*. You may be pretty busy or loaded down carrying stuff sometimes, so an easy to operate gate latch is a real convenience. Try to put it on level ground and in an area with reasonable footing. The portable rail pens are also nice since they can be moved around, even brought into the indoor arena for wet weather use. Due to its many uses, and the safety it affords you and your horses, the round pen is a tool every horse owner should have or at least have access to.

There is also something you have that you're going to have to leave behind when you enter the pen, your voice. You will need to learn to be quiet. For some of you this will be a bigger problem than for others, but duct tape can augment any lack of self-control you may have to deal with. You need to not talk to the horse in the pen for at least the first few sessions. There are several reasons for this that I alluded to earlier, but this can help you so much we must get it clear. I am not against talking to a horse, in general. I talk to my horses a lot. But you should not be talking without saying anything. You should definitely get your horse to understand and respond to the basic word commands such as whoa, back, stand, etc. But as I said before, these are association commands. The language of the horse is non-verbal. The best tool I have for getting you to learn his language quickly is to take away *your* language, which hasn't been working for you anyway. The more you talk, the slower things will progress. Without *your* language to get in the way, you will develop your skills with his language quicker. Just like going to a foreign country will teach you a new language quickly since you *have* to use it. Being quiet will also improve your concentration by taking away the distraction that your jabbering provides. By staying focused and concentrating better, you will become more effective with your interactions with the horse sooner. It works; try it and stick with it.

ITEM: A lady had come to a workshop with a big, rather beautiful, yet obnoxious thoroughbred. The horse was so obnoxious that no one wanted to work with it. So I played with him awhile and sure enough he was a sweetheart. He changed and relaxed and was really quite different in about forty-five minutes. Then the lady came in and did what I did, and got the big guy to be really good for her, too. She was ecstatic. After the workshop I did several private lessons with her and her two horses during the following months, and soon got her working both horses in the pen at liberty together. She was really having fun with this. Then one day she called and asked if I would come to the farm because she was having a few friends over to see how she was doing with her horses. She was going to show off her round pen progress. I said I'd come. Then she told me that one of the people was Gunther Gable-Williams. If you don't recognize the name, he has been the head trainer for the Ringling Bros. Circus for over twenty-five years – long blond hair, has done American Express commercials with a leopard on his shoulders, and so on. He trains horses, as well as big cats, elephants and probably anything else. How would you like to show off to Gunther what you can do with a horse?

When I arrived, there were a few people from the circus and Gunther. We talked a bit and then my host put her big guy in the pen for a few minutes and he was great for her. Then she brought in her appaloosa and proceeded to play with them both together. They were both doing just fine, and she was happy as could be. She stopped in the center of the pen and both

167

horses immediately turned to her and walked up as nice as you please and stood quietly for the next command. She looked at Gunther and grinned. Now Gunther is German, and tends to be a very animated person around people. He laughed and complimented her on her progress, since he had known how much trouble she had had with the horse previously. Then he looked a little puzzled for a bit and asked, in a rather vocal way, "Bonnie, you don't talk to your horses. Why don't I hear you saying anything to the horses?" Gunther knows she likes to talk to the animals and he was fishing for something. Bonnie turned to him and in a sheepish kind of way said, "Dan doesn't let me talk to the horses when I'm playing with them. He says it keeps me focused on their language better, and in fact I really do think it has helped me." Gunther turned to me and raised both his arms with his hands out as if preparing to ask a question. "You don't let your students talk to their horses in your classes?" Now I want you to understand that I had been doing this work for several years with great success, and totally believed in the "no talking" concept. I had seen it produce incredible changes in people and even had many students tell me how much it helped them. Yet here I was facing one of the greatest animal trainers alive, preparing to defend my position on not talking to horses. No pressure here! I said, "That's right, I want them to use their body language so the horse can relate to them better. It also helps the people focus on the horse's language faster." He thought a second, and then walked towards me. "You really don't let them talk in your classes?" he asked again. "No, and I even have duct tape if I need it," I said. Everybody laughed but Gunther. By now he was right in front of me, inches from my face. He put his arms on my shoulders, looked directly into

168

my eyes and with great intensity said, "You are a Master. If you can get these women to shut up you will help their horses so much, you won't believe it." I sighed and laughed all at the same time. Everyone was laughing including Gunther. He wasn't finished.

He said, "I'll tell you a story. Twenty years ago I am in America and training animals for Ringling Bros. Circus. I am doing the big shows and making big money – on top of the world. Then one night I lose my voice. Not a word could I speak. I had to do my show with the big cats and I had no voice. I was concerned, but the show must go on. I went in and did the best show of my life. And I learned that it was not the words that matter. I came out of that ring a different man that night. If you can get people to be quiet and connect with their horses, you will be doing a great service to the horses and their owners." Wow! I felt great! His comments meant a great deal to me then and now. During the short time the circus was in town, I got to visit Gunther and watch his work. We talked a lot and he shared many things with me that I'll value forever. He confirmed much that I knew and opened my eyes to things I didn't know. He is a true dynamic character and a wonderful man. And a pretty good hand with a horse, as well.

A couple of additional points from this story. Where else have you seen a round pen used besides on horse farms? The rings of the circus. But their rings are only a foot high. What keeps the horses in the pen? Their attitudes. If you have trouble with your stallion and you blame it on his gender, figure this: the circus travels with twenty to twenty-four horses. They are seldom stalled but rather tied side by side on a long rail, about forty-eight inches apart. They live, eat, and travel together. And they are all stallions. When you go in a round pen with twelve stallions, they are almost nose to tail all around the pen. What keeps them in? Their attitudes. What keeps them from killing each other as most of you would expect? Socialization. Their attitudes. Finally you keep hearing me talk about the importance of controlling your horse, for your safety and his. How important would you say it is to be in control when you walk into a pen full of tigers or leopards? Your horse can hurt you all right, but at least he won't eat you.

You will also need some smaller and less expensive items for your round pen fun. You will need a halter and lead line,

Whether for fun or problem solving, using multiple horses in the pen together can be great! Each horse needs to be submissive to the handler before mixing horses together. And when you try to play with several at the same time, think how it will keep you focused. I've done six at once. In the circus they do twelve. Stallions! This is Kasty, Sunny and Shadow. Photos by Susan Sexton.

which I bet you already have hanging on the barn wall at home. This is usually about the time the trainer or guy writing the book tells you of the merits of his nuclear powered special halter and hydro electric lead line and how it works better than any other halter in the world. And you can order one by calling … Well, I prefer to let the tack stores sell the tack. And since most of you have very different tastes in tack as well as every other horse related item, I'll suggest a different approach. *You should be able to handle your horse safely with whatever halter and lead line is available.* Some people use very beautiful leather items and some use the cheapest nylon around. Some like rope or string halters, some like flat ones. I like rope halters but I also use flat ones. The halter should fit the horse, not too tight or too loose. It should have no sharp edges and the strap ends should have appropriate loops to secure the loose end. It should not be so old that the buckle is rusted, bent and impossible to loosen. I will suggest you have several different lengths of lead lines to use as we go on; twelve feet, twenty to twenty-five feet and forty feet or so. You can go to any home improvement store and for very little money buy all kinds of rope cut to whatever length you want. It won't be as fancy or feel quite as soft as the really nice cotton ropes, but it will work just fine. Also I have two pet peeves about lead lines; large fasteners and chains. First, I never use a chain on a horse. I might someday, but so far I have always been able to get the horse to respond with no lead or halter, hence negating any reason to add the chain. Moreover, I like to use the movement of the lead line to communicate with the horse and a chain makes for rough and lousy communication. It's heavy, sloppy and is always smacking the horse's head and face. It is a poor substitute for knowledge.

My other pet peeve is the great big clasps or hooks that come on most lead lines. They are a poor idea as well. I always replace them with the smallest clasp I can buy that is easy to work with gloves on. As with the chain, if I am shaking a lead to signal a horse I don't want a steel chain or a big clasp smack-

171

ing him in his face. Would you like it used on you? And to those who would say that the smaller clasp can break, I would suggest you show me a *large clasp* that a horse *cannot* break. The difference is that if the horse breaks the smaller clasp he has probably not pulled hard enough to *hurt himself* or tear down the barn. If he really tries to leave, he's going. For certain training techniques I understand the need for strong clasps, but for most leading or tying they are unnecessary. Use what you like and are comfortable with as long as it does not hurt the horse. It is *what you know* and *how you use the equipment* that will control the horse, not the type of equipment. Many people sell tack simply because it makes money. But there are people like Pat Parelli and Dave Seay who sell some *very good stuff* that is top quality and not often found in the average tack store. My suggestion, if you buy some trainer's halter or lead line, buy it because *you like it,* not because *you need it.* If you *need* it to control your horse it's a *crutch.*

You will also need to get yourself a magic wand. No, actually I'm kidding. It's not magic when you get it, it only becomes magic when you use it. Your magic wand can be an old broken dressage whip, or a broken lunge whip, or whatever you have around the barn that is about three feet long and has some bend and flex to it. I use a Linda Tellington-Jones wand because I like the way it feels. It flexes just right for me and it's the right length. You can use anything you like, and a $25 wand is NOT NECESSARY. I have done some of my best work using somebody's old broken dressage whip. But you will need to modify it exactly to my specifications. At the little end, the one that used to have the popper on it, you will need to attach a plastic bag. This is where you will have to shell out some big bucks. The cheap flimsy bags from most grocery stores are not too good. You need the heavier thicker ones from places like SEARS or the like. People have asked me if I was sponsored by SEARS, when I appeared somewhere using a SEARS bag on my wand. I'm not. You could let your husband buy the new camcorder he has been wanting, so you can get the nice thick white plastic bag it comes in, but that really isn't necessary. You will also need to modify the bag by cutting the bottom open. Failure to do this step will have you end up with a wand with a small parachute on the end and it will greatly impair your effectiveness. You will also need some good packing tape. About eight inches will do. Most bags have handles or holes to put your fingers through when carrying the bag. Twist them, one at a time, so they can be attached to the wand with the packing tape. Wrap the tape tightly around the wand a time or two, then lay one twisted bag handle on the tape and continue to wrap, lay the other handle on over the first one and then a final loop or two of tape to finish it off. Done this way the bag

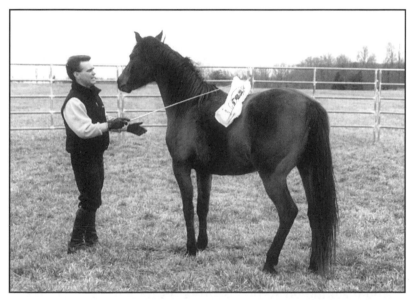

Many people think the wand with the plastic bag makes the horses afraid of the wand. This is a very timid horse that has learned to accept the wand all over her. She could still spook at a plastic bag, but it's not nearly as likely! I shake the bag all around her body and under her between her feet. But I do it untied so she feels free to move. At first she did move a lot. Then she learned. I only helped her learn. I didn't force her. Photo by Susan Sexton.

173

will wear out before it falls off. Just tying it on is usually not enough.

ITEM: I recently ran into a couple that had attended one of my workshops a year or so earlier. They spent fifteen minutes telling me how they had thought I was nuts the first time they saw me discuss using a wand with a plastic bag on it to influence a horse. They expected a disaster. Even after they saw it work on the first horse, they still expected more trouble than results from its use with most horses. Then they began to tell me of horse after horse they have used it on with great success – the most dramatic of which was a very aggressive horse where nothing had seemed to be working. The wand with the plastic bag on it was what let the husband take control and manage the horse, when all else had failed. As I heard them go on and on about the magic wand and how much it had helped them, I interrupted to remind them of their original opinion about how the bag would scare a horse and cause real problems. I said their first opinion was correct. They looked confused. But your current opinion is also correct, I said. The wand can be a tool or a disaster. What allowed the wand to be so helpful to the husband was the knowledge of how to use it correctly. It's not the bag, it's how you use it.

The idea of using a wand with the plastic bag on it as a way to motivate the horse may seem a bit foreign to some of you who have seen other trainers use a rope or lasso in that capacity. The rope is a more common tool. Many of those trainers are cowboys and hence very proficient with a lasso. It's an important skill for any cowboy to have and not an easy skill to master. The few times I have handled a lasso I usually ended up hurting myself with it. But to be honest, I never had the need to learn to use one nor did I have time to develop the skill. I wanted to become effective with my horse, and had no desire to rope

174

cattle. True, it takes very little skill to coil a rope and throw it at the back of a horse, sending him off, reel it in and repeat the process. I did that at first when I started with Sunny. But I did discover a couple of aspects of using the rope that pointed me towards the wand instead.

First, I didn't want to hit the horse and have any physical contact with the animal during the initial steps in the pen. I wanted to motivate him mentally without him ever feeling any discomfort from my touch, if at all possible. Second, and more important, there is a limitation to using a rope that I ran into early on that swayed me away from it. When you throw the rope at the horse to get him to go left, for instance, if he starts left, but then instantly reverses to the right, (and we all know how instantly horses can move) you need to *INSTANTLY* do something to correct his action. Not correct him a half a minute later, but right now. But your rope is lying on the ground and he's running over it. To throw it again you need to reel it in and coil it back up. That takes time. Time you don't have. With the wand you can use it now and use it again a split second later, and again a split second later, and as often as needed. A good horseman with a rope can use it very well, but to someone beginning this activity, the wand is a no-brainer. Safe and simple.

Now for your wardrobe. The women always like this part because I start talking about buying clothes. If you want a "round pen outfit" it's OK, but I'm afraid it's not necessary either. However, you do need to pay attention to what you wear for this activity. Loose clothes can get tangled up as you are running around. Not good. Tight clothes can be hard to move in and you *will* be moving. So wear something comfortable, and not too expensive. It will get dirty, as well as probably get slimed on by the horse. Also, wear layers as you may start out with more clothes on than you end up with. During your round pen fun, you may start to work up a sweat and begin to breathe pretty heavily. You may even need to take off a layer or two of clothes as you warm up because controlling the horse needed more animation from you. Sometimes the round pen is a better workout than aerobics but you feel really good when you're done.

You should probably wear boots to protect yourself in the event of being stepped on by the horse, but I'm not sure any shoe other than a steel-toed work boot does much good with a hoof on top of it. If the footing in the pen is good and deep, that will save you more than any shoe. Good boots are usually excellent, but cheap, clunky heavy boots can hurt your agility, which is a poor trade-off for the slight protection you might get by wearing them. Sometimes I wear running shoes for the agility, but you decide what you prefer. And don't forget, the fundamental purpose of this round pen activity is to eliminate the need for protection by having the horse watch out for you. I have not been stepped on by a horse that I had played with in years. Which does not mean I ignore the risk. I pay attention to the horse and he pays attention to me.

Now that you are mentally prepared, dressed correctly and have your wand and round pen, let's talk about what to do. There are not a lot of specific skills for you to develop as this approach was designed to be as simple as possible. Simple is better. The more complex anything is, the harder it will be for someone to understand, learn and then duplicate. Keep in mind that this is to be a mental exercise involving physical movement, not a physical struggle. The horse is physically superior to you so you will need to make up for that with knowledge and staying one step ahead. You can best do that by "slowing down." What I mean is that if you just run off and start doing one thing after another with a process new to you, it is real easy to get a whirlwind of activity going which you can't control. I want you to *go* slowly and *think* quickly. Anytime you are *going* faster than you are *thinking*, you're in trouble. As I discovered when I first tried to learn this process with Sunny, it is better to stop and re-group than to keep doing and doing, especially if what you were doing was wrong. And you may not realize it was wrong unless you stop and evaluate what you just did by watching the horse. We talked about being patient with the horse. It is equally important for you to be patient with yourself. Understand that we all have limitations and we must accept them without letting them stop us. Slow us down, maybe, but stop us, never. Some of you may be more out of shape than others. You may have to do shorter sessions in the pen at first if your horse is very active, and that's OK. The amount of movement you must use in the pen will be determined by the nature of the horse, not you. A timid, or frantic horse will require much less movement on your part than a stubborn, stoic horse will. You must move as much as needed and no more.

When you take the horse in the pen and turn him loose (from now on I will not say *round pen* but assume when I say *pen* I am referring to a *round pen*), he will do one of several possible things: run around frantically looking for a way out (often calling to other horses as he does), stop and turn his butt to you while he's looking over the fence, walk up to you politely, stop someplace and go to sleep, or run over and attack you. Fortunately the latter only occurs about one out of a thousand or so horses, so don't be too concerned about it, but pay attention with any new horse you do not know. If he were to do anything that *you feel is too aggressive*, you need to get very animated with your wand, waving your arms and *run at the horse*. Remember the old expression "You never get a second chance to make a first impression." Many horses will "try you" if they don't know you. They may run up to you aggressively and try to intimidate you. If you react early and dramatically, you can often overcome a lot of problems, right in the beginning. If the horse tests you, you must respond with all the animation you can generate, while *moving towards the horse*. (You don't want to do any more than necessary, but you must do enough to get the horse to withdraw and move away from you. You can always tone down your energy level if the horse seems to be getting wired or afraid, which would indicate you did too much.) Any backward movement on your part will tell the horse you don't mean it and you're not an alpha. Most of us don't realize how often we back up to get

177

out of the way of a horse's movements. That's a common mistake with horse people. More important is the fact that most of us don't realize what our backing up *SAYS TO THE HORSE*. If the horse moves into your space and you back up, you are telling him you'll be happy to get out of his way. Not something an alpha would say. He should be yielding to you, not the other way around.

Most of you will be going into the pen with your horse – a horse you probably know and may have loved for years. Your actual risk in that situation is seldom much at all. But some of you may end up in the pen with horses you are not familiar with, and who are testing you from the start. Even a horse you *are* familiar with may test you in the pen at first. (If you get a big, resistant reaction from a horse of yours, remember, the resistance you're getting now that he's loose has been there all the time. It's not new, it's just new that you are getting to see it so clearly.) You could find yourself in a situation where the wand/bag is not enough and the horse is not withdrawing from your animation. Again, this is very unusual, but let's talk about the worst possible case scenario first. If you use animation and move at the horse and the horse does not back off, but instead keeps coming, then what do you do? Run for the fence. Yell, wave the wand, but run for it. You must stay safe. If you get hurt, it does neither you nor the horse any good. Also, never let yourself get too close to the rear end of the horse in the beginning, where a kick could be serious. This applies anytime you are playing with a new horse in the pen. I have never had a student hurt in a pen, nor have I been hurt by a horse in the pen. But the first time you aren't watching close enough, it could happen. Always expect the horse to give in and withdraw, but always watch him to be sure he is. (The potential problem of being kicked will be eliminated as you take the horse through the process, but at first you need to be careful.)

    ITEM: In my workshops I always do a demonstration with the first horse, to show everyone exactly how to use the wand and body language, but also to let them see the results it can achieve. They brought in an appaloosa that was obviously a handful since it took two people several minutes to get her *in* the pen. I walked in the pen, explaining to the crowd what I was going to do, but I never got to finish. She interrupted me. Before I ever got a chance to do much of anything, she turned her butt to me and came backwards kicking with both feet. It was close enough that I felt the wind of several kicks. In fact she chased me out of the pen about twelve times in the first thirty minutes. She was a three-year-old filly who was open for business. An attitude with four feet. Many of the people watching got very angry at the horse for her aggression towards me, and rather dangerous behavior. Many of them were frightened and were screaming for me to get out of the pen. It was probably the most intense situation I ever experienced in a workshop. They were relieved each time when I did get out, but grew more and more distressed as I kept climbing back in. I never got mad at the horse because I knew she was acting that way out of her own perceptions about people, probably learned from experience.

Remember the three words I gave you earlier? Patience, Persistence and Consistency. My patience allowed me to be OK with jumping out of the pen and not demanding I accomplish *NOW; we* obviously needed more time. I had thirty people watching to see some results, but *impatience* could have cost me dearly in that situation. Do you understand? Self preservation also came into play a bit as well. If the clinician gets splattered, the workshop would not be considered a success. Persistence is what kept me going back in again and again, to show the horse I had the character of a leader. She could intimidate me for the moment, but I could not let her intimidate me overall. I would not be able to simply ask for this horse's respect; I would really have to *earn* it. Also, the *normal* approach of try-

179

ing to force her to submit had not worked for the numerous trainers that had handled her before me. And lastly, consistency: by staying with the approach that I knew would work eventually, I got her to relax and give in to me. After an incredibly intense forty-five-minute contest of wills, I became her alpha and she approached me softly. I didn't enjoy that session as I enjoy most of the horses I handle, but I was proud of the outcome. I was scared to death several times during the event, and if that sounds less macho than you would expect from someone in my position, then think again. Fear is something to be managed, more than it is to be ignored. Or denied. People who say they are never afraid are either stupid or not in touch with reality. Or both. The crowd that day not only got to see a worse-case-scenario of what a horse can be like, but they also got to see the techniques I teach and that they worked.

Your success with getting the horse to withdraw by creating animation with the wand is based on the horse's make-up and what usually bothers him. That's why I like the wand with the bag on it. It is something that will almost always cause a horse to withdraw and re-evaluate the situation. That's all I want. If you ever get a horse that is totally indifferent to the wand/bag, you may need to resort to another tool. My second choice is a plastic Clorox or milk bottle, with a few rocks in it and the lid on tight. Instead of waving the wand, wave/shake the bottle at the horse to create the needed animation and noise. The noise is more dramatic than the bag, and the animation of a person shaking a bottle is not likely to be familiar to the horse. On rare occasions I have even thrown it at the ground behind the horse. That would be a last resort to get a stubborn horse to move, but you need to do whatever it takes. You may even hold the bottle and the wand in the same hand and use them together. You need to do *enough* to get the horse to yield, no matter how much that may be.

Step One: Getting and Keeping His Attention
What the horse first does when you turn him loose offers your first chance to observe the kind of attitude he has, and

help you decide how to proceed. At liberty, the horse will be less inhibited than when tied or even haltered, so his responses to your directions are a bit more "pure," if you will. If he is still responsive to you when he's free, that's great. Your job may be easier. If he totally ignores you and you have no control at all, you need to see that as a reality check of the horse's attitude. Regardless of what he does, keep in mind that your first task in the pen is to *get* and *keep* his attention. You stay focused on watching where he keeps his attention. You want it to stay on you. If it leaves you for more than a second, get it back. How do you know if you have his attention? Quite simply the horse can focus his attention in as many as four directions at one time. Since he can look in two different directions at once, each eye can be focused on a different stimulus. He can also move his ears all around and even point each ear in a different direction as well. So he can look and listen to four possible "threats" simultaneously. When you are playing with your horse, you must constantly remind him to keep at least *one eye* or *one ear* on you at all times. This is the attention/respect he will pay to his herd leader. A horse will rarely lose track of where his herd leader is. That's the job you are applying for.

This horse is not paying attention. Always get the horse's attention before *you attempt any training. By simply popping the wand (creating animation) you can get the horse's attention and then proceed. Photos by Susan Sexton.*

He may put both eyes and both ears on you occasionally, and that's OK but not necessary. If he starts out by ignoring you, pop the wand in a quick, dramatic motion that will produce a sharp, quick flutter sound and some movement at the same time. This will get the horse to look and maybe even move. If he jumps and moves off, that's OK. You know you got his attention because he reacted to your animation of the bag. If he looks away and takes off around the pen, watch his inside ear, the one closest to you. If he keeps the inside ear pointed at you, but is watching elsewhere, it's OK. Even if he's looking away, if that ear stays pointed to you, you're on track. If he looks at you and his ear goes somewhere else, that's OK too. You must insist on one eye or one ear, at least. More is OK, but no less. If you allow him to *not* pay attention to you, you are telling him you are not that important. As you continue to play with him, do not forget to keep his attention on you. This is critical! If you lose his attention, use sharp, crisp, pops of the wand to get it back. Say nothing verbally. Let your movements and body language do all your talking. At first he may stay focused on you for a couple of seconds, then you may lose his attention. Pop the wand. If he stays focused on something else, such as another horse nearby, he is telling you that he thinks the other horse is more important than you. That is his communication to you, honest and specific. You *must* change that opinion. You must pop the wand again and get his attention back on you. If one little pop doesn't do it, then pop it harder and louder. Do something with the wand and watch him for his response. If he does not focus back on you, do *MORE* with the wand, louder and harder and maybe add waving your other arm as well. Keep escalating your animation until he changes and gives you an eye or an ear. These actions on your part should be quick, precise actions and not vague or "whimpy" in the slightest. Occasionally I will even run at the horse, waving the wand madly as I go, if that is what is needed to get his attention. BUT – and this is critical – when he does give you his attention you must *STOP* being animated *instantly*. That is his reward for doing what you asked – quiet, and the *release of the pressure* you were applying to get the response. Your animation was the pressure on him, his response was to pay attention to you as you requested, and your reward was to remove the pressure as he wished. This simple action is your first act of controlling the horse at liberty. Simple, yet very important in teaching him about your importance to him, and teaching you how to employ the process of rewarding the horse by removing pressure. So subtle, yet so powerful. From this point forward, you will always watch the

To know if you have the horse's attention, he must have at least one eye or one ear on you at all times. This horse is looking away, but the inside ear tells you he's still concerned about you. The handler is "getting quiet." Be still and keep the wand behind you. Photo by Susan Sexton.

horse's attention and if you lose it, get it back. Attempt no training or other work unless you have his attention. It would be a waste of time. And remember what he is saying by taking his attention away from you; if it is not on you then it is on something he deems more important than you. You are less important to him than you need to be. This is one of the most crucial aspects of handling horses I can share with you. Remember that you *are* letting him pay attention to other things, but you are not allowing him to *NOT* pay at least some attention to you, all the time.

ITEM: A lady had called and was bringing a four-
year old Arab gelding over to see if a friend of mine

could get rid of the horse for her. The horse was almost unmanageable in that it didn't lead well at all, was not rideable, and constantly yelled to other horses. He had just been gelded a few months back, and acted more like a stud than most studs. He was never led down the barn aisle even though they always had a chain on him, as he'd charge other horses in their stalls. They put him in an end stall so he didn't have to be led past any other horses to get in the barn. Get the picture? If my friend could get the horse to lead well enough to be given away, that was all right. If she could get it rideable so it could be sold that would be incredible. My friend was going to be out of town when the horse arrived and she asked if I would play with him a bit. I agreed and went to visit the new arrival. Upon reaching his stall, I was impressed at how pretty he was and how totally out of control he was. He was even out of control of *himself* in the stall – to the extent that I had to hook the lead line on a moving horse when I tried to catch him. (The halter was still on because they couldn't take it off. And if they did, they'd never have gotten it back on.) Getting him out of the stall was interesting and involved a lot of very fast moves on my part to avoid being run over. If you are thinking something along the lines of – I wouldn't have let that horse act that way if I were there. I would have shown him who's boss the minute I went in his stall – then you would have started a physical struggle with a nine-hundred pound out-of-control horse in a teeny tiny room. *HIS* room at that. If there is *any other choice*, I will *NOT* start the struggle for control in the stall. In that close proximity, the struggle would likely be more physical than mental, and I could lose. Which would not help him or me.

As I got him outside and headed for the pen, it was apparent that he had no regard for people at all. Which is a strong way of saying I did not have his attention. Every horse on the farm had his attention but not me. The pen was in a corner where two fence lines met from two adjacent pastures. As I got him in the pen all the "civilized" horses came running up to see the "new guy." The horse was all over the pen. I stood still about ten feet in the pen, then popped the wand and waved my arms in a big way each time he almost ran into me. In a couple of minutes he stopped running around and stood still. Except he had his rear end turned to me and was calling to the other horses. I popped the wand to get him to look at me. He jumped and looked at me for about two seconds then turned back to the horses. I did it again, with similar response from him. For the next forty-five minutes I never moved more than a step or two, but continued to ask for his attention by popping the wand. At the end of forty-five minutes he could keep his attention on me for about thirty-second intervals. An eternity for him. Then I walked over to him and attached the lead. I stood by him for a few minutes and each time he called to another horse or tried to turn away, I flipped the lead and popped the wand. He'd jump and circle me, and I stood like a statue waiting for him to settle down. He didn't settle much, but when he seemed to be about as quiet as he was likely to get, I led him back into his stall. All the way I kept asking him to pay attention to me, nothing more. When he tried to run past me, I'd get his attention by popping the wand and he circled around me quite a bit. Once in the stall, I loosened the halter, but when he tried to jerk his head away (some of you knew that was coming, didn't you?) I held on and didn't let him avoid

185

me. After six tries, I took the halter off. He jumped across the stall, looked at me with that "what the heck!" look. Then surprisingly, he walked over to me. I stood with him for a minute, then left.

The next day he was a lot less bothered, and I got the halter on in a minute or so. It wasn't pretty, but it was not bad. When I opened the stall door he started to bolt out, and I flipped the lead and backed him off me. Why did I do it today, but not yesterday? Yesterday he spent an hour giving in to me in the pen. That gave me the leverage I needed to try to control him now. Had he not given in and started to pay attention to me yesterday, I would have not tried to control him in the stall today. Had it gone poorly in the stall, I would have given up on the stall and gone right to the pen only. Once in the pen, I did nothing but ask for his attention, over and over. After about thirty-five minutes I finally asked him to go off for the first time. He did about twenty laps and ended up facing me. We stood still together again for about five minutes, and then I led him back in the barn. He was still a bit distracted, but he was not the same.

The third day he actually came to me in the stall and the halter went on with the second try. He only called to one horse all the way to the pen, and his attention was on me more than not, without me asking for it constantly, even when all the horses came running up. He did a few laps, but most of the time was spent standing quietly next to me. And I kept his attention. When I moved, he moved with me. We were getting connected. Out of the pen I led him over a few obstacles like a wood box and a puddle, and a couple of fence rails. They were all a challenge, but he did it. After each, we'd stop and think about it. He learned fast. When we got to the barn, I walked him past his stall and down the aisle. He snorted a couple of times but that was it. Then we went back in the stall and the halter came off. No struggle and no pulling away. And once the halter was off, he just stood with me and made no effort to leave.

The fourth day I took him down the aisle right off the bat. As we were walking back up the aisle, on a loose lead with his head by my shoulder, his owner walked by us and asked me where her horse was. I said, "You mean this one?" She was beside herself and couldn't believe her eyes. "Where's his chain?" she asked almost at once. "On the hook, where it should be," I replied. My friend returned from her trip and in a few days she was riding the horse nicely. No bucking and no wars. She got the horse doing so well he became a happy show horse with some great new owners, and is a dream to ride now. BUT…that is not the end of the story. Over those first few weeks he became a real pleasure to handle and ride, but he would still call to the other horses from time to time. My friend, who is a brilliant horsewoman and very intuitive, had him checked by another vet and he was found to still be a stallion. He had one left inside and it still worked, very well. After a little prodding, the original vet, "finished" the gelding job, and the calling to the mares went away shortly thereafter. The point is he did not become a nice, manageable horse because he was gelded. He became a pleasure because of the way he was handled.

Step Two: Developing Your Body Language

You are going to develop a language using your body movement, involving a signal and animation that your horse can understand, then an increase in pressure on the horse to reinforce to the horse that he must comply with the request from the signal. Re-read that over and over until it is clear to you, then I'll give you an example to demonstrate. Let's say you are in the pen with the horse facing you (so you have already got his attention) and you want him to go off to your left. You want him to move around the pen to your left. This simple action will require several steps that most people don't fully understand so let's walk through them all, in order. (Also, consider that if the horse is not facing you, you should send him off in the *opposite direction* he is facing. Reason, it is more of an act of submission to turn and walk off than to just walk off. He may have been planning to go that way anyway.) First you need to decide what it is you want the horse to do. This is the most common mistake people make. They haven't clearly decided on the action they want from the horse before they start asking for things to happen. The operative word here is "clearly." And if you are not clear in your mind what exactly it is you want the horse to do, then your body language will be vague and unclear to the horse. You should be able to say, in your mind, clearly and succinctly, exactly what you want him to do; "go that way" for instance. When you "do" whatever signal you create to get that action from the horse, if you are clear in your mind about what you want, he will most likely understand it. If you are not clear, then your body language will confuse the signal and he will be confused in trying to understand it.

Next you will need to devise a signal or cue to give the horse so he can begin to associate that signal with the action he is about to do. In many cases the signal will in itself create a degree of pressure to promote the action, but not always. For instance, word commands mean nothing to the horse until he associates the word with an action. You will need to get him into the action before any association can occur. For a more tactile signal such as a leg yield, the signal itself (pressing on the horse with your leg) produces a pressure that can generate the action from the horse all by itself. A more direct and immediate association will occur.

Going back to our initial request from the horse – "go off to

This series starts with the correct position to send the horse off and keep him going. To reverse his direction you would bring the wand behind you *to change hands as you shift your body position towards the front of the horse, as in the second photo. Then bring out your hand as the signal, followed by using the wand for animation,* but only as much as needed *to get the horse to respond. Were the horse not held, he would have started turning by photo 2 and be reversed by photo 3. (In this series of photos we are holding the horse to more easily show you several positions for your body in relationship to the horse.) Photos by Susan Sexton.*

your left" – you would initiate the action by pointing to your left with your left arm fully extended and finger pointing as well. That is the initial signal; big, bold and dramatic. The horse may go off with only that action on your part. If he did, you would do no more. You asked and he responded. Success. But he may not do as you asked. He may just look at you. He may not understand the signal, hence the lack of response. Or he may understand the signal but doesn't want to comply. That would be defined as an act of resistance on his part. Understand? He might even try to go the opposite way, which would

189

show a greater degree of resistance or perhaps even defiance. You must evaluate each response he gives to each signal you give in order to help you better understand him. Does that make sense? Do not just run into a pen and start running the horse around and around with no thought or planning. And every time you do something, take that opportunity to evaluate where the horse is mentally by watching what he just did in response to your signal. That is communication and that builds strong relationships.

Let's evaluate our options in the above situation if the horse does *NOT* do as asked. You have several "levels" of animation to employ to get the horse to do what he is apparently not eager to do. If I pointed left and he did not go, within a second I would have *already begun to add some animation* (pressure) to ensure his compliance. First, I would begin moving towards him and to my right of him. Pressing on his bubble with the pressure of my movement and because I was going to my right, it would "open the door" for him to go to my left. The pressure on him caused by your approach would be applied such that his going left would reduce it and going right would increase it. Horses like the path of least resistance. Remember, you're an alpha now. Your bubble is more powerful than his; we just have to convince him of that. If moving towards him got him to yield and hence go off to the left, I would do no more. Success. Pointing alone is less pressure than pointing and moving toward the horse. We are escalating the pressure we apply in incremental steps in order to apply only as much pressure as needed to get the response. This initial step will overcome the problem if he didn't understand what you wanted. By changing your position to him, as you maintain the signal (pointing) you are "herding" him into the correct action, helping him to understand what you asked. In short order he will know the signal, and only his attitude will be a problem.

Next I would bring the wand from around behind me or beside and behind me (wherever I ended up holding it after getting his attention in the beginning), and move it to my right

190

to further increase the pressure he was feeling. I would be pointing to my left and holding the wand out to my right, looking like a scarecrow. By now the change in my body position and location, combined with the increasing pressure of the bag/wand would probably be enough to get him to yield and go off the way I asked. Success. Our fundamental goal is to ask and have him yield to our request. If he still hadn't yielded and gone off I would now begin to wave the wand. First a little, but then more and more, in a very animated fashion making lots of noise and movement, and I assure you, it will be a very rare horse that has not left by this point. If he was still resistant I might even run *at* him, waving the wand and my arms, even jumping up and down as I went. This is *really rare to be needed*. The rule to follow is simple; do as little as you can to get the response, but as much as needed. You cannot accept "no response," as that is resistance or maybe even defiance. You must get a response. As soon as you get a response that is at least part of what you asked for, you must back off on the pressure as the reward. Initially you will need to keep some pressure on to continue the movement, but if you got to the point of waving the wand to get him to go, once he's going, try just holding the wand out there but not waving it and see if he doesn't keep going. Eventually you will diminish even the signal needed to get the response as the horse becomes more attentive, submissive, and responsive. For example, if you started by pointing with your arm extended, try extending it less and less until you can just point with your hand or even a finger and the horse takes off as requested. You will be amazed at how little it takes to get a horse to respond once you learn to utilize this approach. It still amazes me sometimes.

Once he is moving, do not make the mistake of changing your position in relationship to him such that you get by or in front of his shoulder. In other words stay behind the horse, driving him forward. You will not be on the "rail" behind him but you will be behind in relationship to the direction he is traveling. You will be going in a small circle while he goes around

This illustration shows an INCORRECT position, as it is giving the horse conflicting signals. Your body is behind the horse telling him to go forward. Your hand and wand positions are telling him to go the other way. Photo by Susan Sexton.

the rail, but you will be facing his rear, not his head. For some reason we have a tendency to rush forward when the horse takes off, and often people get their body positioned in front of the horse and don't even realize they did it. If you do, your body position is telling the horse to go the other way from what your signal is telling him. You are giving him conflicting signals. He will follow your body position and reverse direction. Not what you want. The best way to avoid this error is to have someone coaching you from outside the pen as you play with the horse. They will see it and can point it out to you in case you miss it. This happens at every workshop I teach, so please stay aware of your body position in relationship to the horse and his direction of movement. Stay behind the horse to move him forward, remembering not to get too close to his rear end and risk being kicked.

So, you point and he doesn't go, then you get animated and he takes off as you asked. Now he's going around the pen, what next? Many trainers run the horse through lots and lots of laps to wear him down and get the horse to give in from fatigue. That's better than beating a horse into submission, but it's not what we're after. As he goes around a lap or two, watch for his inside ear to be sure you still have his attention. Anytime you lose his attention, pop the wand or move towards him, or do something animated to get his attention back on you. As you do it, think to yourself, "pay attention to me." That is your primary focus; his attention staying on you. Let him do a lap or maybe even a few laps if he needs to work off a little excess energy, then you're going to ask him to reverse directions. You may also want to remember to breathe during this time where he is moving more than you. Sometimes people get so focused on the horse they forget to do that. I strongly recommend you continue to breathe throughout all your horse activities.

You do not want the horse to get into a pattern of doing dozens and dozens of mindless laps. That will tend to induce the horse to tune you out mentally and stop thinking. He needs to keep alert mentally and paying attention to you. I know it is standard procedure for many round pen trainers to promote the idea of running a horse until he gives up from exhaustion but I disagree with this approach totally. I prefer to do as few laps as possible in the beginning and then more laps later on as the student has developed the skills to extract a benefit from those laps for the horse. Laps in the pen can benefit many areas for you and the horse, including specific task exercises, agility work, teaching gaits, etc. But it will be easier and you will be more effective if you have first developed the appropriate attitude in the horse before attempting more complex tasks and asking for numerous laps. Few laps now, more laps later.

Your next step will be to get him to change directions and reverse. When you are ready to ask him to turn and reverse, you will need to complete several steps, in order. First, be clear in your mind what you want him to do, reverse and go the other way. You must be *clear on what you want before you do any-thing*. Once you are ready, drop your pointing arm and the arm holding the wand, moving them together, *behind your back*. You are going to change hands with the wand but *NOT* in front of you, *behind* you. If you move the wand in front of you to change hands, the wand approaching the horse will take his attention off of you and put it on the bag and possibly even get a dramatic reaction from the horse. You do not want that. If you move it behind you and change hands there, as the wand went behind you it will draw the horse's attention back to you. Since the horse is moving around the pen towards your left you will also need to move your body position to your left and more in front of him, sort of blocking his path, but not directly in front, just be ahead of his shoulder. By the time you have begun the reversal with these first two actions the horse will know something is changing. He will usually give one of two responses; either he will begin to slow or stop, waiting for further direction, which is a display of submission. Or he will bolt forward to get beyond the point where your body position can turn him. The second choice on his part does *not* show submission. He is trying to take control away from you. Be ready for it when it happens. If you sense that he is going to bolt forward (and his body language will tell you if you're listening well enough) move *immediately* farther to your left and bring the wand up towards his face, waving it dramatically. You will cut off his forward movement and block his path to reinforce that you are in charge. You will use the animation of the wand to enforce this. However, don't be surprised if every so often a horse is too quick or too fast and gets past you before you realize it's happening. It will happen. *DO NOT CHASE THE HORSE AROUND THE PEN FROM BEHIND, TRYING TO TURN HIM.* It won't work. You could even drive into a crash into the pen. If you're behind him he will only go forward. Once you have "lost him" by letting him get past you, let go of trying to control him and cross directly to the opposite side of the pen and be waiting for him when he gets there. You can't outrun him, but by cutting across the pen you can "head him off." Begin to get *very animated* in front of him, nearly blocking his path, and reminding him that you are in control. (I said "nearly blocking his path" since if you don't get animated enough, every so often an aggressive horse may try to just "push" you out of his way. Don't get run over! Again this is a *RARE* possibility and usually due to the person not being animated enough, but don't get hurt. Better to back off, regroup and try again.) You should be thinking, "I said go that way!" And mean it! Once he turns, ease back to the center of the pen and keep him going a lap or so.

If he didn't bolt past you, but instead had slowed, await-

In this series the horse is being resistant to the signal and has bolted forward to defy the handler. If this happens, do not chase the horse from behind! Ignore the horse and run directly across the center of the pen and be waiting in front of the horse when he gets to you. Create a lot of animation with the wand while pointing the horse in the direction you want. Be very definite in this situation to affect the horse's attitude. Photos by Susan Sexton.

ing your direction, you would have brought your right arm up to point to the right direction, as you began to move towards him, increasing the pressure. If he turned and went off to the right, you would need to do no more. He may stop and look at you. If your signal was vague, he may be confused. Clarify the request and get him moving. If he stops and looks at you and your signal *was* clear, he may be saying, "Nanner, nanner, I don't have to! Make me!" To which you will respond with more animation from the wand and moving at him in an assertive fashion. Thinking in your head, "I SAID GO THAT WAY!" As soon as he turns and moves off, begin to reduce the animation. Whenever he complies with any request, remove the pressure at once. You must pay attention to your timing during this. If he gives you what you asked and there is no release of pressure, he got no reward and hence no incentive to try the next time. If the pressure stops in time with the action, he will respond sooner next time. And will need less of a signal to get the response. Remember, he is always looking for the release of pressure.

You must continually evaluate each response from the horse as you go, in order to stay ahead of what is happening and judge your progress. Every time you ask for a turn, watch how he responds. Is he quickly and willingly reversing or is he trying to get by you and not turn? Is he resisting or submitting? You are looking for quick responsive actions from him. *The number of laps is irrelevant.* You are evaluating his attitude and response to your direction, not trying to wear him down. I have done many horses in public demonstrations that came in with very poor attitudes and great resistance, yet got them to change in six to ten laps. And do not think they need to turn only once every lap. They may turn four or five times a lap. Do not turn them in the same place each time. No pattern. They turn when you say to turn. A half lap and turn, a quarter lap and turn, a third lap and turn. Laps don't matter. Responses to directions matter. AND, they cannot turn unless you said to turn. Sometimes a horse will try to turn on his own. He may try and try again. And again. This is definite resistance. *Do not let him turn on his own.* Get animated and block his path and turn him back in the direction you last requested.

After a few turns (two to six or so) you should begin to see a change in his responsiveness. He should be learning the signals and becoming willing to cooperate. If his change is only slight, or maybe even none at all that you can see, don't worry. It's OK. Even if he *is* getting very responsive, that does not ensure his attitude is OK yet. This is just the beginning of a process. Allow it to be a process and don't expect it to be a one step event. Your next step is to stop asking for movement and offer him the opportunity to stand still. You do that by doing what I call "getting quiet." That means you stand still in the center of the pen and put the wand behind you. You will need to pay close attention to what you are doing with the wand at this time. Many people forget to pay attention and end up waving the wand around behind themselves unintentionally. This will agitate some horses and give them all kinds of mixed signals. Keep the bag-end on the ground behind your feet and the big end in your hand behind your back. Breathe and relax and get quiet inside and out. Be still. And watch the horse. Follow the horse around the pen with your eyes, but don't keep turning your body, stand still. What you would like to see is the horse stop and turn in and walk over to you politely with his head down. You may see that or you may see the horse continue to run around like crazy, or anything in between. I'll explain and walk you through several options for those scenarios, but first we need to talk about a very important point.

I said, "watch the horse." And I meant, watch the horse all the time. Obviously when you are turning around with him moving, that's easy. But when you stop to "get quiet," since your head can't do the exorcist spin, it's not as easy to watch him constantly. Usually if you turn your head as far as possible one way then swing it to the opposite extreme and pick up the horse again, there will only be a few feet of his movement that you missed. That's OK. If the horse is dangerous, you may wish to watch him every second, but that is rare. Very rare. One more thing about watching the horse. Many of you may have heard a certain big-name trainer who does demos everywhere talk about a means of getting a horse to come to him by turning away from the horse by forty-five degrees and looking at the ground. I disagree with that approach because of potential problems it presents, and I'll explain why. I have three reasons why I feel you should *never look away from a horse you are playing with*, and I think they will make sense to you as well.

First, I have stressed repeatedly that you need to watch the horse to evaluate his responses to your signals, and understand him and best decide what to do next. If you don't watch him, and he does something important, how can you immediately respond as you should to his action? You can't. He is trying to communicate with you so you need to listen. And with horses you listen with your eyes. Watch the horse.

Second, have you ever met someone who would not look you in the eye? How do you feel about that person? Do you trust them? Are they deceptive or unethical? Perhaps. Maybe not. Perhaps they are just very shy and insecure. That could be. But in either case, when you are trying to convince a thousand pound animal that you are worthy to be his leader, do you want to do anything that could be construed as being untrustworthy, or especially timid? *Alphas are never timid.* Watch the horse.

Third, just suppose you are in the pen with a horse that is really dangerous or very aggressive. How long do you want to stand there looking at the ground, not knowing where he is or what he is doing? I think that is a poor plan and could get you hurt. Watch the horse.

I think those three points are sufficient to get you to not look away from any horse you are playing with in the pen, but there are a few other things to consider as well. As you learn to really "read" the horses, you will discover that they will tell you when they are going to come in to you before they actually do it. So if you wait until just the right moment, just before he's coming in and you look away, when he comes in, it looks like a cause and effect rather than the cute trick it is. I have never had a horse that I could not get to come in to me while I looked him in the eye. Never. I look at them as a friend, with firm compassion in my eyes and they seem to be able to tell how I feel. Watch the horse.

Step Three: Get Him To Stop

So you are "quiet" in the middle of the pen and the horse stops and looks over the fence, turning his butt to you. That is not an act of submission, but an act of disrespect. I would send him off again, really soon. Like immediately. Have him do a few laps, reversing direction a couple of times each lap, then get quiet again. He will soon be stopped and at least looking at you. Suppose you get quiet and the horse just keeps going. And going. And going. This is something that has confused and baffled many people, and it's not uncommon. Horses have too often been conditioned to solve any problem by moving their feet, especially when lunged in hundreds of mindless circles. You need to get the moving horse to stop, but it is my belief that you must *let* him stop rather than try to *force* him to stop. Remember the part about horses learning from the removal of pressure, not the application of pressure? Well, we're going to use that concept and their bubble to help stop the horse that can't stop on his own. Here's how.

When you "get quiet" and offer the horse the chance to come in, you will evaluate his attitude by what he does next. This horse stopped and turned his butt, showing no respect for the handler. Do not accept this, but send him off again. Photo by Susan Sexton.

You're standing in the middle of the pen with a horse doing lots of mindless laps around you. You want him to stop and come in respectfully, but he just keeps going. The *normal* approach would be to let him "get it out of his system" and eventually he'll stop. True, he will stop, sometime, but what is going on in his mind as he is continues to circle in the meantime? More important, what is *causing* him to continue to circle in the first place? Remember, horses never do something for nothing, they only do something because of something. What is the "something" that is keeping him moving? What got him moving when you started? Pressure. You applied pressure and he moved. Now the pressure is constant so he's still going to try to get away from the pressure. As long as there is no release of pressure, he keeps going. But you're not doing anything, you're just standing still. Where's the pressure coming from? Him. His bubble. His perception of you as a

199

possible threat is putting pressure on his oversized bubble, and he is responding to that pressure by moving and moving and moving. Looking for a way to get the pressure off, but it isn't happening, so he just keeps going. And unfortunately that tends to *increase* his bubble, making the situation worse. He is working himself into a frenzy, and he can't help himself. I cannot tell you how often I have had people talk about this problem in the round pen. It can even escalate into the horse going over or through the pen and create real problems. It can also create extreme stress resulting in colic, lameness and other physical problems. Here's how to deal with it.

Since the pen is a constant size, say sixty feet in diameter, and his bubble is so big that the pressure is constant and keeping him moving, how big is his bubble? At least thirty feet. Maybe more. You need to adjust something so as to get the pressure on his bubble to be intermittent, thereby giving him a chance to feel the release he so wants, and help him find a place to stop. Try this. As you stand in the center, face one place on the fence, perhaps the gate. Keep your body facing that spot as you watch the horse go around you. But each time the horse comes out from going behind you, take a step backwards toward the fence. As you get closer to the fence, make the steps smaller, but keep working your way backwards. Notice what happens. As you get more and more off center in the pen, the pressure on the horse will increase behind you at the same time it is decreasing in front of you. This is due to the change in your proximity to the horse and that effect on his bubble. Closer to you means more pressure, farther away means less. You may even see him speed up dramatically as he passes behind you to avoid the intense pressure of being "trapped" between you and the fence. He will often slow down across the pen where the pressure is least. It is a very interesting process to watch. You will see the bubble of the horse as clear as day. He will usually stop as he approaches the increasing pressure nearing you. Going clockwise it would be near the three to four o'clock position. Going counter clockwise it would be near the nine to eight

If this were a horse that didn't want to stop, but kept going and going, you would want to stop him, not let him run it out. *Each time he came out from behind you to about where this horse is standing, you would take a step or two BACKWARDS. As you get more and more off center, you will change the pressure on the horse (which is what's keeping him going) and* get him to stop without forcing him to stop. *Photos by Susan Sexton.*

o'clock position. Occasionally they will stop across the pen where the pressure is least, but that is not most common. They feel the pressure building, then reducing, as they move and they look for the release of it. You set up a way for them to find what you wanted them to do – stop. You didn't force it, but you got what you wanted. You got the horse to stop. And they got what they wanted – a release of the pressure they were feeling. Win-win. With no crash and burn either. If this is not clear, try drawing it on a piece of paper.

Now comes the hard part. The horse has stopped, perhaps not walked up to you, but at least he stopped running around the pen. This next step will be very difficult for you but you *MUST DO IT AT ALL COSTS*.... Wait.... Do nothing.... Stay quiet.... Be still.... Don't *DO* anything at all! I know this may contradict what you have seen before with other round pen

201

methods, but try it. It is time to leave the horse alone and let him have time to digest what just transpired. This is what I refer to as "letting" things happen instead of "making" things happen. If you want to be technical, you *are* making things happen by applying the process, but you are also *letting* things happen within the process, at the horse's pace. By allowing him the time to think and digest things as you go, you minimize his frustration and hence his stress. And often you get to watch him change right in front of your eyes.

ITEM: When I got back from attending my first few round pen clinics I was anxious to get Sunny in the pen and apply my new-found knowledge. I had not yet actually worked with a horse in the pen, but I had watched a lot. It had looked simple enough. As I entered the pen for the first time, I had no clue about several important factors that were going to affect Sunny and me greatly over the next few weeks. I will discuss each of them with you at the end of this story, so you can avoid the anxiety and frustration I experienced with Sunny. Since I was *on my own,* I spent a lot of time in the pen just trying to figure out what I wanted to get Sunny to do. I'd wave the wand and send him off, but he was very resistant. You can also understand that I was pretty unsure of what I was after as well as how to do it. My signals were vague and my timing was poor because I was trying to do something I had never done before. I'd seen several very good round pen trainers make it look very easy, but applying it on my own by myself was quite different. So I would run Sunny around a bit then stop and try to remember what to do next. I knew I wanted him to come in to me, but he was just staying off by the rail. Can you understand that since it wasn't going the way it had looked when the expert did it, I was lost? And confused. And frustrated. For quite a few days, my best efforts only produced a sweaty horse and a lot of frustration. Then, as I stood in the center of the pen with Sunny facing me from the rail, while I was trying to decide what to do next, he put his head down, worked his mouth and walked over to me. This was the first time he had ever done that. I was baffled. He did just what I had wanted him to do, but I wasn't actually doing anything to get it. Or was I? We had both stopped moving several minutes earlier and I wasn't actually *doing* anything when he came in. Maybe my giving him time to think about it was what he needed all along. Maybe just standing in the center of the pen going from command to command was not what he envisioned an alpha to be like. Maybe just constantly *demanding* he respond was less fair than asking for something and then *waiting* for him to respond. As this realization began to sink in, I started to separate each thing I did with Sunny with a big pause between each. I found I was able to keep my thoughts more organized and Sunny began to change faster and faster. By pausing between each step, I could better tell what worked and what didn't. It helped me learn faster by letting me separate things into cause and effect. *If you don't wait for the effect, how can you tell what you caused?* It also helped Sunny as well, and he began to calm down a lot. I had heard people say things like "don't do too much," or "give him time to think" but that was so vague that it never really clicked as to how to apply it. And I will honestly admit to you that had I not had this breakthrough with Sunny, I would never have succeeded with Kasty when I got to her. This simple step saved Kasty's life and let me become a better trainer. It was that important to her. After I had been doing OK with her for a while, one of her previous trainers who had had little success with her, came to watch what I was doing. After about a half hour he said, "You're doing a heck of a lot less than I ever did with her, that's all." But that was the difference. Too much is too much. For Kasty, even slightly too much was more than she could handle. We all have a certain amount of stress we can handle, and beyond that, things can go bad very quickly. Sometimes less work is more effective.

I mentioned several important factors at the beginning of this story and I want to go over each for you right now. First, for a person to *learn* to do something as they try to *do* it with a horse that hasn't done it can be very difficult. A beginning rider needs a well-trained horse. A green horse needs a well-trained rider. A beginning rider on a green horse is a common, yet often tragic, mistake. If you want to learn dressage, take lessons on a dressage horse, not a barely rideable four-year-old that knows nothing. When a person is handling a horse, at least one of them needs to know what's going on. If I had had a coach to accelerate my learning curve during my efforts with Sunny, I would have been much better off. So would Sunny.

Second, Sunny was more difficult for me than he would have been for a stranger because he knew me and we had a history together. He had considered me *NOT* to be an alpha for some time now, and I would have to change his opinion. For me to have done my first round pen work with a strange horse would have been easier than Sunny. Your first efforts after reading this book will most likely be with your horse. Don't worry about it, but just realize that you will have to try harder due to your history with the horse. You may also tend to take the horse for granted, and not be as thorough as you would with an unknown horse. Don't. And most important, remember to be patient with yourself as well as the horse.

Next, consider how my lack of understanding of the *process* gave me very little help in trying to organize my thoughts about what I was trying to accomplish in the pen. I wanted

Sunny to go around in circles and then come to me. Those are the physical steps, but it's the mental process that matters. I had been watching the actions, signals and the mechanics of the clinicians, but had picked up very little understanding of the horse and how the process affects him. Not to mention my lack of knowledge regarding what to look for from the horse that would let me evaluate what was happening as we progressed. That's why this book spent so much time getting you to understand the horse and the process, before I started telling you about the steps to *DO*. What you *do* is only important as far as you can evaluate what you accomplished by what you did. In other words, the horse's reactions are what really matter, not the laps he did or where you stood.

Finally, *watching* something is not like *doing* it. That is true of almost everything involving horses. And part of the difference is *perspective*. It looks and feels very different in the pen with a horse reacting to your every move than it does watching someone with lots of experience make it look easy. It's not hard, but it does require thinking and effort on your part. The better the clinician, the easier it looks. And the more that will deceive a beginner. That's why in my workshops I do very little with the horses. It is a better teacher to have the people who come to the workshop do almost all the handling of the horses. They make mistakes and you will learn more from watching others make and then correct the same mistakes you will make than you could ever learn from watching someone make it look too easy.

For each thing you ask the horse to do, you must then give the horse time to figure it out. The pattern here is to do something, in this case control the horse's movement at liberty, then ask him to stop and be submissive. That's a lot at one time. Now let him alone and watch to see what he does. He will tell you how he feels and how much he is willing to go along with your idea of being his alpha. But you need to wait for him to tell you. Patience. For the horse that would not stop running around, this is not necessary, it is *critical*. That was Kasty. In spades. This quiet time between activities will accomplish several good things if you can be patient. It will let the horse figure out what you want, eliminating his frustration. Horses, like people, don't handle frustration well. Don't frustrate your horse. Some horses get real excited when thinking and figuring out new things. This can get them stressed. The pause between activities lets them have a time to relax. A relaxed horse is a safer horse. And most important, letting your horse have some quiet time to relax *while you are handling him* gets him to associate *being with you* with *being relaxed*. You become a calming force for him, rather than a reason to get wired. I cannot impress upon you too much how effective this tool is for you. Be committed to spending time, lots of time, simply being with your horse, while he is paying attention to you, yet having to do nothing. Just relax. Remember alphas are always alphas. It will be time well spent *for you both*. People tend to be too proactive with horses and the horses suffer because of it. We won't make that mistake.

Step Four: Evaluating Your Results

There are several key signs to watch for once you let the horse stop. In fact some of them may have already appeared during the exercises. You want to see the horse working his mouth, or licking his lips. This action on his part is directly related to his thought process. If you do something with the horse and his mouth is shut tight, *he didn't get it, or he's resisting what you want*. Do it again. I cannot stress enough that you must watch for the mouth movement. It is such an important indicator of the horse's progress you cannot overlook it.

There are other expressions of body language that will help you evaluate the horse as you go. Is he flipping his head up as he runs around the pen? A sure sign of resistance. Is he looking away from you as he goes, or does he keep his head straight? Looking away indicates he'd rather avoid you than submit to you. (Unless he has a physical problem that keeps him in a crooked frame as he moves. We'll discuss this more in the chapter "Physical.") The head getting lower is an indicator that he is relaxing and not stressed. Anytime you can lower the head, which I also call flattening out the top line, you are going in the right direction. A relaxed horse is always better off than a wired horse. If his tail is ringing around, he is not happy, and is perhaps nervous. If his ears are pointed back he is getting ticked off and you had better change something quickly. If he cocks up one rear foot while he's standing, he is

A better response would be that the horse at least looks at you. He's still on the rails, but a look is better than ignoring you. Photo by Susan Sexton.

getting relaxed and not preparing to flee. And of course, if he turns away from you and kicks in the air in your direction, that is what I call the infamous "Horsy Finger," with its obvious show of disrespect. All in all, there are a lot of tell-tale signs that indicate the horse's mental and emotional state. If you can learn to read the signs, you become a much more effective handler and have fewer surprises from the horse.

Lastly I would ask you to really look at the horse's eyes and body as the two best overall indicators of his condition. His body can become tight and ready to explode in an instant when he feels threatened. But even beyond that, there are more simple subtle things to "read" as you learn to listen to your horse. If he is going to move, he will turn an eye or an ear in the direction he is thinking of going before he goes that way. He can't take a step anywhere until he shifts his weight and gets ready to take the step. Learn to see his preparation to leave by where his eye or ear goes and how he shifts his weight, so you know he's going before he actually goes. Again, so much of what he does he will communicate to you before he does it, if you can only develop your skill at understanding his body language. And most important of all are his eyes. Their eyes will tell it all. Just as in people, their eyes are the windows to their soul. If the eyes look wide, and frantic, you are in trouble. If you can get the eyes to look soft the body will be likewise. But don't forget, the other important aspect to their eyes: they are reading your body language and looking in your eyes all the while too. Everything you do is read by them and assumed to have been intended. Even the way you *feel* will be obvious to them from your body language, so be sure *you* stay aware of your emotions. This is not likely a form of communication you are used to or perhaps even comfortable with yet, but it can help you so much with your horse, you need to develop your abilities with it. Remember, your horse is trying to communicate with you the only way he knows how. You need to become a good listener.

Overall the key factor to watch for as far as evaluating your progress with the horse in the pen is his attitude towards you. And that is displayed by his responsiveness or lack of responsiveness, including resistance or perhaps even defiance as you ask him to do things. When you ask him to reverse directions does he begin his turn quickly *as you are asking*, or does he continue on his way and only turn when you get more animated and demand the response? Does he respond to the signal alone or does he require several levels of increasing animation before he submits and gives you what you asked for? Initially he will likely be resistant, but as you continue, he will become more and more responsive, requiring less and less on your part to get the response. You will get to the point where you feel that the horse is reading your mind and commencing his response as you begin to ask for that response. The extended arm as a signal will give way to a pointing finger producing equal response. And a simple shift of your weight or turn of your head can reverse the horse. You will begin to communicate on his level. As you build his trust and respect, *everything* will get easier and faster. Remember, every action you get from his body is an expression of the attitude in his mind. This is a mental exercise for you both.

Step Five: Knowing When You've Waited Long Enough

You ask the horse to go off and he does, then you reverse him a few times and you get quiet. He stops and turns towards you but does not walk up to you. You're looking at him and he's looking at you and nothing seems to be happening. Or is it? I said you need to pause after each series of actions in order for him to digest what just transpired. Look at him closely. Is his head a bit twitchy and are his eyes and ears moving around a bit? Is he shifting his weight back and forth from leg to leg? Is he raising and then lowering his head or looking from side to side? Is he snorting or changing his respiration? Is he twitching any muscles in his shoulder or neck? Is his mouth chewing? Any of these signs indicate there *IS* something going on and you should wait a bit longer. These are very subtle signs but they are indicative of thinking on his part. He's still thinking about what you're doing. As long as he's thinking, it's OK to wait. If you err at first, err by giving him more time than needed. Don't err by being in too much of a hurry. That will help you both. In my workshops I almost always have to *slow people down*. I rarely have to speed them up to do more.

You want the horse to walk over to you and touch you gently, indicating his respect for you and asking to join your herd. But he's standing out by the rail and just looking at you. There are several ways you can approach this situation, and the *normal* approach would be to send the horse off again and again, since he didn't do what you asked for. I would not say that is incorrect if you did it, but I would ask you to think about *why* he didn't come on in. If you said, "Because he was being bad," then you need to re-read this book. If you said, "Because he wasn't ready," then you are more on track. So *why* wasn't he ready? Could be he doesn't trust you enough yet. Could be he is not sure you are really an alpha. Could be he's had some bad experiences with people before and he's not taking any chances. Could be he's stubborn as heck and wants to be in charge. All in all, he doesn't trust you yet or you haven't earned his respect. Notice I didn't offer "He doesn't understand what you want" as a choice? Be-

If he stops and turns to face you, that's better yet. But note his head is still high, so he's telling you he's not sure about you yet. Photo by Susan Sexton.

cause he *does* understand this process; it's as natural to him as breathing. If he doesn't come in, it is because he's not ready to and the reasons may take you awhile to figure out. The more frequently you use this process and the more different horses you use it on, the better you will become at understanding what the horse is displaying. The best way to work through whatever is bothering him is to repeat the process and then wait to see what happens. He will make it clear to you sooner or later.

If he stops and looks at you and gets very relaxed and his body becomes quite still and quiet, it is a safe bet that he is not doing any heavy thinking and hence not likely to change any further. If you see the horse assume this really relaxed, totally inanimate posture, you need to move on. Do something. We'll discuss several options of exactly what to do later. But for now you need to be able to tell if you should wait or get on to another step. If he looks dead, but standing up, you waited too long. You cannot become alpha by boring the horse into submission. Most people *DO NOT HAVE THIS PROBLEM.*

If he looks a bit relaxed, but is still fidgeting, he may be ready to come in to you. You really don't want to *do something* a few seconds before he was going to give you what you had been asking for all along. Before he comes in, he will almost always start working his mouth and chewing. He will also usually lower his head as if to sniff the ground. He may also look from side to side. He will shift his weight so the front foot that is further back is lightened and ready to step. And he may do all that but only

210

Your goal is to be patient and give him time to decide to drop his head (usually coinciding with chewing), turning in to you and then walking up to touch you gently. When he does, be sure to WAIT. Don't DO anything! That's the reward. Photos by Susan Sexton.

take one little tiny step, instead of walking all the way in to you. Don't despair, he's trying. After he takes that little step, be still and take a deep breath to let him know you are relaxed and he will keep trying. Every step is a "try" and Ray Hunt says, "You must reward the slightest try." His reward is "quiet."

The bottom line on waiting is very simple: if you think he's still thinking, there's no harm in giving him a few more seconds to decide what to do. If you think he's going to sleep, you'd better move on because he isn't likely to change any further at this stage. And this process is all about change, not staying where you are.

Step Six: Getting Him To Come In To You:

Your goal is to get him to willingly come in to you and touch you gently, asking to join your herd. That act shows a degree of submission and respect. Yet so far he has turned his butt to you and you sent him off for that. Then he ran and ran around the pen, but you got him to stop by moving off center and getting the pressure on his bubble to become intermittent. Then he stopped, but did not come in. He just stood there look-

211

ing at you. The best you have gotten from him so far is to stop, turn and face you, but not walk in. Now what? Now you have several choices of what to do. And in most situations there is not a right choice and a wrong choice; there are simply "choices." This is where a good horse person will begin to really think. This is where the approach I'm talking about becomes less cut and dried, less black and white. Also a bit harder to explain with only words. The accompanying pictures will help, so please refer to them to be clear in what we're doing.

You could always send the horse off again. This is the primary action of many trainers, and used over and over. It would not be wrong, but I prefer to vary what I am doing so as to not bore or stagnate the horse, as well as to provide me with additional actions to observe and evaluate the horse. Too much constant send him off, send him off, can condition the horse to stay away from you, the opposite of what we want. Also, some horses respond well to certain actions and not well to others. I like to do what works the best, easiest and quickest. I don't want to do the same thing over and over if it's not getting the result I'm after. That requires me to be flexible and to think as we go. Remember, do something, watch for the result and then adjust as you go.

If you didn't want to send the horse off again, you could just wait awhile. By awhile I mean a few seconds to a minute or so, not five minutes. He will be evaluating you as you wait, and if he thinks you're too passive, you will lose ground by waiting too long. But in many situations in my workshops, I let people wait a bit longer just to see what happens. And believe me, the people are always real quick to want to *DO* something. For the person to stop doing for ten seconds may seem like an eternity. Yet often as we simply wait, it is common for the horse to change and walk in, even after he had been standing for a couple of minutes. If he was up tight and nervous, or didn't trust you enough, then standing and waiting may let him relax and see you as a leader but not a threat, and then decide to come in. Your ability to observe and adjust as you go is your best tool in deciding what you do next.

Before I go to the next possibility, I'd like you to consider the following idea: when a horse's feet are stuck (he doesn't want to move) it indicates his mind is stuck. Let me explain that a bit further. If the horse went around the pen and when you got quiet, he slowed quickly, turned in to you and walked up politely and touched you with his nose, it would indicate that he trusted you and was willing to be submissive to you. He decided you were OK and then acted upon his judgment by coming in. If he didn't come in it could be because of several possible reasons, but all would indicate a degree of resistance or indecision on his part. Unwillingness to make a decision, either because he is still too stubborn to give in or because he is unsure enough about things to relax and trust you, are what I call being "stuck." Mentally stuck. But remember, what moves his feet? His mind. So if his feet are not moving what is stopping them? His mind. He's stuck mentally. Two ways to get him unstuck: do some exercise (such as send him off, etc.) to change his thinking, OR simply get him to move his feet. If you free up his feet to where they are moving easily and softly, his mind will free up as well. It can work both ways. Free the mind to move the feet or move the feet to free up the mind. They are interconnected in such a way that understanding and being able to use this concept will help you immensely. Here's how you can do that.

Suppose the horse is facing you, but still standing by the rail. He doesn't seem to be very active with a lot of thought going on, so you doubt he's likely to walk on in to you. Try moving your body around him to one side. In other words, take a few steps to your left or right. Either way could be fine. Take only a couple to three steps at a time and watch the horse. If he takes off around the pen, you got into an area he was uncomfortable about and you will need to remember that situation to work on as you go. If he did leave, then go back to the center and get quiet, asking him to stop. If he stops quickly, it was no big deal. If he is going around in a frantic fashion, it *was* a big

213

deal and you will need to get him stopped by moving off center and start over. Remember which side of the horse you were on and which way you moved. It matters.

In most cases the horse will not run off but instead he will watch you. What you want is for him to move his feet. You want him to stay facing you as you circle him, by turning his body as you go. Always facing you. A horse facing you shows respect. Some horses will let you walk all the way around, almost behind them and watch you with their head cranked around, but never move their feet. That would be a horse whose mind is really stuck, often a stubborn horse, but possibly a horse that does not trust people. All you are doing is gently and quietly moving around the horse, you may be ten to fifteen feet away or more, and trying to get him to turn and follow your movements with his body. Often you will see the horse leaning and leaning, but appearing as if his feet were nailed to the ground. You need to break through this resistance but not with force. You need to get the horse to move on his own, not make him move, if at all possible. (I have found that if you help a horse figure something out on his own rather than just forcing some response, it makes a more lasting impact. If I couldn't get the horse to free up and move with this gentle pressure, then I would make him move by sending him off. You cannot accept "no response" as an option for the horse. Most horses will respond without being made to if you will only try a softer approach first.) If you move to your left and he doesn't move, try going back around to the right. Sometimes a horse will turn to one side with no problem, yet on the other side he will be stuck in cement. That means you need to spend a lot of time on the "stuck" side to get him over that. Failure to work through the resistance on the problem side will often result in serious problems later. When you least expect them. Remember, the horse never does something for nothing.

ITEM: She was a very tall lady with a very tall horse. About five-foot-ten and nearly seventeen hands respectively. The horse was really cute with a lot of

214

personality, but very pushy with the owner. She rode English and had ridden for years. She came to the workshop "just to see what it was all about." She said she didn't have any problems with her horse. In the round pen handling he did very well, but took a lot of time to come in to her. He was also very bothered anytime she got near his right shoulder. I pointed it out to her several times and even discussed it with the group as she neared his shoulder and got the reaction. The reaction was that he'd move so as to put her back on his left side. She didn't mind being on the left so it was not a problem to her. My take on the situation was quite different. If she sees he doesn't want her on his right and simply goes back to his left, she is *avoiding* the situation. Besides the obvious non-alpha-like behavior of letting the horse control the situation, things you avoid with your horse usually come back and bite you in the butt later. If she lets him put her back on his left, who is in charge? You got it, he is. She adapts to avoid what he doesn't like and he gets her to *not* do what he doesn't like. A lot of control being exercised there but all of it in the wrong direction. I kept bringing it up to her and finally she said in a rather challenging tone, "If it's such big deal, how come it hasn't been a problem in the two years I've had him and how would it show up if it did become one?" The answer to her first question is that she'd been lucky. She had also been trying to *avoid* any trouble areas so she had probably done that pretty well. The answer to the second question was that since he was so bothered by someone being around his right shoulder/withers, if some day she was leading or riding and something came into that area rather quickly, the horse could over react and cause a problem. She shrugged off my comments as unrealistic and we moved on. I have long since learned that *you can lead a student to knowledge but you can't make her think.* The next day we were practicing getting on and off from both sides of the horse– something I strongly recommend to everyone. She was having trouble getting the horse to stand still to mount from the right side (surprise, surprise), and he was going around and around her. I suggested she hold up a minute and I would help her with him when I finished with the person I was helping with a saddle. She persisted. Everyone else was mounted and she was getting angry. Again I called to her to wait, but she kept fussing with the horse and trying to get on. I told her to stop, but she finally grabbed on and tried to swing into the saddle. The horse literally exploded upward and she went flying about ten feet in the air. Fortunately she landed on her butt and only her pride was hurt, but it was very dramatic. No sooner had she hit the ground than someone spoke up and shouted, "That is exactly what you warned us about yesterday with him not wanting her near his right side, isn't it?" It was. He even tried to warn her repeatedly today by trying not to let her get in the area he was troubled by. Her previous avoidance of a trouble spot, compounded by her refusal to listen to her horse almost got her hurt. I see it often. *I'm going to do this, horse, whether you like it or not.* Not too bright and not too safe. Horses never do something for nothing. Don't confuse what I just said to refer to understanding what caused that behavior in the horse. You'll probably never figure that out in a million years. It's unimportant. What is important is that you notice it, and then take action to correct it. Not avoid it. To answer the next question… If a horse doesn't want you near some part of his body, you *MUST* go there

216

a lot, but in small, gentle steps that he can cope with. Using the leverage you have as his alpha, get him to accept you closer and closer to that area, until you are there. Do this untied, preferably in the pen. He has a bubble about that spot on his body. You break down that bubble by applying, then removing pressure to that area. Once you can get to the area, stay there a few seconds and then leave that area (releasing the pressure of being there). In a short period of time he will lose the problem altogether.

As you move around the horse, let's say you take a few steps and are about even with his right shoulder. He turns towards you with just a slight step. Stop moving and be still. Your movement, as subtle as it was, put pressure on him from a different angle and he yielded by turning to you. When he turned toward you, *HE* took the pressure off so

If he didn't approach you, so you approached him, you may end up standing next to him and he seems stuck. The feet aren't moving. Simply step to the side, parallel to his body. His head should turn to you, and then he should step towards you. Gauge your moving to keep his focus on you: too fast and he'll leave; too slow and you aren't likely to get a response. Trial and error will teach you very quickly! Photos by Susan Sexton.

you don't have to back up. You did have to stop moving to avoid putting the pressure back on too soon. Wait for a bit and watch for the horse to work his mouth, or sigh, or lower his head, or shake his head, indicating he is thinking and he got it. He's changing his attitude and starting to relax. If there are none of the above actions present, you need to keep trying because he isn't getting it yet. If you are deliberate and patient, he will change for you. By simply changing your position in relationship to the horse, that change in pressure as the horse perceives it, can cause him to move. You may move very little or you may move quite a bit, but the goal is to get the horse to move his feet by you changing your location in the pen. You want him to turn and face you wherever you go. Each time he turns, you stop moving. You will start out moving until he turns, then stop. As he becomes more and more responsive, you will be able to literally run around him and have him spin to follow you. That may take a few weeks, but it's really fun to do.

Right about now it is common for someone to think about this idea of the horse being loose (you walk around him and no matter where you move, he continually faces you) and ask, "What happens if you want to get to the back of the horse? If he keeps turning, you won't be able to get to his rear end." A logical point, but there is a simple solution. I can't really explain it very well but this is how it works. If the horse is free, he will face you out of respect. If you touch him and begin to move around him as you touch, he will not move. If you stand by his head and touch his neck, as you start moving down his side, touching his body as you go, he will stand still. If he didn't, then one quick animated movement, perhaps raising your hands towards his head as he began to turn, would stop him in his tracks. If you moved around him to his rear, and stopped touching him he will stay still. If you want him to face you, simply back up a step or two and he will turn to you. If any of this doesn't work, then you are either moving too erratically or he doesn't respect you enough yet.

As you really study the horse you may notice the horse that isn't moving his feet may also be tense and nervous. Horses that are not free with their feet are usually tight and stiff in their overall motion. They may be stubborn or afraid, and either is a problem. Fearful horses tend to be quick and erratic in how they move. They also tend to stay still but then bolt forward with unnecessary speed, overreacting to things. Stuck and then exploding with movement. Their mind is in fear and then panic. Often they will continue to do fast, erratic laps in the pen and not want to stop. This can be dangerous in the real world, but usually not difficult to help a horse through. The timid horse that tends to be stuck, then almost explosive in movement, needs to learn to move in smaller increments. He needs to learn that he can move without the panic, and develop confidence in himself. (Please understand something: a timid or fearful horse may never be a really brave horse. But it could be a *braver* horse, so that is your goal.) As you patiently get him to begin to loosen up, and move his feet in smaller controlled actions, you will also notice a softening of his entire demeanor and a change in his overall appearance. He will relax and his eyes will soften. And the stiff, locked up appearance will transcend into an easy, free moving horse. All because you were able to get him to move his feet. And think.

Another option for you to use on a horse that stopped but did not come in to you would be to approach the horse. Just walk up to him. Your goal being to again get him to move his feet, and free up his mind. But there is a lot more to it than that. Remember the bubble. If the horse is not trusting of you, and perhaps either timid or stubborn and not willing to give in, he will have a big bubble regarding your approaching him. You need to walk towards him in a moderate natural fashion. Not too fast, not too slow. You're going to approach the horse with the same technique you would use to catch a horse that didn't want to be caught. Let's go over how to use this bubble idea to catch a horse and you'll understand its application in the round pen work.

Suppose you had a new horse somebody just brought to your farm, it was in a hundred foot square paddock, and was not anxious to be caught. You could try the old *tiptoe up to it and hope it didn't run off* approach. That seldom works. People do it because they think they won't run the horse off by approaching slowly. Logical to people, backwards by horse standards. As a prey animal, the horse spent fifty million years learning *NOT* to let anything sneak up on him. Predators moved very carefully, trying to go undetected until they could pounce on their prey. The horse knows you are a predator, and when you begin to act like one by moving so slowly, you cause the horse to be more on guard. You are creating the exact opposite response that you wished because of a misunderstanding.

You could get the carrots/apples/treats/grain, etc. and try to lure the horse to you and then catch it. But what happens when you don't have the carrots/grain/etc.? What lures the horse in without those aids? You could try to rope it. Can you throw a lasso? I can't. If you caught it with the lasso, could you stop the horse if he tried to leave? Really tried to leave. Probably not. In fact, every time you try to restrict the physical movement of the horse with contact, the natural response from the horse is to resist and get free. He associates his freedom of movement with being safe from predators. So the more you try to force the reduction of movement in the horse, the more he is likely to struggle to move. Again, your actions tend to create the exact opposite response from the horse that you were after, due to your misunderstanding.

You could get six to ten friends and try to herd the horse into a corner and then grab it. If it didn't want to be grabbed (and it usually doesn't), it might run over you. And again you would be appearing to the horse as a predator trying to get him, and his instinctive reaction would be to avoid being gotten. Those are all *normal* ways of trying to catch a horse. Pretty poor at best, but it is all that most people know. Let's try something less *normal,* but more effective.

The horse is against the far side of the paddock. You walk into the paddock with a halter and lead in hand. (And I know there is no chain on the lead, right?) And you walk calmly and gently towards the horse. Not timid and not aggressive. As you go, you pay extremely close attention to the horse, looking for any sign of movement. Any reaction to your approach, if you will. Your timing is crucial here, so stay with me. You are *NOT* sneaking, but just walking in a calm, gentle fashion. As you approach the horse, you will eventually hit his bubble, the place where he is no longer comfortable with you getting any closer. The point where he begins to feel that if you keep coming he will need to flee. As you near his bubble, he will react by raising his head, or leaning away, or shifting his weight, or backing up, or twitching his muscles in his neck or shoulder, etc. Unless you are moving way too fast, he will communicate several indicators of his *intent to leave* before he *actually leaves*. Usually the raising of the head is the easiest telltale sign to see, but watch for them all. As you hit his bubble (and you will know by his indicating it with the signals we just listed), you must stop and take a half step backward instantly, *BEFORE HE IS PRESSURED INTO MOVING HIS FEET.* By stopping your forward movement and backing off just that little bit, you take the pressure off the horse. If you are too late in reacting he will leave. If your timing is perfect, he will not move his feet. The horse will grade you on your ability to pay attention to him and react accordingly. If he moves his feet you failed. (Remember we talked about the relationship between the movement of the horse's feet and his mind being free and working? The other aspect to this relationship is that if you *control* the movement of the feet, you control the mind, and hence control the horse. If you can approach him without him moving his feet *you* have controlled *him* without any contact.) If you can find his bubble and get a reaction, yet back off without him moving, you get an A. The hard part will be that each time you hit the bubble and then back off, you will want to go on forward again. *DON'T.* Wait. Wait for a signal from him that he's OK with this. The

221

signal? He moves his mouth, drops his head, sighs, etc. Once he does that, walk forward again. Watch for the bubble and continue as before, stopping each time he reacts and backing off a half step. Then again, wait. Watch for the signal of his mouth moving or head dropping etc. before you go on. Why only a half step back? Simple. If you move and he reacts and you go forward a step and back up a step, then do it again and again, you aren't progressing. Stalemate. You need to be getting closer, hence one step forward, one-half step back. That's progress. Your goal is to get next to the horse, not to catch him. With some horses it will be slower than others. You progress as fast as the horse can accept it. No faster.

In this process of approach and retreat you are applying pressure and then removing the pressure. You are controlling the horse by not letting him leave. He could leave, but since he will only react to something, you can control the situation by controlling the amount of pressure he feels. Your proximity, your approach increases pressure on him. Too much pressure, he leaves. You lose. Just enough to get closer and closer, not letting him leave, and you both win. You win because you get next to the horse with no struggle. He wins because he learned to trust you while avoiding a struggle. And he also begins to realize that you can control him, even when at a distance, untied – enhancing his respect for you. When you first try this you may get the horse to run off a few times. Don't worry. We all do that in the beginning. Some horses are SOOOO sensitive that it is really not easy to do. But the really sensitive horses make you better. Pay attention to the horse and work on your timing. It always works. Always. I didn't say how fast it works, but it *is* faster than struggling to catch the horse every time you go out to get him. The longest I have ever taken to catch one was forty-five minutes. Usually it's less than ten. But consider this important fact: after you catch him once this way, the next time you show up it will take you less time. The next time it will take you less yet. Usually in two to three visits the horse will approach you and not wait to be caught. I see people that have a struggle with catching their horse almost as often as not. The typical comment is, "Sometimes he's OK, but when he doesn't want to be caught he just runs off." Sounds like the horse has the person figured out more than the other way around. Yet those same people won't spend a couple of sessions of ten to twenty minutes to solve the situation once and for all. They just keep dealing with the problem over and over, making excuses as they go. You decide which approach is faster and better in the long run. So simple, yet so powerful.

Eventually you will end up standing next to the horse that didn't want to be caught. At this time it is *normal* to want to get the rope around the horse as quick as possible. Don't. I've been in situations where I spent twenty minutes getting up next to the horse, winning his trust, and being ever so careful not to let him leave, only to have the observers yell out, *"GET HIM!"* as soon as I get within reach of him. What do you think the horse was expecting from me once I got next to him? He was probably expecting to get caught. Try something different; don't throw the rope around his neck, don't grab him, don't even touch him. Just stand there quietly with him and don't put the lead on or anything. After thirty seconds to a minute, do something else he doesn't expect, walk away. Turn slowly and gently and take six or eight steps away from him. Then stop, and turn back to face him. I bet he will be looking at you as you walk off. Do you realize that by being close to him you put a degree of pressure on him? Do you realize that by walking away you took that pressure off? Wait for just a minute and then walk back to him, watching for his bubble (although it may be gone), and be ready to react if needed. Again, don't touch him, just stay there next to him and be quiet and relaxed. Breathe and be still. He'll like that. Repeat the process of walking away and walking back a few times but each time you turn to leave, do it slowly and gently. Usually in three to five of these visits he will begin to think you're OK, and he will really relax. He will also begin to associate you with the release of pressure he so likes. Then he will usually do something quite amazing to most

223

people; eventually when you turn to walk away he will go with you. He will willingly follow you with no signal or contact. He will have decided he would rather be with you than be alone. A big decision. Walk a few steps and then gently stop. He will stop too. Wait a few seconds then walk again. Again he will follow. Notice how his head will get lower and lower as this all takes place. The low head carriage means he is getting relaxed. After he walks with you two or three times, stop and gently put the halter on his head. You just caught a horse that didn't want to be caught, by making it a good deal for him. No struggle and no force. All you did was to understand his perspective on things and adjust your approach. And one last point to use. Once you have the halter on him, *DO NOT* grab it to pull him along nor grab the buckle under the halter, nor do you pull the rope tight. You will hold the lead two to three feet from the buckle and walk off exactly as you did before the halter was on the horse. You want the horse to follow you by choice as he just did rather than because the lead is on. We'll go into leading more later.

Now that you've used "the pressure on the bubble" concept to catch the loose horse in the paddock, let's go back to the round pen horse that hasn't come up to us yet and use the bubble concept on him also. If you walk straight up to a horse that is loose and you don't pay attention to the bubble, you will most likely watch him trot off away from you into the sunset. After controlling the horse in the pen by sending him off in both directions a few times, he may be concerned about you approaching him and feel safer running away. You need to alter that pattern of behavior. You approach the horse and watch for the bubble. When he starts to react (don't wait until he has already left.) you back off a half step, and then wait. Don't forget the *wait* part. Keep approaching and then waiting until you are next to him just as outlined above. Then gently walk away a few steps. As with the earlier action of you moving around the horse, your goal is to get him to move his feet, and turn with your movement, even to follow you. By calmly and gently applying pressure with your approach, then taking that pressure off, you can get him to give up his bubble (indicating a lowering of his resistance) and join you. If he lets you approach but doesn't go with you when you walk off, his feet are stuck. Which tells you what about his mind? It's stuck too. He's still concerned about you and can't give in to you, yet. Mentally he's stuck. Your job is to slowly and gently move in one direction, watching for a change in him. What kind of change? A step. Maybe even a lean, which precedes a step. The more you do this, watching for the slightest movements and changes in the horse, the more subtle details you will begin to notice. You will begin to see things in the horse you never noticed before. And *everything he does matters*. You want to work towards getting him to take a step, and then to be able to walk freely and relaxed with you *AS YOU MOVE*. You want him to become your shadow. Wherever you go, it goes. That's what you want from the horse. You will need to move around one side and then to the other. Each side of the horse may offer a very different reaction to your movement. Pay attention to that. If you can't get him to move on one side, go to the other side and try again. If he moves there, then keep working with the good side until he moves very freely. Then keep alternating by going back to the weak side and eventually you'll get that side freed up as well. He needs to be free moving on both sides eventually.

Have you ever noticed that horses don't always do what you want? That's probably one of the reasons you bought this book. Well, the "pressure on the bubble" alone is not always enough to get some horses to let go of their resistance and join you. They may be too afraid, or too stubborn, or just too loaded down with all the mental baggage from a lot of previous bad experiences with people. You *WILL NEVER FIGURE OUT WHAT CAUSED THEM TO BE THE WAY THEY ARE*. It never ceases to amaze me how much effort people will put into worrying and trying to figure that out. But the reality you *DO HAVE TO DEAL WITH,* is that this is the way this horse is today. Whatever problems or traumas he has had to get him to what he is now, is all history. Now your responsibility is to try to help him over that. You may occasionally have a horse that is so stuck that his feet aren't moving, no matter how much you work on his bubble. OK, next step. We will actually touch him. I don't like to touch the horse right at the start, for several reasons. One, it's what he's used to; people fussing all over him. Not very alpha like. Two, I want him to come to me and ask to be in my herd with no physical coercion. Three, the longer I wait to touch him, the more it will matter when I do. And I want him to notice my touch and appreciate it. And never take it for granted. If you constantly keep grabbing the horse and touching the horse, he begins to associate your touch with a struggle and something to avoid. If you wait until he is almost longing for it, it will be far more important when it gets there. For an alpha to rub on a lesser horse is a big deal, not taken lightly. For this situation, how we touch him will be very specific and with exact purpose.

You get up next to him and he's stuck. He's still paying attention to you (you didn't forget that you should have been watching for his attention *ALL THIS TIME* did you?) but he just won't move or follow you. Let's help him to move and let's see just how much resistance is in this horse. Say you are standing to the left of his head, his left side, facing his head, so your left shoulder is by his head and your right shoulder is by his shoulder. Got the picture? Put your left hand on his face just above his nose so your thumb is on one side and your fingers are on the other. Your thumb will be near you. He may even resist you putting your hand up there. If he does, just keep trying to catch his head with your hand but don't get violent or struggle. Be persistent but not aggressive. If he turns to run off, remember, you can't stop him. So make his leaving your idea, and send him off. If he stays with you submissively, he gets to relax. If he gets an attitude, he has to run off by himself. If he runs off, go back to getting him to stop and face you and approach him again. VERY IMPORTANT POINT. *Any time he does anything displaying attitude and you take control back by sending him off or enforcing your will in some other way, be prepared for a change in the horse shortly after that interaction.* The horse may have been stuck and would not come in. You got close and tried to get your hand on his head, he took off and you sent him around. Now you get quiet and he stops, turns in and walks right up to you like a perfect gentleman. A big change and you think, Where did that come from? It came from you asserting yourself and acting like an alpha. Taking charge and not letting him take control. And not being physical about it. This is mental, not physical. Many people will be handling a horse in a workshop and the horse will be demonstrating some serious attitude and the handler will be getting upset or mad at the resistant behavior. I welcome the display of the resistance, because when he shows it and you respond correctly, he will change. Sometimes you have to really put pressure on a horse a bit to *GET HIM TO DISPLAY SOME UNWANTED BEHAVIOR,* in order to really get the horse to change. You have to peel the layers off of onion, so to speak, to get to the heart of the horse.

So you get him stopped and approach his head, standing on his left. You go back to putting your hand on his face and now he lets you. You will be contacting the horse at two levels, asking for submission in each. I'll explain. Just putting your hand on his head took a certain amount of submission from the horse. That was the first level of submission you *did not get* when you first tried to put your hand on his face, and he took off. So just the fact that he now accepted your hand is an act of submission greater than where he was a minute ago. Level one accomplished. You need to keep your hand there for a minute or so, but not *DO* anything with it. You are asking for, and getting, a small degree of submission from the horse by his accepting your hand *being there*. Next, you want to progress to level two of submission. Now you take your hand and *ask* the horse to move by actually applying pressure with your hand to the horse's head. Let's say you take a step back and around to his shoulder, asking him to turn towards you with his front end as you move. You want a step from the front feet of the horse, turning in your direction. One step is an act of submission. Do not squeeze his face, just use a firm but polite grip with your hand. You may get the step. You may get the head and neck to bend around but no movement of his feet. Or, he may jerk his head away and try to avoid you. Let's evaluate each possibility.

If he gives you the step you asked for and moves his feet, turn him just a bit and then stop, but *do not let go of his face*. You were asking for the turn with pressure, but you had been asking for a degree of submission by just having him accept your hand there before you ever asked for the step. Understand? Once he takes the step, you release the pressure but only go back to level one submission, which means he still accepts your hand. If he were to try to jerk his head away, you try to keep your hand on it, but if he gets away, send him off. Go back through the previous scenario; get him stopped, get next to him and then get your hand back on his head. Eventually, usually in a few tries, his resistance will begin to fade away and you will

If the horse is really stuck, you may need to help him to get his feet moving by actual contact. Place your hand on his nose (not squeezing) and ask him to accept it being there. If he does that, you have got level one submission. Then ask him (by applying some pressure) to turn or back as you wish. Do not stop asking until he moves his feet and takes a step. If he gives you what you asked for, that is level two submission. And if his attitude is still resistant, he'll jerk his head away as in the last photo. Your response to that would be to send him off.

Photos by Susan Sexton.

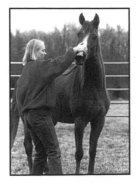

feel a softness in his movements that can only be described as wonderful. He will begin to yield to you with only an ounce or two of pressure. You will move a thousand pound horse around as if he weighed nothing. And as you work with the horse with your hand on his head, remember this: whatever resistance *you feel in your hand* is *the amount of resistance in the horse's mind.* If you are pushing and pushing on his head to get him to move, his attitude is not submissive to you. You are *physically feeling his resistance.* Conversely, when he will move, yielding to your hand with almost no pressure at all from you, he has given in and is willing to do what you ask. You have made progress by changing his attitude towards you. Great progress.

If he were bending his neck but not taking the step, he is *still resisting.* If the feet are stuck, the mind is stuck. If his feet won't move, he is resistant. Keep turning and asking for the step until he gives you a step. When he moves his feet, he has given in to you, and even the slightest step needs to be rewarded. How would you reward the step? By releasing the pressure. Again, not taking your hand away, just releasing the pressure you used on his face to ask for the turn. *Once you ask for something from the horse, you cannot stop asking until you get at least some of what you asked for.* If you ask him to do something and then stop asking before he does it, you are telling him he does not need to submit when you ask. You are undermining your own authority with the horse. Persistence. Many people think since his neck bent, he gave in and they release the pressure. Not true. The movement of his feet are your guide to judge submission. If he didn't move his feet, he didn't submit and is stuck mentally.

Lastly, if he jerks his head away and leaves, do not get upset. Do not overreact, just send him off, but do it instantly. Remember, we do not refer to unwanted behavior as bad, and therefore prejudice our actions with unhelpful emotions. He did what he thought was best from his point of view. Or at worst, what he thought he could get away with. We just need to change his view on things. Obviously, this act would indi-

229

cate resistance, and you would go back to moving him off around the pen, turn him a few times and then get quiet. You will always do something and then go back to being quiet and wait. That is your pattern. He will learn to like and appreciate you being quiet. He will begin to respect you and pay attention to you. And you will begin to need to do less and less to influence him.

STEP 7: Getting Him To Follow You

Throughout all of the interactions discussed above, your goals should include:

1) Getting and keeping the horse's attention
2) Getting the horse to move off in the direction you specify
3) Seeing that he not reverse except at your signal
4) Seeing that he responds quickly when asked to reverse by your signal
5) Constantly evaluating his attitude by watching his responses
6) Getting him to stop moving by getting quiet yourself
7) Getting him to allow you to approach him without his moving
8) Getting him to turn, remaining facing you as you move around him
9) Getting him to come in to you, and be relaxed and submissive with you
10) Being able to walk away from the horse and have him willingly follow you

Let's talk about number ten a bit. When you first got quiet and asked the horse to stop moving, you were also offering him the opportunity to join your herd and come be with you. The only stipulation was that you run your herd. Some horses are really looking for leadership and will come in very soon. If the horse is not running around like a rocket after you got quiet, or stuck on the rail with his feet planted in cement, he may come in right away. When the horse turns off the rail early on and heads for you in the middle, be sure to watch "how" he's approaching you. Some horses are a bit pushy around people (because it always worked for them in the past) and they will come in, but with the intent of taking over the herd, not assimilating into it. If the horse comes in real fast with his head way up, be ready to get very animated and send him off dramatically. That is not indicative of a submissive approach. Once you send him off, have him do a lap or two and maybe turn him with greater frequency. By coming in fast with his head up high, he is showing a non-submissive attitude toward you, even though he did come in. You need to change that attitude. How? Turn him a lot more often. A half lap and reverse. A quarter lap then reverse. A third lap then reverse. Maybe even reverse, then reverse again. Think about it. Each time you reverse him you are taking control of him. He is submitting to you. That is the pattern you must enforce; you ask, he submits. You're in charge.

After some combination of the above scenarios takes place, you will end up with a horse standing next to you, in a reasonably calm fashion. Remember to wait after each action you take. The less relaxed the horse is, the longer you need to wait between actions in order to let him calm down. Now you need to evaluate how submissive he is and how much control do you really have with him loose. You do that by moving away from him and seeing if he'll follow you. Initially you will need to move away softly and gently, to make it easy for him to go with you. If you duck away quickly or in a very animated fashion, he may mistake your animation as a signal for him to leave. You need to be clear that you want him with you without giving any signal to come. Don't let that confuse you, because I know it sounds contradictory on the surface. You want him to go with you because he wants to, not in response to any signal. For him to want to be with you, he has to believe you are his best option. He must trust you and feel safe with you. Just the same as if a horse in the wild saw his herd start to move, he would be moving right with them in an instant. He not only wants to be with them, he needs to.

Another way to get his feet moving and get him connected to you is to walk into his space. Shown with a halter and lead, it can also be done when the horse is free. Stand beside the horse and move into his space at his head, NOT HIS SHOULDER. He should turn softly and yield to your approach. Just get a single step at first and build

until you can run around him as fast as you can go, to get him spinning. And when you stop, he should stop instantly. You can reverse the process and turn him the other way, moving to you. His response tells you all about his attitude towards you. Photos by Susan Sexton.

If you move off and he stays put, he's stuck. Mentally and physically. Go back and try using pressure on his bubble and get his feet to move. You could also use the hand on his face approach we discussed earlier. Another tool I use that works well once you are next to the horse (either he came to you or you were able to approach him successfully) is to stand by his head and simply walk through his head expecting him to move out of your way. If you bump into the horse or if he tries to lift his head over you to avoid moving his feet, he is not submissive to you yet. He's stuck. Let me explain further. As you walk into the horse's "space" at his head, he should yield his bubble to yours and gently turn away. You don't want to initiate your movement with too much animation so as to send him off, just walk in expecting him to yield away from you. If he turns away softly, you're on the right path. If not, here's what you do.

As you approach him, you should see his head begin to turn away almost as soon as you move forward. He should be paying attention to you almost constantly by now, so there should be almost no lag time between your moving and his response. Any lag time shows a lack of attention, hence a lack of respect. If he is not yielding as you move forward, bring up your hands towards the side of his head as if to push his head away. I often have students (especially if they are a bit nervous around a particular horse) put one hand in front of their face with the palm facing the horse. The other hand can hold the wand behind their back. This is to keep you from getting bumped in the face by the horse, as well as give you something to control the horse with if he resists. He may resist by not moving so you would need to move him. Remember, if you ask for something, you can't accept not getting it. If you actually got to the point of contacting the horse with your hand, the *normal* approach would be to smack the horse with your hand to move him. Don't. Instead, you should bring the wand up behind your head so the bag is near or above his face using the animation to get his withdrawal rather than using force. This *will* get him to yield his space and turn away. He may run off, and that's OK, but you'd rather have him just turn away a step or two. This is the part where your judgment comes in; use only enough animation to get the yield, and no more. Enough is enough and any more is too much.

If he just plants his feet and tries to raise his head over your approach to avoid you, that is also an act of resistance. As you approach, if his head goes up, raise your hand to keep his head from being able to pass over you, thereby controlling the situation. Keep moving forward and get him to yield to you, adding movement from the wand behind you if needed. Now this does take timing and concentration on your part, but it's very easy. Try having another person watching as you do it so they can coach you from a different perspective on how you did. If you make an error and use too much animation and the horse runs off, it isn't the end of the world. Just regroup and try it again. You want to get to where the horse will softly and politely yield to any approach you make into his space. His feet should move easily and freely, not fast and erratic. You should also focus on being calm yourself as you do this. Often people get tense when they try to do things with a horse in such close proximity. Which is exactly why you need to do this. So you can become effective and comfortable controlling your horse as close as need be. And not relying on force to do it. He needs to develop his confidence in you, but you also need to develop your confidence in you. The best tool to help anyone's confidence is to help them become more effective. The more effective you become, the more you will relax and be natural in your movements. The more you relax, the more confidence your horse will develop in you. Another win-win scenario.

Using some combination of the pressure techniques we've discussed so far, you will be able to get the horse to free up his feet (and his mind) and begin to move softly and responsively in the pen. You will soon get to the point where if you walk off, he will follow. You stop and he stops. You have just acquired a thousand pound shadow. This is the moment you have been working towards with all the exercises we've discussed so far. The moment where the horse gives himself up to you and asks to join your herd. When that happens, I know you will want to go ape, petting him all over and talking to him in baby talk telling him what a "Goooood Booooy he is," etc. Don't. This is an exercise in discipline for you as well as him. Not that it is bad to say "good boy," and soon enough you will. But for now realize that those words coming from you would signify an emotional response from you, and your emotions are what need to be checked for a while. We've all done too much with our horses based on emotion, and not done that well. We need to recognize, perhaps even enjoy our emotions, but retain our good judgment. Be it fear, or anger, or what I call the "lovey dovey syndrome" we must learn to deal with our emotions around the

When the horse's attitude is getting where you want it, you will lead (walk) and he will simply follow – without signal or command. He is choosing to be with you! You lead him with his mind. And when you add a halter and lead line, nothing will change. The lead will be loose and draped because it's giving him the freedom to choose. He is following you, not the lead. The lead is simply another way to communicate with him. Photos by Susan Sexton.

horses. They seem to be so good at evoking such powerful emotional responses from us, which is no doubt a great part of our attraction to them in the first place.

This situation of getting connected to a horse in a way that is so fundamental to a horse can bring forth some strong emotions in us at the same time. I have had very troubled horses in my workshops or demonstrations, where I spent a lot of time getting the horse to trust me and come in to me. I watched the horse struggle with trusting me or not and then finally giving in and walking over to me. Many times it may have been the first real positive connection the horse ever had with a person. Then I moved and he moved with me, and it gives you such a magical feeling that's hard to explain. When it first happens for you, if you feel a little emotional, don't feel alone, it happens all the time. I've had grown men walk out of the pen after the horse came in like that, and seen their big grin accompanied by a little dampness in the eyes. A big, burly cowboy once described it very well. He had come to the workshop very skeptical of getting anywhere with his aggressive stallion. He'd tried forcing the big horse, only to start war after war. In forty minutes in the pen, he got the horse to do everything he asked and follow him softly all over. A horse he could rarely catch before. As this big guy walked out of the pen with his stallion gently following, he looked at me and said with a tear on his cheek, "I don't think I've ever felt that close to a horse before. It was really nice. Thank you."

Our emotions are part of what make humans so special. When I talk about not letting your emotions interfere with your horse's best interest, I am not at all suggesting you deny or ignore your emotions. Rather, I am asking you to recognize your emotions and enjoy them without letting them create problems for you. *Emotional responses* to horse situations are usually not very good choices for the horse or the person. Fear can destroy our ability to act effectively and eliminate any possibility of success. Anger can get us to do things we will regret almost immediately and often create further obstacles even more difficult to overcome later. And being too "lovey dovey" is a way of patronizing our emotions at the expense of the best interest of the horse. These three emotions cause us too many problems that are usually avoidable. Be aware of your emotions and recognize their effect on you. That is the best step to eliminating the problem.

But there is one more emotion that I want to mention briefly, and it is not easy since I have no adequate word for it. It is the feeling you get when you see a horse running free and it gives you a tingle inside. It is the feeling you get when you see the picture in a magazine of the beautiful little foal and

For those that like to start a horse at two or three, I say you're missing all the FUN! And a very big opportunity! If the mom has been through the round pen process, then mom and baby go in the round pen before the foal is a week old! Just a couple of minutes and no big stress. Think of the impression it makes on the foal to see mom submissive and responsive to you. By the time of weaning this foal will lead like a ten year old. By the way, this fillie, Lexi, was orphaned at birth, and Kasty has become her surrogate mom. If the mom has never been in the round pen, don't do this with the foal. You may not have mom's respect and the maternal instinct can kick in. Photo by Susan Sexton.

his mom in a green grassy valley. It's the feeling you get when you think about *your horse* and that you can't wait to see him after work today. It's the feeling you get when you walk in the barn and he nickers at you and turns to say hello. It's the feeling you get when you touch him, and smell him and look in his big soft eyes. It's the feeling you get when you ride and he shares his power with you, letting you do things you could never do without him. It's the feeling I get when I think of Raj and how he opened up the incredible world of horses to a man that didn't have a clue. It's the feeling I get when I think of an incredible day in the snow covered mountains of Colorado when Shazi helped me see what I was missing, even though it was right in front of me. It's the feeling I get when I think of a pitch-black night in the mountains when I had to trust Cisgo and just let go of my fears. And it's the feeling I get every time I climb on Sunny bareback and think of how this incredible animal has so changed my life and indirectly the lives of so many other people and horses, in so many ways. Even though I have no word for this feeling, I know it is the reason we have horses in the first place. It's why that first horseman knew he just had to ride one of those magnificent creatures. It's why they will no doubt be a part of human history forever. And it is one of the best feelings I have ever experienced. This emotion is to be treasured and relished for all it's worth.

SECTION 2 – TRANSITION

I was doing a demonstration at a major horse show a few years back, and the horse I was given to use was pretty rank. He was really aggressive at first, but as frequently happens, he changed quite quickly and ended up being a great demonstration of the effectiveness of what I teach. Afterwards, there was the usual crowd of people with comments and individual questions, and I always try to hang around and talk to as many people as time permits. The third or fourth woman that approached me said she had been doing round pen work with her horse for a few months, and he was great in the pen but as soon as she took him out he reverted right back to the pushy, obnoxious horse he had been before the round pen work. Then in a rather confrontational tone she stated, "That round pen stuff is a cute gimmick, but it doesn't do much for real people with real horse problems." She was obviously frustrated and wanted to vent that frustration on me. The rest of the crowd was very quiet now and listening intently for my reply. The question was actually a very reasonable one and one that has popped up repeatedly for me. I have met many people that saw a clinician do something in the round pen and went home to duplicate what they saw. They went through the motions and got *some response* from the horse but overall they never saw any significant change in their horse's behavior as the result of what they did in the round pen. Hence that was a very reasonable question for her to ask. Sort of the equivalent of "I tried it but it didn't work for me."

"I understand perfectly what you're saying, and unfortunately you are quite right based on your experience," I replied. That was not what she expected from me and now the crowd was *really quiet.* I went on, "And I doubt it's even your fault that you didn't see the changes you wanted or hoped for. But it's not because it doesn't work, it's because you weren't given a complete picture of everything involved with the process. The work you do with a horse in the round pen is only the tip of the iceberg, so to speak. It's a place to start, it's not a conclusion. Often people are led to believe that the round pen is their salvation. You were, as many others have been, shown a few pieces to a puzzle without being shown the entire picture you're trying to assemble. There were several important pieces to the puzzle that you had not been shown, so getting the final result was unobtainable for you. For example, had you been given a better understanding of the way the horse thinks, and how the round pen activities affect his thinking, that would have helped you. Had you understood going in that the round pen work actually solves very little on its own, you would have had a more

239

realistic expectation of what you were after. Understanding that the round pen is simply a controlled environment that allows you to quickly and safely change a horse's attitude about you would have been of great help to you overall. And perhaps most important, knowing that the change in the horse's attitude would provide you the *leverage* you need to *transition* his initial submissiveness in the round pen into real world behavior improvements would have created a very different and more effective mind-set within you. And one more thing. Had you been shown *how to transition* your round pen results into ways to change what you did with the horse as you *left the round pen*, you would have gotten the results that have eluded you so far." The crowd was still quiet, but now at least they were nodding a lot. The lady said I had made sense but then asked, "How does that transition you talk about work?" I'm glad you asked.

We have devoted a lot of space in this book discussing things that help you understand both how your horse works and how you need to adapt your approach to be more effective with him. The round pen is a step in a process, but it is not the first step. The first step is to understand the horse. The next step is to understand the process of changing the horse's attitude. Only then should the round pen be brought into use. It is the next step. The work you do in the pen will change the horse's attitude while it also *develops your communication skills with the horse.* The latter is as important as the prior. It is the improvement of *your communication skills* that you sharpen while doing the round pen work that will *afford you the ability* to maintain and even expand on the change you get with the horse in the pen, once you leave the pen. A child doesn't learn math in school just to know math. The child learns math because of how the knowledge of math can help him in so many important areas of his life long after school is over. What I did with Sunny in the round pen changed both him and me. His attitude change achieved by our interactions in the pen gave me the leverage to influence him. But the development of my communication skills and the improvement of my ability to understand him that occurred *while I was working on his attitude* is what allowed me to become more effective with him in every aspect of our lives from then on. That education of me was what enabled me to transition the control over Sunny I developed in the safety of the round pen into similar control in the real world environments outside the pen. I call it *transition*. This is an area of understanding I see very much overlooked by many trainers and is the basic cause of the lady's question I just discussed.

The way I demonstrate transition in my workshops is by several leading exercises we do after each horse has been through the round pen process. I should also add, that having put a horse in the pen once, and gotten him to

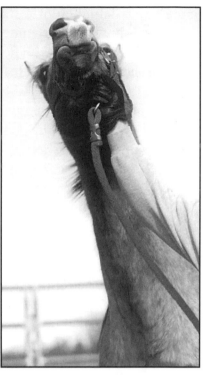

This photo illustrates how many people lead by hanging on the buckle or the halter itself. It also illustrates how most horses feel about this approach! Photo by Susan Sexton.

approach you or at least complete some part of the desired response outlined earlier, is not the end. I believe the round pen exercises are a valid tool for ongoing use with every horse. But once you have had some success in the pen, it is time to continue that approach outside the pen as you return the horse to his stall or pasture on the lead line. The halter and lead line are *THE* primary tools we use to control horses from the ground. To start with a definition, let me say that leading a horse is not dragging a horse around on the end of a rope. Nor should it be a horse dragging you around on the end of a rope. That sounds more like a definition of a struggle. When we earlier got the horse to walk with us around the pen with no halter or line in place, we were leading with no physical connection, and that is how we should continue to lead the horse. I am not suggesting that you forgo the halter and lead line from now on with your horse. But I am suggesting that you try to lead the horse with his mind as you did in the pen, and not *rely on the rope*. Also, remember what I said was the first step in getting control of the horse? Turn him loose. We need to employ that same approach as we use a line. Let me explain.

So how do you turn him loose while there is a line on him? Leave the line loose or draped. No pressure. You maintain a loose lead. When you put a halter and line on your horse, many people feel the need to take hold of the horse. In other words, grab the halter or the clasp where the line attaches or at least pull on the line. All of those actions apply pressure to the horse and the natural tendency is for the horse to pull back, or resist the pressure. Even the innocent resting of your arm on the line under the horse's chin will require that the horse *exert a resistance equal to the weight of your arm* in order to keep his head where it was before you grabbed on. We spent all that effort in the pen trying to get the resistance out of the horse and now you already started putting it right back. Do you understand? If you apply constant pressure he will initiate constant resistance. You didn't need to pull to lead him when there was no halter on the horse, and you don't need to pull now. I know the idea of having to hold on to the horse when the lead is on comes from the idea of maintaining control. It goes back to the misconception that you *have* control when the line is on and you don't if it isn't. So you hang on. Remember, if he really wants to leave, you can't stop him by holding on the line, so don't try. By offering the horse a bit of freedom with the loose line, you do not initiate any resistance from him. The loose line offers you several advantages that you don't have if the line is tight. Let's discuss each advantage the loose line offers.

When the horse becomes responsive, try using longer and longer leads. Try backing or turning the horse at greater and greater distances using less and less pressure. If the lead stays tight for more than a second it means things are getting physical and you probably made a mistake. Photo by Susan Sexton.

Let's go to a worse case scenario first. The horse blows up and bolts off while you're holding his line. We already said you can't stop him with a line, but if you have a tight grip on the halter or line when he blows up, you have no time to react before you are drawn into the crisis by his movement. The instant he moves is the same instant that movement will begin to jerk you into his panic. I have seen numerous people with torn up hands or dislocated shoulders because they didn't have even a split second to get free when their horse bolted. They got hurt before they could react and they had too tight a contact on the horse and it cost them dearly. What would a looser line have caused to be different? Very simple. It would have given them a bit of time to react before they would be dragged into the crisis. If you are holding the clasp under the halter, the instant the horse moves, you are moving too. And we all know how quickly and violently horses can move. If you were holding the line with two or three feet of slack between the clasp and your hand, that two to three feet of slack would translate into a split second of warning for you before you would be feeling your arm jerked out of its socket. Perhaps just enough time to let go and avoid the crisis. Think about it.

Suppose the horse does something you don't like while you're leading him and you need to generate some animation to discipline the horse. Perhaps you just need to get his attention back on you after a brief lapse in his thinking. Try getting animated while you are tightly holding his halter or the clasp under it. You are in immediate contact with him and that begins to create a physical struggle at once. He pulls back, jerking you all over the place. You lose. On the other hand, suppose you are holding the line with a few feet of slack in it. You can flip the line up and down or back and forth and be very animated without the strong contact you really want to avoid. And a loose line can create a lot of animation with little effort on your part. Even more important is that by giving the horse a little freedom with the loose line it will *allow* him to back away from you when you get animated. Remember that one of the best ways to discipline a horse is to get him to back up. That demonstrates him yielding to you. Exactly what you want. If you get animated while holding a tight grip on him and he tries to back up, he is instantly in contact with you, which he can perceive as you saying *don't back up* after you just got animated telling him *to back up*. Contradictory signals. If you ask him to back up you have to *let him back up* when he tries.

There is also the possibility that the horse could be doing something more serious than just not paying attention and you need to really get after him to change his behavior, and fast. You may need to give him a physical shot to get him to realize you mean business. Now, so I don't get misunderstood about this, I will explain exactly what I mean here. You have heard me saying over and over I don't want to hit the horse. And I don't. But one of the fundamentals I discussed earlier was the idea of using a signal and animation to get a response from the horse. If very little signal or animation gets the horse to do as you wanted, then no additional effort would be needed.

244

If the horse did not respond as you wanted, you would escalate the animation until you got a response. You cannot accept no response. So if the horse does not respond to a little flip of the lead, then you will need to flip it a lot harder. You do a bit more and a bit more until he complies. Sometimes it will not be enough to just flip the line. If that is the case it is also indicating that you have not accomplished enough of an attitude change in the round pen or his attitude would be better and you would not be facing this situation in the first place. But at the moment you need to get the horse to respond and a quick trip into the pen

This time the handler walks off, not paying attention to her horse who is obviously not paying attention to her. *In a second the lead will get tight and things will get physical. She may win or she may lose. She would have been better off to stay focused and notice when she lost the horse's attention and get it back. Then move away. Make it mental, not physical! Photo by Susan Sexton.*

may not be an option now. You need to jerk the heck out of the horse and ring his bell in order to make your point.

With a loose lead you can give the horse a much harder jerk than you ever could from an initial position of tight contact. Try it. Have someone hold a line and you grab on right next to their hand and jerk real hard. Then hold the line three feet from their hand with the line very slack and draped. But before you jerk this time, make sure they have a glove on or are holding on with both hands. Now jerk again with the same amount of force you used before. The difference will be amazing to you. The point being, the tighter the contact you have on the horse the less you can really do. A loose line is a great deal more effective than a tight line. And safer to boot.

As you begin to practice leading your horse on a loose line, try to maintain the same attitude about getting him to follow you that you had before the line was on him. Try not to use the line but rather to use your movements to get him to follow. Remember to apply pressure by your bubble as you approach him or animation of the line. And when he responds, you must remember to release the pressure at once as the reward. Try standing by his head and simply backing up one step, expecting him to back up as you do. If he doesn't back up, he is not paying close enough attention or he is not respectful enough. Go back to the pen and work on attitude. You could also try the step back and if he doesn't comply add a little animation to enforce your request. You want it to be as if you and he were dancing and he was letting you lead. If two dancers tried to dance as they both tried to lead there would be no dancing, only a struggle. That's why the round pen is used to change his attitude and let you lead the dance. Now that you have his attitude where you need it, you can dance without the struggle. But dancing also involves a precise degree of communication. By you understanding how to communicate through body language, you can effectively "lead" the dance with your horse in a fashion he can understand. You can apply slight pressure to induce a response and then remove that pressure to reward his compliance. This is the basis for transition – using the same approach you used in the pen, but adapted to the real world outside the pen. Same approach, different techniques and tools.

Speaking of working outside the pen, let me share with you an idea for dealing with things that don't go as planned when you get outside the pen. Let me start by suggesting you consider three areas to work in and quantify the amount of control each area will offer you. The first area will be the round pen. You will have more control in the round pen than anywhere else. As a controlled environment, less can go wrong in the pen than anywhere else. This is your security blanket, so to speak.

The second area would be an arena, indoor or outdoor, but it will be much larger than the pen. It will probably offer more serious distractions and just because it's bigger, more can go wrong in it. The fence or walls offer some limitations, but not as safe as the pen.

The third area to work in is "out there." The real world. All those places that have no limits. Those places that have all the dangers and distractions that cause horses to get in trouble and test our ability to maintain control. This is where we want to ride. But it may not be the best place to start riding. I suggest you start in the round pen. I always start in the pen if at all possible. If everything is going well in the pen then proceed to area two. If all goes well there, then head out into area three. If at any time things start to fall apart, don't panic, just regress to the previous area, and regroup. Try again in a safer area. Work on things until you have the control you need, then proceed to the next area. I have seen this approach used by many and it offers a logical progression of difficulty with ways to adjust for problems. And there are always problems. Don't fear them; use them to learn and improve. But in order to do that, you must have some means to control the situations that give you trouble as they arise. Most people don't and that's why they get more afraid or get hurt.

For example, let's say you have a new horse and he's really full of himself. You play with him in the pen and he's doing very well. You attach his halter and lead him around the pen with no effort. Then you lead him out of the pen into the main arena and he begins to feel a bit distracted but is still OK. You should really focus on keeping his attention at this point and let this scenario tell you that he will probably be more distracted if you take him to a show or some big event. As the dynamics of the area increase, it is reasonable to anticipate a decrease in the level of control you have over him, based on the change you observed. You need to work with him in the pen and then in the arena until there is little or no difference between his responsiveness in each. And if the loss of control was dramatic upon leaving the pen, then you know you *really* need to do more in the pen before you try taking the horse somewhere exciting. Does that make sense?

Before we leave this "How To" chapter, I want to give you a few ideas on other uses for the round pen, especially relating to this three area approach. Let's suppose you have a horse that seems clumsy and trips a lot. I hear people complain about this often and it can make a rider become very uneasy on the horse. They say things like, "He trips over shadows." Assuming there is no serious physical problem, it is often a matter of the horse not paying attention to where his feet are. You can help him with this very simply. Put the horse in the pen and run him around a little, turning him and getting him to pay attention to you as usual. Then get a few cavalletti or simple fence boards and lay them around the pen like spokes of a wheel. Two or three are fine to start. Use no specific spacing, just put them out there. I know there are some very good books on uses of cavalletti and specific spacing, etc., but for this exercise, forget the books. How many inches apart is the log from the rock out on the trail? Who cares, they are all different. The purpose of this is to get the horse to know where his feet are at all times and develop the ability to adjust his stride for anything that comes along. It is not to develop any particular length of stride.

With the boards or cavalletti in place at no particular intervals, send the horse off as before but now he must jump or step over the obstacles as he goes around. He must also pay attention to you as he does it, since you are directing his movements. You can also reverse him at any time, adding another challenge to his ability to stay focused. As he goes over a cavalletti, you may reverse him right back over it again. He will bump into them at first, but soon he will start thinking and watching where he puts his feet. After a few minutes, stop and let him relax while you rearrange the cavalletti into a different pattern. Try again. You can continue the process by adding more

Use the horse, untied, in the round pen for problem solving. This mare took a vet, a ferrier and two helpers over three hours to shoe her before I got her. A war! It took about four hours of handling during one week to get her to trust me enough to do this with each foot. Her next shoeing took me and a ferrier an hour and five minutes for four shoes. And not even a struggle. Remember, untied! They need the freedom to move. Photo by Susan Sexton.

cavalletti or raising the cavalletti into small jumps, or turn them into X's or other odd shapes. You can replace the boards with a plastic tarp or a water box, or anything else you can think of that is different, yet safe. A few weeks of this and I've seen some dramatic changes in horses that were considered poor under saddle. It is true that some horses are far more coordinated than others. All you can do is give your horse the opportunities to, as the Army says, "Be all that he can be." He may surprise you. This is an excellent way to get a horse to begin jumping. By starting his jumping at liberty, he only has to deal with the jumping. When you start a horse jumping while the student is learning to jump at the same time, the horse has to deal with the jumps and the changing balance of the rider. Even a good rider is a weight liability to a beginning jumper, so I prefer to begin at liberty. Once the horse has a bit of experience jumping at liberty, then adding a rider to keep the horse collected and work on other specifics is a good plan. It does let the horse deal with things one step at a time, and I prefer that approach.

For a different but common problem, let's suppose you have a horse that's hard to shoe. You may ask what does that have to do with a round pen? Everything. The hard-to-shoe horse is either afraid, due to abuse, or just an example of a bad attitude that he's made work for himself all too often. Do you now see that you will need some leverage to deal with the situation? Most people would go back to trying to hold or tie the horse as a start. I disagree. I would start by turning the horse loose again, and taking all the pressure off. Start by putting the horse in the pen and going through the process. Once the horse is responsive and attentive, and coming up to you freely, you have the leverage needed to address the situation. Notice I didn't say "address the problem." The hard-to-shoe is not the problem, it is a situation. The problem is the attitude that allowed the situation in the first place. You addressed the problem already. Now you have the leverage you need to address the situation. To add one more point: if a really good horse had a terrible experience being shod, then the good horse may now be a butt to shoe. This situation is probably fear based, but you still need leverage to get a horse to deal with something he sees as fearful. Restraining or holding a fearful horse tends to exaggerate his fear and you want to diminish it. Fear creates a bigger bubble. You diminish the bubble (hence the fear) by applying and removing pressure to it.

Once the horse comes in and stands by you in the pen, you will touch the horse and walk around his body, touching him as you go. Circle him a few times in no particular pattern, until he's OK with it. Then ask him to give you a hoof. If he resists and perhaps even jerks it away and runs off, *SEND HIM OFF*. Remember, you can't stop him so don't waste time trying to do what you can't. Make his leaving your idea. Send him out of the herd he just tried to join. Then stop and wait

250

for him to return to you and then do nothing. Wait again. Let him relax and then gently ask for a different foot. Assume he has a bubble about you picking up the foot and approach the foot with the same approach and retreat we used to catch him in the first place. Let him do as much as he can, but if that is only a slight part of what you requested, you must reward that slight try as well. He may lift a hoof with great tension in his body, showing his concern. Take the hoof and then put it right back down before there is a problem. Give him a chance to succeed and build on that. Go slow and be patient. Also be consistent and be persistent. It may take a day or it may take a half hour over ten days. But you will prevail. How long do you work any one day? That will depend on how good your timing is. And how patient you are. If your timing is off, he'll get wired. If you go too fast, he'll get wired. If you go at a pace he is OK with, you could do this an hour or more and he'd be just fine at the end. His mental state *at the end of a lesson* will tell you if you were doing well. Try short sessions at first, but as you get better, the length of the sessions will matter less and less. This approach can be used to solve almost any problem, as long as you can facilitate a way to apply pressure to get a response and then release the pressure as needed.

Why is it important to do this in the pen? Because you will have more leverage with the horse in that environment than anywhere else. By simple association on the part of the horse, you will be safer and more effective in the pen. Use that advantage. Any time a problem arises, resort to the best environment you have available to solve that situation. And every time you help your horse through something that has troubled him, he will get braver and stronger. Your position in his mind will also get better as he associates you with his success. Your leverage to get him to do things will increase in direct proportion to his confidence in you. And as your mind gets more adept at using what you've learned, you will be able to solve bigger and bigger situations with less and less effort.

SECTION 3 – UNDER SADDLE

Finally, we get to the place where we are going to get on and ride. Most people just "get on" with little or no preparation, and both the horse and rider suffer for it. I hope to see that change. Riding a horse is fantastic, but most people have no idea how much fun a horse can be on the ground. You may find this surprising but at one point just after I got Shazi, a trainer suggested I could benefit from doing some ground-work with my horse. My reply was something to the effect of, "I have a dog to play with on the ground. I bought the horse to ride." Talk about "ignorance on fire." I was an inferno! But I didn't know what I didn't know, so my perspective was hurting my possibility. Make sense? Today I am not sure whether I prefer riding or doing liberty work. I think riding would still edge out as my favorite, but there are days I don't ride, and I have a ball with the horses on the ground. But the main point is that *I am a much more effective rider because of what I have learned on the ground.* And what I can *do on the ground* helps me have a better horse when I do get on.

It is not my intent to try to teach any *discipline* of riding in this book. There are many excellent instructors that have more expertise than I with individual types of riding. And they need to work with you in an ongoing fashion so as to coach you and polish both you and your horse into the best possible *team* that you can become. My goal with this book is to better prepare you mentally for riding by giving you a different mind-set about the process of riding. But before we get into that I do want to offer a couple of things for you to consider as you look for a riding instructor to work with. I say this as someone who has watched a lot of riding instructors with their students, and been impressed with both good and bad at what I saw.

When I was working as a corporate trainer and motivational speaker, my job was to do a class that would change people's behaviors and hence their performance in business. My value to the companies that hired me was determined by monitoring the *improvement in sales and other activities* of the people I worked with for 90-180 days *after I was there*. In other words I was paid based on the results I produced. Some riding instructors would starve given that system of earning. You should be getting better and better as the lessons go on. You should not be stagnate. If you are not progressing you may need another instructor. I've seen that a lot. But the instructor may be just fine and the trouble is really you. That's a hard pill to swallow but reality makes an honest guide. If you don't listen and you don't practice then don't blame the instructor. And there is another possible reason for a lack of improvement – the horse. Horses, like people, are unique and as diverse as any group on earth. If your horse has done all he is capable of and you want to do more, then it's not fair to him to keep going. Or, what I see all too often is when someone buys a horse, and they see a particular class in a show, they tell their instructor, "I want to win the so-and-so class on my horse Fluffy next summer." Well, you need to see if Fluffy is really suitable for that class, before you do anything. If Fluffy is a soft relaxed western horse and the class you like is a class for hot English horses, don't bother. Either do classes that the horse is suited for or change horses. Now some horses can do almost anything, even classes at opposite ends of the spectrum. If you are fortunate to have a horse like that, go for it. But you don't go to a tractor pull in a Corvette and you don't enter a sports car race in a four by four. Be fair to your horse. Be fair with your instructor. And be honest with yourself.

One of my pet peeves with riding instructors is screaming and ridiculing students. I am not talking about being loud to be heard, although even that should not be continual. If there is a lot going on, a bit of yelling may be appropriate to be heard. I am referring to people that harass and criticize students and then call themselves instructors. If you have to be yelled at continually, then you need an attitude adjustment or another hobby. Riding a horse while being yelled at does not do any good for the horse either. Remember my example of changing the word "wrong" to "troubling" as a way to improve the nature of a question? Instructors should be asking the right questions in the right way so as to empower the student, not belittle them. Often instructors who resort to these techniques are really insecure with their own abilities and should be avoided.

As your training progresses, be constantly aware of both you and your horse as to how you feel during lessons. It is normal to be nervous and even a bit tense in a lesson. That's OK. A good instructor will keep pushing you to bigger and better achievements. If cantering bothers you, then you need to canter some to get it better. Breathe, pay attention, and try. Don't worry about how you look, as most people always do, worry about what you're thinking. If you're thinking about paying attention and trying, you will look better and better. And one last thing on this topic, keep asking yourself, "Are we having fun?" Isn't that what this horse stuff is all about? And the "we" refers to you *and your horse*. If your horse is a mental wreck, then I don't like what you are doing. If you aren't enjoying the process of improving your riding (not that every lesson will be fun, they won't), then stop taking lessons and go trail riding or sell the horse or change whatever *is* the problem. Some people forget that *they* are paying the bill here. Money is power. If you aren't happy, take your money somewhere else. And since I mentioned money, add this to your list of things to remember – the most expensive instructors are not always the best. If you want to "win at all costs" then you probably want the most expensive instructor because they will go along with your philosophy. A good instructor will be honest with you and sometimes tell you things you don't want to hear. Like "this horse is not suitable for the class you want." That's the kind of instructor you want. Bottom line, have fun. If it stops being fun, something needs to change.

So what do we want to discuss here about using what we've done on the ground once we get on the horse. Well, most of what we need to do has already been accomplished; now we just need to focus it. As you began to play with your horse in the pen at liberty, you were forced to "let go" of him. Then you began to try to influence him from a position where you first thought you had no control. Next you began to understand what it takes to use soft pressure to really influence his attitude, and you got to see how soft and responsive he could become in return. You grew more effective at "reading" the horse's communication to you so as to understand *his* perspective and allow you to adapt your behavior to his needs. Hopefully you got quieter and more relaxed around him as you began to see him become more submissive and responsive to you. And you found out that the equipment is not the savior you thought it was, but more of a crutch that got in the way. Now you're ready to get on.

When you first get on, I think it should be in the pen. Area of most control, remember? As you start to get on, what is the horse doing? Remember, watch the horse. If he gets bothered and real tense, maybe this is not the right time to get on. More important, *why is he getting bothered*? Him getting bothered is his way of telling you he has a bubble about what you're doing. Pay attention to it. You would break down the bubble by applying and then releasing pressure. Let's take a specific example.

Suppose as you step up in the saddle, the horse walks off. This is not uncommon but I consider it a behavior needing change. When he walked off without you asking him, what was he paying attention to? Not you. But it should be you, shouldn't it? So let's discuss a technique to get the horse's attention back on you at the same time we remind him we can still take control of him if needed. In the pen on the ground we did that by sending him off; making him move. That brought his attention back on you and got him to yield to your signal. Now that we are going to be on him we need a bit of a different approach, *but the fundamentals are the same*. But as usual, there is a little understanding needed to precede our actually doing anything with the horse.

We mentioned earlier that for you to get in trouble around a horse he has to move his feet. All of the things we *don't want a horse to do* relate to moving his feet; bucking, rearing, striking, kicking, running away with you, stepping on you, slamming you against the stall wall, etc. The list goes on and on, but you get the point. Control the feet, you control the horse. There is a basic technique that goes right to the heart of the horse's movement and will let you take control in most situations under saddle. It's called a one-rein stop. Our first example is a horse walking off with you as you mount. Not real dangerous, but not desirable either. The one-rein stop will solve that. Suppose our situation was the horse going into a trot when all we wanted was a walk? Use the one-rein stop. Suppose the horse was running away with you? Use the one-rein stop. This is the tool I used to control Sunny after we did the round pen work, and it can solve a myriad of other situations as well. It combines two movements that take the horse "out of gear," so to speak. The power of the horse comes from his rear end, and yet one simple position change can disable the horse incredibly. That position is when one back leg steps through and across in front of the other back leg. It's called "disengaging the hind quarters." Once he has a back leg crossed over he can't kick. He can't rear. He can't buck. He can't strike. He can't run off with you. He has only one option open; step on over and *uncross the legs*. The most important aspect of this action is that *HE KNOWS HE'S OUT OF GEAR TOO.*

The one-rein stop is done by first turning the horse's head to one side by pulling on the rein. One rein, not both, hence the name, one-rein stop. As his head comes around, you will apply a pressure to his flank, which will cause him to disengage his hind-quarters and step across with his back end. He has just lost control to you and he knows it. It can stop the runaway, but you can't use it on a runaway unless he has already learned it. Remember when Sunny ran away with me in the first clinic I did? And the clinician was yelling for me to "do a one-rein stop, pull his head around!" Well, his idea was good but it often doesn't work well if the first application is done in a real serious situation. It needs to be applied to the horse in various lev-

256

els beginning at a standstill, not a gallop. Disengaging the hind-quarters is the most underestimated tool in the horse world.

As you step up on the side of the horse, standing in one stirrup only, if the horse walks off you will apply the one-rein stop from there. You will hang on to the saddle, maybe even lean over it a bit for security, and if you are on the horse's left use your left hand to pull the horse's head around to the left. At the same time, touch his flank with your toe and get him to disengage his hind-quarters to his right. He will now be in a tight circle or spin to his left. Most horses do this in a slow, awkward fashion but some can actually spin quite quickly, so be prepared and hang on. You do not need to keep touching his flank once he starts to turn, but you will keep his head around until he stops moving on his own. When he stops and yields to you, pause a second and then release his head. He will then either walk off again or he'll stand still. If he walks off, repeat the process. If he stands nicely, just stay there on the side of the saddle and wait. Remember, just as on the ground, you do something and then wait to see what the horse does in order to decide what you need to do next; always giving him time to figure out what you want. Repeat this process over and over until you can step up in a stirrup and he doesn't move. It usually doesn't take long unless the horse had been a long time runaway like Sunny. Sunny took awhile. Most horses learn this quickly. Repeat this from the other side.

Once you can step up on a stirrup and he doesn't leave, then swing your leg over and into the saddle. He should stand still. If he walks off, pick up one rein and turn his head to the side as you put your heel into his flank and disengage his hind-quarters. It usually doesn't take a lot, so don't jerk the heck out of his head with the rein nor kick the heck out of him with your heel. Just do it firmly and with intent but without anger or malice. Only now you have a new option to you. Now that you are on the horse you can turn him either way. Left this time, then right. No pattern, and change direction often. He won't know which side will be next. It will force him to pay attention to you. (There's that phrase again – Pay attention.) How nice would it be to be able to get on your horse and have him stand still until you wanted to go? Yes, even Arabs and Thoroughbreds. Most people can't get their horse to stand well at all because they are always doing something on the horse and never let the horse understand that it's OK to just stand still. This took a long time with Sunny and even today he still reverts back once in awhile. But he's a lot more fun today the way he is now than when I adapted to getting on a moving horse.

So now you're on, sitting still and the horse is not going anywhere. Stay still for several minutes. He should not leave until you ask for it. If he does walk off, use the one-rein stop and remind him. (Don't try to get him to be still for ten minutes the first day, it may be too much to ask. Work up to it gradually. It took several days before Sunny stood for one minute. At that time it felt like an hour on him and I was ecstatic.) After he stands still for a few minutes, you are ready to ask him to walk off. All you want is a walk. If he goes into a trot or canter, use the one-rein stop and turn him in the circle. Alternate sides as before. Once he stops, release him and wait to let him digest what you just did. Then try it again. Walk. Do this in both directions of the pen. Once he walks only, then ask for the trot. Again, you want a trot, nothing else. Any change on his part causes a one-rein stop. You will notice he is getting more and more responsive to you as this goes on. It will take less and less effort on your part to get him turning. And by the time you have done this standing to mount, and then sitting on the horse, then at the walk, then at the trot, he will have learned the message. Pay attention and you can control him under saddle. And by the time you get to canter or gallop, he will know it and respond to it. And whenever he tests you under saddle, you will take control back by using this technique. That's why Sunny has not run away with me since that first ride with the halter in the mountains of Colorado. He has tried. He has gotten excited and gone faster than I wanted. But I was always able to get him slowed down, without depending on the bit or anything else.

Riding should be fun. It should be like dancing, not like wrestling. You will find that the more you *do* to control your horse, the more you will *have to do*. As I said about controlling the horse at liberty, do as much as you need to get the response, but as little as possible. If it took two pounds of pressure on a rein today, you should try one pound tomorrow. And your goal should be to get it done with an ounce or two. And as with the ground work, the pressure is not what matters, it is the release of the pressure that teaches the horse. The reason so many horses are so hard mouthed, so to speak, is because they were never given a proper release as a reward. The rider pulled and they learned to pull back – the exact opposite of what all this is about. Everything we discussed about liberty work and using pressure and its release will apply directly to everything you do under saddle to control the horse. If you feel constant pressure on a lead line on the ground, *you* made a mistake. If you feel constant pressure on a rein while riding *you* made a mistake. Now there is one qualifier for that last statement and it needs explaining.

Most people ride with way too much contact on the horse's mouth. How can I prove that? Easy. Some people ride their horse with nothing on his head, no bridle or halter, which equals *no contact*. If they can do it, then it's been done and is doable. To be more specific, when I rode Sunny at first, I held on tight to keep control. What did he do? He ran away with me all the time. So I *proved* that wasn't working, didn't I? When I rode him in a halter with a loose rein, i.e., no constant contact, he became responsive and stopped running away with me. The riding with a loose rein was the second step in the process of gaining control – the first step having been to change his attitude to be submissive *before* I got back on. With a scared rider on top of a powerful horse, to say you have more control if you let go of him is not going to make any sense. And the scared rider should not be on the horse yet anyway. But the point is, you start with the attitude and then worry about the reins. Then you will need less rein, leg, spur or any other aid to control the horse. And any aid (we could substitute the words signal or cue or *communication*) will get results without being a struggle. You will lead a soft responsive horse and you will ride a soft responsive horse. You will practice doing less and less to get more and more. If you listen intently when I speak, I could communicate with a whisper. If I shouted all the time, you would learn to ignore me and I'd have trouble even getting your attention. Too many of us are continually shouting at our horses with our signals and we wonder why they aren't listening. Constant contact is the same as shouting.

Several points are important here. We need something to signal or communicate with the horse while on his back, and the reins seem to be the best tool we've found. Pulling on the reins is necessary but the pulling is not what matters; it is the release of the pull that matters. Due to a horse's natural sensitivity, you can *decrease* the amount you have to pull by being very specific with the *timing* of your release. Release at the earliest possible instant of response and the horse will learn faster. Your goal should be to be so careful about your release that the horse begins to require less and less pull to create a meaningful signal. As you use your reins to signal or communicate, simultaneously add a word command and seat or leg cues to install those in the horse's repertoire of commands. Leg and seat may be taught without reins in many situations; but for most people I have worked with, this approach is reasonable, safe and understandable. Remember that the horse will associate your words with whatever is going on as you say them. If every time he gets scared he hears you say "Easy boy, easy boy," he will learn to be afraid as he hears "Easy boy."

We get horses to ride. And then we ride them for a purpose. And usually that purpose requires us to be able to communicate certain things to the horse and get specific responses. Whether that purpose is dressage, jumping, barrel racing, showing or any other activity, it can all be boiled down to the process listed above. Understand your horse, learn to communicate with him, gain his respect by becoming his alpha, and *THEN*

GET ON AND RIDE. You will not be able to ride the same after you have learned the other first, because you will better understand him and he will better understand you. And that will help take the struggle out of your riding. With most horses the change will be dramatic. Horses with more long-term problems or baggage will take longer, but the result will be even more dramatic. Extremely stubborn horses like Sunny, or desperately insecure horses like Kasty may require ongoing effort with even greater levels of consistency. But you will see the results and enjoy the process as well. If you are taking lessons for your purpose, they will make more sense and you will implement new ideas faster and easier using what was outlined above. And you will have fun with your horse, which is really all that matters about riding.

CHAPTER 9

The Physical Horse

I must begin this chapter by telling you that I am not a veterinarian, nor a medical doctor of any sort. I do work with a lot of horses with physical problems of various kinds using a BioScan, which I will explain shortly. What I am going to tell you in this chapter is based on my experience and the experience of others I have learned from. The knowledge we all depend on daily is the combination of what we have studied and the experiences we have lived. Each can be a quality teacher. Many people have little formal education, yet possess great capabilities due to years of experience. Many people have achieved the uppermost levels of educational study, and draw their abilities from that arena. Yet, in either situation, the most powerful advantage anyone can possess is that of having an open mind. As I have repeatedly stated throughout this book, if we are willing to accept what is *normal* as being optimum, we doom ourselves to a very limited existence. I am so very fortunate to have been associated with some of the finest horse people around and been allowed to experience their many different perspectives. This is not going to be a technical, medical discussion, but a natural look at the reality of the physical problems we all face with our horses; as well as ways to understand the causes, relationships and solutions to some of those problems.

Since many of the ideas I will share with you may seem different, I need to explain what the BioScan is and how it works. This is not meant to be a commercial for BioScan, as much as it is a way for you to understand how I arrived at some of the conclusions I have made. Much of what I am about to share is less the result of any great wisdom on my part as it is the result of me having access to an incredible tool, as yet unavailable to many. I will tell you right up front that I have been using the BioScan for six years now, with great success and I believe in its abilities without question. I have used it on over 2200 horses, and the results speak for themselves. But for now I would like you to understand the reality of what BioScan can and cannot do.

BioScan is a two-part system. The first part is a device called a BioFind that allows me to go over the body of the horse externally and determine any place there is some abnormality present. It uses principles found in the same physiology that allows us to feel pain when we are injured, yet translates that into an audible signal to alert us to problems in various areas of the horse. It is quite specific and quite accurate. If you stop to consider how often you can have several people, even trained veterinarians, studying a horse and offering totally different opinions on what they see as the problem, you will understand the value of something that is less dependent on interpretation. If three BioScan people go over a horse, they will find basically the same results because they are getting a measured response from the tissue. They are not having to interpret to help the horse, although the BioFind can be used to interpret in many situations. This lack of the need to interpret anything is why the BioScan can be so effective in the hands of an individual without medical training. And in the hands of a good veterinarian it, can be an incredible tool.

Another aspect to using the BioScan is the fact that we train people to scan the *entire horse* regardless of the *apparent trouble.* Let me explain further. When your horse displays a problem, let's say, a front leg lameness, that lameness is often *not the problem* but rather the *result of other problems* in the horse. Of the 2200 horses I have scanned there were virtually *none of them* that had only one problem. Horses by their very nature as prey animals need to keep going. In the wild, if they can't go with the herd, they know they are vulnerable. They will keep going as best they can even when they're hurt or injured. They will *compensate* to incredible lengths to keep going at all costs. Their survival depends on their ability to move. To think that your domestic horse is any different is a serious mistake. When we scan a horse, every time the scanner goes off we put a mark on the horse with a water crayon to document the location of each problem. By the time we finish, there are marks all over the horse that draw muscles, outline joints or skeletal problems, indicate acupuncture points relating to internal problems, etc. The list goes on. But what this visual display offers is a very accurate method of *understanding* what's going on in this horse in its *totality* rather than a more limited perspective. It may not be just the individual problems you see but the relationship of numerous problems that provides the greatest insights. On so many occasions after I scanned a horse, the trainer has become excited, saying things like, "I knew there was something wrong with that shoulder but we could never find it. I knew it. I knew it."

It is very common for people to say things like, "Tell me where the problem is. Is it the hock or the stifle or the hip?" Remember how I kept saying be careful what question you ask because it affects the answer? Asking to find *the problem* sets you up to consider the *first problem* that is discovered to be the cause. Which means once you find *a problem* you stop looking. How do you know that the horse does not have a hock *and* a stifle problem? In fact if a perfectly healthy horse got kicked in the hock (and you saw it happen so you *KNOW* it is in the hock) within two to three day1s he could develop a stifle problem on the opposite side, simply because of the way a horse will compensate. Now he has two problems from one situation. If the two problems are not solved, the rear end will get worse until there is compensation to the front end, causing soreness and problems there as well. Now there are three problems. And on and on. I have worked with so many horses in this situation it is incredible. This caused that and then that caused something else over here, and now the poor horse is a wreck. But he's still trying. You or I would have probably just given up and said, "The heck with it. I quit."

The above scenario of multiple problems is the main reason why it is so often difficult to pinpoint problems from a conventional external evaluation. The two or three people watching the horse and coming up with different opinions are often seeing different things that are really there. Each responds to what he or she sees. Or, the combination of several problems can create a movement in the horse that may seem to indicate something else altogether. In the past six years I have worked with some of the best veterinarians and trainers around, and I try to learn from them all. I have watched them study a horse's movement in order to assess the condition of the horse, and it often amazes me that they are so good at it. Some vets are almost psychic in that ability. But it's not easy and it's also not an exact science. You might think I would be pretty good at watching a horse move and tell you what's wrong, after all the people and horses I've worked with. But I'm not. Like anyone else, if it's obvious I'm great, but often I just don't know. A few weeks ago I was with some very good people working with some very expensive horses and everyone was watching this particular horse trot out to determine the nature of the lameness. Everyone had an opinion, mostly differing in nature. I was silent until a rather cynical veterinarian that I didn't know turned to me and said, "You're the hot-shot from out of town here, so what do you think?" Several of the other people whom I knew laughed, waiting for some snappy comeback from me. As I looked at the vet I had a realization that surprised even me. As I said to him, "I haven't a clue from watching the horse," it dawned on me *WHY* I never got very good at this. I continued, "I'm not too good at this because it's never been important to me. I don't have to try to guess at what is going on by observing because I'm so used to having the BioScan and it tells me exactly what's going on without the speculation." If you inject the hock when the horse has a stifle problem, you are not only not addressing the issue, but you may be starting a whole new issue. And you may not need to have done the injection anyway.

265

Once I scan a horse and mark each problem that shows up today, I then go back over the horse and use a *light therapy* on each area that I marked. That may seem totally foreign to many of you, as it did to me six years ago. Let me explain further. I will use two specific wavelengths of light (around 660nm red and around 880nm infrared) to stimulate those areas of the body. And for you to understand this we first need to talk a bit about healing in general. Healing is an internal process. By that I mean, when you cut your finger, it grows back together. If you bruise your arm, it heals as well. Your body – and the body of all other animals such as horses – heals using complex systems that we are only beginning to understand. When I say we, I am referring to human doctors and scientists, not myself. I understand the basics because some very learned people put the complexities into simple concepts I could grasp. Think of it this way; healing is a bio-chemical change in the body. Something goes wrong and the body initiates action to correct the problem. Sometimes it works better than others. Doctors can help the process along and facilitate great changes, but it is the body that actually heals.

It was considered many years ago that light could have healing properties for living tissue. In the past forty to fifty years great strides have been made in understanding how this works, but suffice it to say that it has been scientifically shown that certain wavelengths of light (red and infrared) can produce physiological changes in living tissue. Those changes will vary depending on the type of tissue involved and the nature of the problem present. Healing is also considered a pro-active condition, meaning it requires the expenditure of energy to generate the changes we call healing. You may be dormant as your body heals, but your body is *very active* when healing. Remember your mom saying, "Eat your soup to keep up your strength," when you were sick? That was to provide fuel for the body to heal. When you use a light source on a living tissue, that light energy can be absorbed directly into the tissue and not only stimulate the healing responses, but provide energy at a cellular level to help things progress more quickly. The first time I heard this discussed my response was, "Yea, right." Now six years later, I often see the same look of "yea right" in someone's eyes as I explain it to them. The difference for me is what I've seen and learned in the six years; what using light therapy on 2200 horses, numerous dogs and especially myself has taught me. I did not come into this BioScan work with an open mind. Perhaps the biggest advantage I have achieved in six years of work is allowing myself to become more open-minded – never to ignore honest skepticism, but never to let that skepticism prevent education or progress.

During those six years I have worked on million-dollar horses and back yard ponies. I have worked on horses suffering from colic to bowed tendons, and from some mysterious lameness to a simple lack of performance at their given task. In many cases I was the last resort after many dollars and many tears had produced little benefit. People grasping at straws will try anything. Sometimes my BioScan was the last act of a desperate horse lover trying to help their animal. I never cared about any of that. I only cared about being able to help. In many cases the results were "Oh my God" dramatic. Often they were far more subtle, but still of great importance. And to a few horses that were out of options, the BioScan was a life or death chance. Whether it was a horse going to the National Championships or just a horse that was lame, to the owner it was very important. It's always important when it's *your horse*.

A few more points to make before we move on. First, light as a therapy is non-drug and non-invasive. *I am not against the use of drugs*. But I am very much against *any unnecessary use of drugs*. In short, if you can solve a problem without a drug, why use the drug? Next, one of the reasons light is often so fast acting and so effective is because we use it very *specifically*. By that I mean we use the light on the very location that the scanner indicated a problem. *Nowhere else.* How often does a drug or other therapy travel throughout the entire body to treat a single specific location? Treating specifically focuses the body's resources on the problem only, hence the response is often so much quicker. And lastly, I have been training people to use the BioScan for years now. I have trained veterinarians but mostly ordinary people like you and me. BioScan can never replace a good veterinarian, but it can open doors to the horse owner and to vets that were before unavailable. And much of what it has provided me has helped me develop the understanding of the physical horse and his problems that I am about to share with you.

There are several common problem areas that I want to discuss and we'll start with the feet. The horse's hooves are his base for all his movements. The importance of correct shoeing is talked about, but few of us really pay enough attention to it because of our perspective or misunderstanding. Did you ever get a pebble in your shoe? Of course. Did it bother you? Of course. And when you finally got to a place where you could stop and take it out, how big was it? Pretty tiny, right? That tiny little pebble had been bugging the devil out of you and now you see it and it's so tiny. Well think about what you did to *compensate* for that pebble being there. If it was on the outer edge of your shoe, did you turn your foot to the inside and try to keep the pressure off of that area? Of course. When you turn your foot in, what happens to your ankle? And your knee? Suppose you had to walk that unnatural way for a while. Could your ankle get sore? Then would you expand the compensation to protect the foot and the ankle? Of course. If the problem persisted, could the abnormal way you are now moving continue to escalate the problem to other areas of your body, such as lower back, hips and even your neck? Bet on it. All because of a pebble. Remember the old story about "for the loss of a nail... the loss of a shoe... the loss of a horse... the loss of the war"? It is true today but more in physical problems than wars.

How long do you think it would it take for you to make some other part of your body (besides your foot) sore from the pebble changing how you walk? How long does your horse go between farrier visits? Good point, but it is not just the pebble that can be the problem. The *angles* at which the hoof is trimmed is critical. Many of you know that but do you understand that the side to side angles (inside of the hoof high or low and outside of the hoof high or low) are just as important as the front to rear angles (toe too long or short and heel too long or short)? In the above pebble problem, you would lean your foot off the pebble, which would overload the other side of the foot and change the natural alignment of the entire leg going all the way up into the shoulder or hip. Which means a poor shoeing job can cause problems in areas far removed from the foot. And how would you tell?

The front-to-rear angle of the hoof can affect the alignment of the legs, but due to the fore and aft movement of the legs, the shape of the hoof (such as length of toe) changes the point at which the hoof "breaks over" and leaves the ground. This can affect the length of stride and the timing of the stride as to front-to-rear overlap. When you hear your horse's rear feet hitting his front feet, check the hoof angles. And also of great importance, the front-to-rear angles can overly stress the suspension system of the legs, the tendons. Low heels can cause major tendon failures from undue stress. The more severe the angle problem the sooner trouble can occur.

It is not my intent to teach anyone about correct farrier work; you can do volumes on just that topic. I would like you to understand the importance of correct feet and have a little awareness of what needs to be considered. The feet are the foundation of your horse. You know how sore feet can bother you, and you probably don't have to run around carrying someone on your back. And don't let someone tell you that since his feet aren't sore the shoeing is OK. Poor shoeing can create problems all over the horse. One last thing. For those of you that don't shoe your horses, think of this. For fifty million years who shod the horses? No one. If you ever get to see a slow motion film of the side view of a running horse and how the hoof hits the ground, you would see a great deal of flex in the hoof during the impact. That flexing of the hoof is the initial phase of shock absorption in the anatomy of the horse. Not unlike you running in Reeboks. The running shoe takes up the initial shock. Running in cowboy boots is a lot less comfortable. The greater the distance, the worse the problem. When we put a steel shoe on the hoof we constrict that flexing and eliminate the natural initial shock absorption. That additional concussion must now be absorbed by the rest of the suspension system throughout the leg. I'm not telling you to run your horses barefoot. (Many of you could, with additional considerations thrown in.) What I am suggesting is that if you don't use shoes, you do need consistent and correct trimming to protect the proper angles.

Why can't you run your horses barefoot? Primarily because of a lack of toughness. In nature, horses cover ground from day one after birth. Wild horses roam over vast areas, but mostly walking. Lots of walking. This continual movement tends to "trim" the feet to the natural angles needed in an ongoing fashion. It also tends to toughen the hooves a lot. A horse with weak hooves could break a hoof, go lame and die. He would not pass his weak feet on to future generations. Today that horse would survive and pass on a negative trait – weak hooves. The more confined the horse, the more the need for shoes. The more area the horse covers daily, the less the need for shoeing. Many folks disagree, but fifty million years of survival is a strong argument. And by the way, many of those horses lived in rough rocky areas, so don't say it's dependent on soft terrain. Our horse today is not as tough as his ancestors, so we must take better care of him. And breeding great big horses with tiny little feet to achieve some desired look is cruel and debilitating to the horse. Barefoot or shod, the angles *MUST BE CORRECT*. Neglecting your horse's feet is pure cruelty.

Any discussion of the physical horse must discuss saddles. Go into any tack shop and you will see so many different saddles in both style and function that it's incredible. Unfortunately, the importance of the saddle is often taken too much for granted. And the ramifications of that indifference can be grave for the horse and you. We all talk about saddle fit, but do we understand it and the problems it creates? I see a lot of misunderstanding about it. For example, does a poor fitting saddle cause a sore back? It might, but it *might not*. So to assume the saddle is OK since the back isn't sore is inaccurate. Why? Go back to the pebble in the shoe. You will adjust your movement to avoid the pain caused by the pebble. Where will that make you sore? We don't know, but as we discussed, it could be a lot of places *besides the foot*. Let's say that a particular saddle doesn't fit well and pinches the horse's back on one side a bit. The horse will flex his back to avoid that pain. It may not cause his back to be sore, but *it will affect the alignment of his body as he travels.* The head and neck is the primary balance tool of the horse, and anything that inhibits the ability of the horse to freely use his head and neck will limit his ability to perform. Let the horse move for any length of time with a poor fitting saddle, forcing him to alter his natural pattern of movement and he will develop neck problems. Once his neck starts to get sore and he further alters his natural pattern of movement to compensate for that trouble, other parts of his body will become sore as well.

If he were able to flex his back avoiding the saddle problem and not affect his neck, it could affect his hips, or lumbar region. Ever experience any lumbar pain? Really hurts, doesn't it? Could that cause him to stiffen his movement? Bet on it. If the rear gets really sore, he'll begin compensating to the front and it will get sore as well. And the effects on his alignment may begin to show. Where we are vertical in our alignment (spine running top to bottom) the horse is linear (spine running front to rear). As you ride your horse you see him pulling a bit to the left with his head carried off to that side. Remember the part about "a horse never does something for nothing, he only does something for something"? You see him tilted a bit left so you pull the reins to straighten him back up. As you "straighten him back up" you are causing him to further unbalance himself, since he was off to the left to protect himself from the pain he feels. He reduced the pain by carrying his head to the left and you force his head back to the right. He's straight, but he hurts more that way. The problems escalate.

And sometimes it's our own ego that contributes to the problem. In many disciplines of riding, people can win saddles at big events. Often the saddle is engraved with the event name and date. And too often if someone wins a saddle that proclaims their victory, *they are going to ride in that saddle.* If it doesn't fit, then just add another pad or two. Or three, or four. Don't laugh. I've seen it all too often. Think of it this way. If you went into a shoe store and closed your eyes, walked over to a shelf and picked up a pair of shoes without even seeing them, what are the odds that they would fit your feet? Slim to none, right? Same odds that winning a saddle will get you a saddle you can use on *your horse.*

But you really like it and it's really pretty, so on go three or four pads and blankets. That will make it OK, right? Suppose you wear a size six boot and the pair you picked up with your eyes closed in the store are nines. You love them, but the store only has nines. You'd buy them anyway and just wear four pairs of socks, right? I doubt it. But consider this: when you use three or four pads, the saddle is way off the horse and will tend to slide around a lot, wouldn't it? The solution to that, crank the girth really tight. Now the extra pads are spreading your legs too wide, decreasing your ability to feel the horse and him feel you, your center of gravity is too high, and the saddle hurts the horse and the too-tight girth is causing additional discomfort. Because he's so uncomfortable, he starts to carry his head too high. You can't have that so you add a tie-down to hold his head where you want it. Now he can't put his head where he wants and he ends up carrying it to the left. You crank it back to the right, and maybe add a more severe bit to keep it there. He now has a very unnatural curve to his neck so he is having trouble balancing himself very well. One shoulder has become very sore so one lead is hard to get, much less keep. His hips are carrying too much of his weight so his canter has deteriorated and his collection is weak.

At this point he is showing a lot of resistance so you go to a more severe bit and add a chain on the tie-down. The horse is getting to be a real handful to ride or even handle and his performance is way down. Everything is becoming a struggle and you are considering selling the horse. He really has a bad attitude. *Where did the attitude come from?* From pain. It could have started from a poor fitting saddle or a poor shoeing job or a fall, or a kick, or overwork, or dozens of other possibilities or combinations of them all. But it did come from something, it was not just a sudden desire on the part of the horse to become a butt-head. You may think the scenario outlined above is far fetched, but I'm here to tell you it is all too common. And even in a more subtle degree it is cruel to the horse. We are too quick to blame the horse rather than to understand the horse. Finding physical problems and pinpointing their locations are critical to a fair evaluation of any horse's performance. Often when I am asked to work with a horse with a really resistant attitude, I will BioScan him first. And I usually find some problems. In fact, a horse that's very fit but has an attitude will often develop physical problems as a result of the struggles he incurs with people over his attitude. It goes both ways. If the horse has some physical problems, I want to address them first, before I do any training. If I find no physical problems, then I *KNOW* I am dealing with an attitude. I consider it unfair to try to re-train a horse that has an attitude due to pain. We must first address the pain issue.

Before we leave saddles, I want to dispel another myth or two. "A small saddle puts too much pressure on the back and is not good." Wrong. I ride in a dressage saddle and use a single half-inch thick synthetic pad. The saddles fit the horses and no back problems occur. (Note I said *saddles* and *horses,* not *saddle* and *horses.* I have three horses and two of them can use the same saddle. The third cannot. Her back is very different. Economics is not an excuse for hurting a horse by using one saddle on several horses. If you can't afford a saddle for each horse, if needed, then you need fewer horses.) Remember I am riding hundreds of miles over rough terrain, not a dozen laps around an arena. Most endurance saddles are not very large. In fact a long saddle may cause the horse discomfort if the lower corners overlap the shoulders or hips and impair movement there. This is often true in Arabs with western saddles, but can occur on any smaller horse: quarter horses, Morgans, Pasos, etc.

How about "A western saddle puts your feet too far forward and limits riding position." I hear this a lot from English riders. Also untrue. There are western saddles that are garbage and there are western saddles that are flawless. This country was built on western saddles. If you watch a good rider in a good western saddle, his body position is just right. And he can do the same dressage movements that any dressage rider can do. I've seen Ray Hunt, Buck Branaman, Pat Parelli, Dave Seay and many more do incredible things on horseback in western saddles. Western riders tend to *do* a lot on their horses (such as working cattle) that requires skill and communication at the top level of horsemanship. I recently obtained a video series done in the late forties and fifties by Monty Foreman, a brilliant horseman. It was transferred from film to video and is a bit rough by today's standards for video. His discussion of saddles and rider position are as on target as anyone I've seen today. I learned things watching a fifty-year old western tape.

To choose a saddle you need to consider three things: 1) does it fit my horse, 2) does it fit my body and position me where I need to be, and 3) does it look good. In *that* order of importance. Many people apply the order backwards and it costs them greatly. If you see discoloring of the hair under the saddle area or chaffing at the girth, then that is a dead give-away of a problem there. But because you don't see any of that, do not assume the saddle is OK. If in doubt get competent help. But finding *competent help* can be a whole other issue in and of itself, can't it?

While we are talking about saddles, let's talk about the other equipment people use on horses, starting with bits. Throughout this book you have heard me make numerous comments about the failure of certain bits to stop Sunny during his runaway period. And I now ride him in a snaffle bit or halter with no bit. I am *NOT SAYING I AM AGAINST USING BITS*. The bit is an excellent communication tool for directing a horse. It is not for hurting a horse into submission. There are so many different designs of bits that I can't name even a small percentage. Some are very good and some are just plain cruel. But the bit is of little importance compared to the knowledge directing the hands on the end of the reins. The same can be said of spurs, crops and most other equipment. I would ask you to stop and evaluate any piece of equipment you are intending to use on a horse to see if it involves pain or communication. Slight pressure, even to the point of some discomfort, is not excessive nor abusive to a horse, providing the timing of the release of that pressure is done correctly. And fundamentally, using pain on a horse will create a resistance that produces physical stress and problems in that horse. This will impair performance and lead to additional physical trouble. Use equipment wisely, not with indifference.

Since we are talking about physical problems and injuries, we need to discuss the definition of training, conditioning, rest and therapy. These terms are bounced around so much that I think a little clarification is in order. Training relates to teaching something to the horse, such as an activity or movement or skill. It is mental. Conditioning is getting the horse to be stronger and more fit to perform the activity. It's physical. Rest allows the horse to regenerate his energy and overall body condition to his "ready to go" state. Rest has both physical and mental benefits. Therapy is to actively *do* something to the horse to repair a problem or injury. This also has both physical and mental benefits.

You start *training* a barrel racing horse by walking the pattern hundreds and hundreds of times so he gets the pattern in his head. Then you trot it a few hundred times. And only after the mental process of training is started do you begin *conditioning*. Now the physical work starts. Ignore this sequence and you'll get horses that bolt and run with speed that is not manageable. Less control. Less efficiency. Less success. And between all the training and conditioning there must be adequate *rest*. Not enough rest creates chronic fatigue. Fatigue causes mental and physical stress. Physical stress causes breakdowns of anatomical structures, starting with simple sore muscles, and escalating into more serious problems. Mental stress causes tightness and less natural movements. Increasing breakdowns. The horse begins to perform poorly. Since you can't find a specific problem, you decide on the magic cure-all, rest. Better late than never, but rest alone is often not enough to remedy serious physical problems. You give the horse thirty days off and he looks better, so it's back to work. Question: how much of the improvement is due to his healing and how much is due to his getting used to the problem and adjusting? Both are occurring, but evaluating the results is difficult at best.

Therapy requires a couple of factors that we often don't have, which then eliminates or negates the use of therapy. First you have to recognize that there is a problem. Then you have to *know* what and where it or *they* are. Remember, injecting the hock for a stifle problem is not good. Also, do you select a therapy for its optimum results or its short-term gain? "Doc, we need the horse to race this Friday. Can't you just give him a shot or something?" Lots of compassion there. And don't be too quick to blame the veterinarian. If the trainer wants the shot and the vet says no, he'll just call another vet. Veterinarians have bills to pay like everyone else. They work long hours and most are not rich. And they have to deal with difficult decisions day in and day out. The problem is not the vet; it's the attitude of the trainer.

Now to where all this overlaps gets a bit more interesting. Training is an ongoing process, but once a horse learns something, it takes much less effort to keep him sharp. The more technical the skill the more effort needed. A race-horse needs less work than say a dressage horse to stay *mentally* sharp for his sport. Conditioning is critical for both. So is rest and when problems arise, so is therapy. Follow this: I was recently working on a top-level thoroughbred race-horse a few weeks before a major stakes race. A multi-million dollar horse getting ready for a big money race. The horse had been racing for a year or more and was physically a wreck. The trainer had a specific training schedule that he didn't want to change. Many trainers are very inflexible. I suggested the horse needed to be "not worked for a week or so," BioScanned every day, treated at least twice a day and walked a lot. I was met with great resistance. "He needs to be in training. The race is in two weeks," they said. I asked, "How's he doing in training?" "Not worth a damn," was the reply "Doesn't he know how to walk in the gate and run around a circle? He has won a few big races you said." "Yea he has, but he needs to be in training to win," came back again. I was getting frustrated. "Injury does more to impair performance than a slight decrease in training. He can't do well if he's hurting. He's not training well if he's hurting. He needs to heal to win. He can't heal if he never gets time off *and* therapy. A fit, strong horse does not lose his condition in a few days or weeks. It takes much longer than that to deteriorate. He does not need training, and he does not need conditioning. He needs to heal and get healthy. And he's also mentally stressed and that is taking a toll as well. A lot of walking will get him stretching his legs and relieving his stall stress too. But it's your call." The owner had been listening and there was a conference held moments later. The horse had done poorly in his previous three races. Result? He didn't get worked for a week and was walked and scanned as suggested. He was second by a nose in the race. Far better than the odds makers had put him. Training schedules are great, but once a problem arises, the program needs to be adjusted for the situation. Always consider training, conditioning, rest and therapy and what each encompasses.

In discussing the physical aspects of the modern horse, I would be remiss were I not to discuss the common obsession we have with size. Today in the horse world, many people are constantly looking for and trying to breed bigger and bigger horses. We Americans are known for always wanting bigger and bigger. Like with our cars in the 70s we found out that bigger is *NOT* always better. I do not fully understand this intense passion for bigger horses and its illogical foundation. Most people like horses because of their beauty and athletic ability. I do understand that a big beautiful horse can be *very majestic* and if you want a big horse because you like that look, that's fine. A big horse is a truly majestic creature, drawing awe from those around him. But there are several factors which come into play if you are looking for an athletic horse, and size is not always the advantage many people believe it to be.

- Bigger horses have more mass to move, hence are less likely to be as quick and agile as smaller horses. Agility is a prime factor in the ability of any athlete. Why are big, very athletic horses so expensive? Because they are not that common.

- Science has proven that as an animal gets larger, its proportion of internal mass increases faster than its surface area increases. This is important in affecting how an animal dissipates heat; internals generate heat and surface area dissipates heat. A smaller horse can stay cooler longer under physical stress.

- If you are looking for speed, remember that there are only two things that can increase the speed of a horse, more strides per minute and longer strides. A bigger horse has longer strides (usually), but as limbs get longer and heavier, physics show us that they cannot move as quickly, hence fewer strides per minute. That's why many animals such as foxes are only slightly slower than a horse and yet dramatically smaller proportionally. One of the most successful Arab race-horses (circle track racing, not endurance racing) was a horse named Monarch. He was barely 14 2 hands tall yet often won by ten to twenty lengths.

- Larger horses create greater load on their limbs during the impact segment of each stride, which can cause more injuries. This increased loading (stress) does not increase

278

arithmetically, but geometrically as weight increases. In other words, a smaller horse is less likely to break down. The same physics apply in humans. How often do you see a 250-pound gymnast or runner?

- Bigger horses are harder to get on and worse to fall from. You don't have as far to fall when you come off a smaller horse.
- Smaller horses fit under low trees and through tight places without scraping you off.
- Throughout history, people like Napoleon and Attila the Hun conquered vast lands riding small, 14 3 hand horses. Even in this country, the Indians used to ride the cavalry into the ground over and over. The cavalry imported the first large thoroughbreds from England to run down the Indians out west. It didn't work. In a short spurt on moderate terrain, the big horses were OK, but for any distance or over the rougher terrain, the Indian ponies always out-performed the cavalry mounts. The Indian ponies were about 14 hands.
- Bigger horses take longer to brush, clip and wash.

Lameness – the word all horse owners fear, yet often an idea that we allow to confuse how we care for our horses. Let me explain. Often when I ask someone how their horse is, they will respond with, "He's fine, not lame at all." The problem is that we too often incorrectly associate "healthy" with "sound." Unsound would mean a health problem, but sound does not mean healthy! There are many problems that you could develop, such as tuberculosis, cancer, AIDS, hardening of the arteries, etc., that are serious, even life-threatening, yet will they cause you to limp? NO! The same is true of the horse. He can be in serious trouble, health wise, and yet show no sign of lameness. We need to keep that in mind as we evaluate the condition of our horses. I have BioScanned many horses that were doing OK and surprised the owner by finding numerous physical problems. They were further surprised when, after treating those problems, the performance and also the attitude of the horse improved noticeably. What you don't know CAN hurt you. And your horse!

Physically speaking the horse is a true dichotomy, incredibly powerful, quick and fast; able to convert minimal grasses into incredible energy – yet also so vulnerable to injury and illness. You have no doubt said or heard someone else say something like, "One piece of barbed wire in the entire pasture and the horse will find it." Or, "One nail in the barn and he'll cut himself on it." Or even, "He was fine this morning, but now he's as lame as can be and I don't see a nick on him." All of those common scenarios point to the fragile nature of our beloved horses in the current environment. Yet most of the physical problems we see so often are more our fault than theirs. Fifty million years of experience taught the horse how to survive in his *natural world*. Barbed wire, nails and confinement were not part of that education. It is our responsibility to protect them from the risks we subject them to. We need to remember that they tend to keep going, even when hurt, and not allow that to hurt them further. I see as much frustration in the horse world from people dealing with physical problems as I do with behavior problems. Both can be frustrating and stressful, not to mention expensive. But the more we know and the more open we keep our minds, the better off we will be. So will our horses.

CHAPTER 10

Reality. Now What?

We have been talking about the reality of the horse and hopefully given you a better understanding of his world. In order to help tie it all together for you a bit more I want to go over a few more points for clarification. We need to take what we have discussed and apply it so as to create a better relationship with our horses. To learn something and then not apply it is a waste.

Spooking. If I were to say to you that it is rare for anyone to get hurt by the spooking of a horse, I would get a lot of argument from a lot of you with scars to prove me wrong. Yet it's true. How long does it take for a horse to spook? About three-tenths of a second. Just the same as no one dies from a snakebite, no one is usually hurt by the initial act of the horse spooking. It's the after effects of the snakebite, namely the venom doing its thing that kills. And it's the after effects of the spooking that get you hurt as well. If the horse jumps and then settles down without running off or over you, the spook is a minimal inconvenience. If you can't deal with that, sell the horse and buy a cat. If the horse does run off or over you as the *result of being spooked,* that can get you hurt. You change that situation by creating a more respectful attitude in the horse, *before the spooking,* not by overreacting to the horse's spooking. If the horse spooks and you overact, the horse will begin to be more dramatic in spooking as he learns to expect your agitation every time he gets startled. If you become his alpha, he will still spook, but less often and he will not run over you if he does. He will spook and look to see your reaction. If you don't react, he will follow your lead and tend to settle down as well. Which horse in the herd never gets run into? The Alpha. Try it, it works.

Communication. I have suggested you stop talking to your horse for a while to improve your communication skills in his language. This always gets a lot of resistance, until it's tried. If you really want to learn Spanish, go live somewhere they speak Spanish, and you have to *stop depending on English*. If you really want to learn "horse," stop relying on words. Watch the horse. If you doubt the effectiveness of the horse's language consider this: if you brought a Russian, a Chinaman, a Mexican and you into a room and each of you spoke only your language, ordering lunch would be a real problem. Yet put a Russian horse, a Chinese horse, a Mexican horse and your horse in a pasture, and they will communicate without effort. Who has the more universal language after all? Also, you can seldom talk yourself out of a problem that you behaved your way into. Actions speak louder than words.

Inconsistency. One of the saddest things I have seen in the past years traveling around the U.S. is the lack of consistency we force on horses. Different people handle horses in different ways. Even the same person is often very inconsistent in how they handle the same horse. There are many reasons for this, from being distracted by other things when you are around the horse, to ignorance about what horses need, to allowing your emotions to interfere with doing what's best for your horse. Horses are traded from person to person, moved from place to place and handled in every possible different way from babying to abuse; offering no stability or consistency to the horse. And if the horse reacts poorly or has any problems, the situation can be aggravated greatly. I am not opposed to selling a horse; in fact I have frequently recommended selling to clients when the horse they had was a poor match for their needs or ability. But many horses are sold because of some problem, either physical or behavioral, that could have been corrected if the people had only had more information and cared more. They get sold from owner to owner and their baggage relating to people increases with every move and change in environment. Imagine if you were a slave, subject to the whims of beings much wiser and different from you, and having total control over your destiny. They didn't speak your language or understand your needs. They were nice to you one time and then cruel the next. And they often seemed to not know the difference. You could be taken from your family and friends to a new strange place at a moment's notice. Do you get the idea? I'm not at all suggesting we should turn all the horses loose to be free. I am just saying we should try to be more benevolent owners, caring for the horse based not only on our wishes, but his needs as well.

The Three Categories of Knowledge. As we go through life we all deal with three basic categories of knowledge. Understanding that the three categories exist can help us avoid the pitfalls they often present. The first category of knowledge is the knowledge *we know*. We know all the stuff we take for granted because, simply, *we know we know*. The second category of knowledge is the knowledge *we know we don't know*. These items are more troublesome, yet not often a real crisis. For instance if someone around you was to be injured and you are not medically trained, *you know you don't know* what to do, so you call 911 and get someone that *does know* what's needed. You deal with the situation effectively. The third category of knowledge is what *you don't know you don't know*. For horse people, these are the things that come around, sneak up on you and bite you in the butt all through life. Often, if you don't know you don't know, you don't even seek help because you accept the situation as *normal*. And if you did seek help, how could you ask the right questions when you don't know you don't know? Would you even know to ask questions? That was my quandary when I got Sunny. I didn't know what I didn't know. Ignorance with horses is not bliss, it's just plain dangerous.

Competition. Many of you compete with your horses in a wide range of events. I told you that I have enjoyed endurance racing, but I have also done pony express races as well as hunt courses, etc. I also told you that I spent most of my life, from my teenage years to just recently, racing cars and motorcycles.

283

I loved it all. I never raced at Indy or Daytona but I won a lot in the lower levels of racing that are the grass roots of the sport. Showing horses at local or regional shows is a far cry from being National or World Champion, but it's a lot of fun just the same. One thing I learned early on in my racing was that people get very emotional about it. Driving a car at 150mph with thirty other cars fighting for position right next to you is without a doubt an emotional situation. During those situations people tend to get carried away sometimes and make mistakes. I won more races by helping pressure the other guy into a mistake than I did by having the fastest car. But occasionally I made the mistake. And then it was I that wrecked or broke the car. And I was the one that had to pay for it both in losing the race and the dollars for the repair costs.

When I started to race endurance, I discovered a whole new dimension to consider, and I almost discovered it too late. When the car breaks, I pay. When the horse breaks because I made a mistake and went too fast or tried too hard, we both pay. And that was a cost I couldn't accept. I had to err on the more conservative side when there was the possibility of injury to a horse at stake. I understand that as the money gets bigger, the choices become more difficult. But we are talking about living, breathing and feeling animals here, not machines. Martin Luther King Jr. once said, "It's a good thing God told us to *love* each other and not *like* each other, because there are just some people you can't *like*." People that have no compassion for the horse once competition comes into play are people I cannot like. Nor respect.

Understanding. This whole book has been about understanding. But often what we humans do is to wish to be understood. We want our horse to understand what we want them to do. We continually talk, yell, push, pull, jerk, tug, beat and bribe them into the actions we want. A wise man once said, "Seek first to understand and only then seek to be understood." He was talking about people, but it applies in our relationship with our horses as well.

People. We are such complex creatures with so much mental brilliance and yet so emotionally fragile. We get an idea in our mind, and we proceed as if it were reality. We think our fantasy has power. It doesn't. In fact, it limits us greatly. We want a trainer to fix the horse so he's always fine. Won't happen. The other day I took Sunny out for some photos. He had been ridden but a few times in four months and not out in the open areas for even longer. He was a bit of a butt. By the next day he was going nicely again. Your horse and you have a relationship; he thinks, feels and sometimes even changes. He is not a motorcycle that stays the same over and over. Just as we often don't put enough effort into keeping our relationships with fellow humans on track, we don't even think we need to with our horses. We do. We need to pay attention to keeping the relationship healthy and on solid ground every time we see our horse. Your relationship with your horse is not unlike your relationship with your spouse, you need to work at it if you want it to be as good as it can, and to last. If you are willing to settle for much less, then you needn't try as hard. But either way, you must understand it is an ongoing situation, dynamic and evolving, never static.

As you begin to interact with your horse, truly trying to understand him, try to remember that what *he does* is far less important than what *you do in response* to what he did. Don't be angry when he doesn't do as you wish. View his action as an opportunity to improve the relationship. Try to go beyond and look for the why that caused it. Don't be afraid to stop and regroup and especially give the horse time to think. Remember the man that kept sawing and sawing on the tree, day after day. When asked by someone why he didn't stop and sharpen the saw, he said he was too busy sawing. Don't be so busy "doing" something with your horse that you can't stop to re-evaluate your process. And maybe change the approach.

Beware of unchallenged beliefs. Don't accept things because they are *normal*. If a belief is good it will withstand a challenge. If it needs replacing, it won't. Instead of deciding what to do *to* your horse, consider what you can do *with* your horse. He'll appreciate that. Never get too sure of yourself. Horses have a magical way of giving us an *ego enema* just when we need it. Sunny can even smile when he does it.

In closing I want to thank you for caring enough to read this book, and I hope it has given you new ideas and caused you to think. In all honesty, the only reason I learned what I put forth in this book is because at one point in my life I was desperately in need of help with my horse. In the middle of all the crises, which at the time seemed so overwhelming, I had no idea of the changes forthcoming. Sunny was never as bad a horse as he was portrayed by so many people. Their ignorance was as great as mine. I was so very fortunate to have the opportunities I have had allowing me to learn what I did. So was Sunny. Sunny was not unlike so many horses I have worked with since. He was just doing what seemed best to him and adapting to the people around him. He was just being a horse. Exceptionally stubborn and pushy, perhaps, but just a horse nonetheless. There are more people problems than horse problems. But the horse needs understanding people to solve those problems. Be one of those people. Your horse will thank you. So will I. And as your awareness and understanding begins to grow and change, you will begin to feel more and more connected with your horse. It will be different between you. You may even have trouble explaining it. Others will see you with your horse and say "you've got the gift" or call it "magic." But by that time you will understand that FINDING THE MAGIC means knowing there is no magic. It's just that you've learned to understand the reality of that incredible, magnificent creature we call the horse. And it doesn't get any better than that.

For information about hosting or attending a Dan Sumerel Training Workshop near you, call or write:

Sumerel Training System
24 Mulberry Circle
Lynchburg, VA 24502

(804) 237-2012